First World War
and Army of Occupation
War Diary
France, Belgium and Germany

41 DIVISION
124 Infantry Brigade,
Brigade Machine Gun Company
and Brigade Trench Mortar Battery
16 June 1916 - 31 August 1916

WO95/2644/3

The Naval & Military Press Ltd
www.nmarchive.com
Published in association with The National Archives

Published by

The Naval & Military Press Ltd

Unit 10 Ridgewood Industrial Park,

Uckfield, East Sussex,

TN22 5QE England

Tel: +44 (0) 1825 749494

www.naval-military-press.com

www.nmarchive.com

This diary has been reprinted in facsimile from the original. Any imperfections are inevitably reproduced and the quality may fall short of modern type and cartographic standards.

© Crown Copyright
Images reproduced by permission of The National Archives, London, England, 2015.

Contents

Document type	Place/Title	Date From	Date To
Heading	WO95/2644/4		
Heading	41st Division 124th Infy Bde 124th Machine Gun Coy. Jun 1916-1917 Oct To Italy Nov 1917.		
War Diary	Grantham	16/06/1916	30/06/1916
War Diary	Papot	01/07/1916	05/07/1916
War Diary		03/07/1916	04/07/1916
War Diary	Papot	05/07/1916	12/07/1916
War Diary		11/07/1916	12/08/1916
War Diary		11/08/1916	16/08/1916
War Diary		15/08/1916	31/08/1916
Miscellaneous	Relief No 1. dt 5/8/16.	05/08/1916	05/08/1916
Miscellaneous	Relief No 2. dt 10/8/16.	10/08/1916	10/08/1916
Miscellaneous	Relief No 3 dt 14/8/16.	14/08/1916	14/08/1916
Operation(al) Order(s)	Relief Order No. 4. d/-15/8/16.	15/08/1916	15/08/1916
War Diary		01/09/1916	15/09/1916
War Diary		13/09/1916	14/09/1916
War Diary	In the field	15/09/1916	30/09/1916
War Diary		08/09/1916	30/09/1916
Miscellaneous	Appendix I.		
Miscellaneous	Appendix II		
War Diary	In the field	01/10/1916	04/11/1916
War Diary		03/11/1916	14/11/1916
War Diary		13/11/1916	14/11/1916
War Diary		13/11/1916	15/11/1916
War Diary		14/11/1916	16/11/1916
War Diary		15/11/1916	18/11/1916
War Diary	In the field	18/11/1916	20/11/1916
War Diary		19/11/1916	22/11/1916
War Diary	In the field	22/11/1916	01/12/1916
Miscellaneous	Operation Orders by Lieut. J.W. Lawson Cmdg. 124 M.G. Coy.	03/11/1916	03/11/1916
Operation(al) Order(s)	Operation Orders No. 17 by Major W.H. Davis. Cmdg. No. 24 M.G. Coy.	09/11/1916	09/11/1916
Operation(al) Order(s)	Operation Order No 19 by Major W.H. Davis Cmdg. 124 M.G. Coy.		
Operation(al) Order(s)	Operation Order No 21 by Major W.H. Davis Cmdg Metaphon.		
War Diary	In the field	01/12/1916	06/12/1916
War Diary	In the field	05/12/1916	08/12/1916
War Diary	In the field	07/12/1916	09/12/1916
War Diary	In the field	08/12/1916	12/12/1916
War Diary		11/12/1916	11/12/1916
War Diary	In the field	12/12/1916	15/12/1916
War Diary		14/12/1916	15/12/1916
War Diary	In the field	15/12/1916	01/01/1917
War Diary	In the field	31/12/1916	31/12/1916
Operation(al) Order(s)	Operation Order No. 22 by Major W.H. Davis Commanding 124th. Machine Gun Company.	03/12/1916	03/12/1916
Operation(al) Order(s)	Operation Order No. 23 by Major W.H. Davis Commanding 124th. Machine Gun Company.		

Operation(al) Order(s)	Operation Order No. 25 by Major W.H. Davis Commanding 124th. Machine Gun Company.		
Operation(al) Order(s)	Operation Order No. 26 by Major W.H. Davis Commanding 124th. Machine Gun Company.		
Operation(al) Order(s)	Operation Order No. 27 by Major W.H. Davis Commanding 124th. Machine Gun Company.		
War Diary	In the field	01/01/1917	07/01/1917
War Diary	In the field	06/01/1917	31/01/1917
Operation(al) Order(s)	Operation Order No. 28. by Major W.H. Davis Commanding 124th. Machine Gun Company.		
Operation(al) Order(s)	Operation Order No. 29. by Major W.H. Davis Commanding 124th. Machine Gun Company.		
Operation(al) Order(s)	Operation Order No. 30 by Major W.H. Davis Commanding Metaphor.		
Operation(al) Order(s)	Operation Order No. 31 by Major W.H. Davis Commanding 124th. Machine Gun Company.		
Operation(al) Order(s)	Operation Order No. 32 by Major W.H. Davis Commanding 124th. Machine Gun Company.		
Operation(al) Order(s)	Operation Order No. 33 by Major W.H. Davis, Commanding Metaphor.	19/01/1917	19/01/1917
Operation(al) Order(s)	Operation Order No. 34 by Major W.H. Davis Commanding 124th. Machine Gun Company.		
War Diary	In the field	31/01/1917	11/02/1917
War Diary		10/02/1917	10/02/1917
War Diary	In the field	11/02/1917	14/02/1917
War Diary		13/02/1917	13/02/1917
War Diary		11/02/1917	11/02/1917
War Diary	In the field	14/02/1917	16/02/1917
War Diary		15/02/1917	19/02/1917
War Diary		18/02/1917	19/02/1917
War Diary	In the field	19/02/1917	20/02/1917
War Diary		19/02/1917	20/02/1917
War Diary	In the field	20/02/1917	21/02/1917
War Diary		20/02/1917	20/02/1917
War Diary	In the field	21/02/1917	22/02/1917
War Diary	In the field	21/02/1917	23/02/1917
War Diary		22/02/1917	23/02/1917
War Diary	In the field	23/02/1917	26/02/1917
War Diary	In the field	25/02/1917	27/02/1917
War Diary	In the field	26/02/1917	28/02/1917
Operation(al) Order(s)	Operation Order No. 35 by Major W.H. Davis Commanding 124th. Machine Gun Company.		
Operation(al) Order(s)	Operation Order No. 36 by Major W.H. Davis Commanding 124th. Machine Gun Company.		
Operation(al) Order(s)	Operation Order No. 39. by Major W.H. Davis Commanding 124th. Machine Gun Company.	20/02/1917	20/02/1917
Operation(al) Order(s)	Additions to O.O. No. 39.		
Operation(al) Order(s)	Operation Order No. 44. by Major W.H. Davis, Commanding 124th. Machine Gun Compy.		
War Diary	Field	01/03/1917	10/03/1917
War Diary		09/03/1917	10/03/1917
War Diary	Field	09/03/1917	13/03/1917
War Diary		12/03/1917	13/03/1917
War Diary	Field	13/03/1917	15/03/1917
War Diary		14/03/1917	31/03/1917

Type	Description	Start	End
Miscellaneous	Operation Order No. by Major W.H. Davis Commanding 124th. Machine Gun Company.		
Miscellaneous	From O.C. 124 M.G. Comp.	01/05/1917	01/05/1917
War Diary	Field Steenvoorde.	01/04/1917	06/04/1917
War Diary	Field	06/04/1917	06/04/1917
War Diary	Micmac Camp	06/04/1917	06/04/1917
War Diary	H.31.B.3.4.	07/04/1917	10/04/1917
War Diary	Field Voormezeele	11/04/1917	18/04/1917
War Diary		17/04/1917	17/04/1917
War Diary	Field Voormezeele	18/04/1917	19/04/1917
War Diary	Field Reninghheist	20/04/1917	25/04/1917
War Diary	Voormezeele	25/04/1917	28/04/1917
War Diary		27/04/1917	28/04/1917
War Diary	Voormezeele	28/04/1917	30/04/1917
Operation(al) Order(s)	Operation Order No. 143. by Lieut. J.W. Lawson, Commanding 124th. Machine Gun Company.	11/04/1917	11/04/1917
Operation(al) Order(s)	Operation Order No. 44 by Lieut. J.W. Lawson, Commanding Metaphor.	17/04/1917	17/04/1917
Operation(al) Order(s)	Operation Order No. 45 by Lieut. J.W. Lawson, Commanding Metaphor.	22/04/1917	22/04/1917
Map	Map of German Trenches Corrected to 1st April, 1917.		
War Diary	Voormezeele	30/04/1917	03/05/1917
War Diary	Reninghelst.	03/05/1917	18/05/1917
War Diary	Ganspette Training Area.	19/05/1917	31/05/1917
War Diary	Arneke	01/06/1917	01/06/1917
War Diary	Reninghelst	02/06/1917	30/06/1917
War Diary	Meteren	01/07/1917	22/07/1917
War Diary	Trenches Bluff Sector.	22/07/1917	26/07/1917
War Diary		25/07/1917	25/07/1917
War Diary	Trenches Bluff Sector	28/07/1917	09/08/1917
War Diary	Ridge Wood	10/08/1917	10/08/1917
War Diary	Trenches Bluff Sector.	11/08/1917	15/08/1917
War Diary	Ridge Wood	16/08/1917	17/08/1917
War Diary	Thieushouk	17/08/1917	18/08/1917
War Diary	Mont-Des-Cats.	19/08/1917	24/08/1917
War Diary	Staple.	25/08/1917	25/08/1917
War Diary	St. Martins-Ul-Laert.	26/08/1917	30/08/1917
War Diary	Tattinghem.	31/08/1917	31/08/1917
War Diary	St. Martins Ul-Laert.	31/08/1917	31/08/1917
Operation(al) Order(s)	Operation Order No. 53. by O. Commanding 124 Coy. M.G.C. Ref. 124 I.B. O.O. 128.	14/08/1917	14/08/1917
War Diary	Tatinghem Training Area	01/09/1917	14/09/1917
War Diary	Wallen Cappel Area	14/09/1917	16/09/1917
War Diary	Ridge Wood	17/09/1917	19/09/1917
War Diary	Shrewsbury Forest	19/09/1917	25/09/1917
War Diary	Borre	25/09/1917	25/09/1917
War Diary	Hazebrouck Area.	26/09/1917	30/09/1917
Map	Messages Map		
Miscellaneous	Message Form.		
War Diary	Ghyvelde	01/10/1917	08/10/1917
War Diary	Coxyde Bains	09/10/1917	17/10/1917
War Diary	Nieuport Bains Sector.	18/10/1917	28/10/1917
War Diary	Teteghem	29/10/1917	31/10/1917
Heading	WO95/2644/5		
Heading	41st Division 124th Infy Bde Trench Mortar Bty Jly-Aug 1916		

War Diary		01/07/1916	31/07/1916
Miscellaneous	To:- 41st Division A.	28/08/1916	28/08/1916
War Diary		01/08/1916	29/08/1916
Operation(al) Order(s)	21st. Battalion King's Royal Rifle Corps Operation Order No. 15. Appendix 4.	22/12/1917	22/12/1917
Miscellaneous	Company of report sent to 124 IB 21/8/16.	21/08/1916	21/08/1916
Miscellaneous	Handed over by 124 TMB No. 70th Bde. TMB	16/08/1916	16/08/1916
War Diary		30/08/1916	31/08/1916

W095/26992/4

41ST DIVISION
124TH INFY BDE

124TH MACHINE GUN COY.
JUN 1916-FEB 1918
1917 OCT

To 1 THLY. NOV 1917

41
I. TONE
JULY
of 124th Machine Gun Company

WAR DIARY
or
INTELLIGENCE SUMMARY
(Erase heading not required.)

Army Form C. 2118.

Vols 1 & 2

Place	Date	Hour	Summary of Events and Information	Remarks and references to Appendices
GRANTHAM	16/6/16	5.45am	124 M.g. Coy left GRANTHAM for service overseas	
		11.15pm	Arrived SOUTHAMPTON	
		1 pm	Left SOUTHAMPTON in 2 parties	
		2½ pm		
	17/6/16	7am 11am	disembarked at le HAVRE. Proceeded to Rest Camp No 2.	
	18/6/16	18.14pm	entrained at HAVRE	
	19/6/16	18.30pm	arrived at STEENWERCKE. Proceeded to Billets at PAPOT.	
	20/6/16	10 pm	Inspected by G.O.C. 41st Division	
	21/6/16 to 24/6/16		Officers N.C.O.s & Men in Trenches from U.15.c.40 to U.28.c.55. (Tunnel Mogo Sr 9/405 Pt of Shaft - 26 1/10000 for instruction	
	24/6/16			
	27/6/16		Relieved 6 Guns of 10th M.G. Battery in Subsidiary line. (Sec 2 & post of Sec 4)	
	28/6/16 to 30/6/16		Taking of Men on to Trenches proceeded on normal lines	

124th M.G. Coy

Army Form C. 2118.

WAR DIARY
or
INTELLIGENCE SUMMARY
(Erase heading not required.)

Instructions regarding War Diaries and Intelligence Summaries are contained in F. S. Regs., Part II. and the Staff Manual respectively. Title Pages will be prepared in manuscript.

Place	Date	Hour	Summary of Events and Information	Remarks and references to Appendices
PAPOT	17/7/16	7.30 a.m.	6 guns of 124 M.G. Coy in Inbredary line (U.14.d.8.2½ U.14.c.6½.½ U.20.a.5¾. 1 Bogus Trench Map. ST YVES Horse U.20.c.6½. 2½ Oxford Circus Part of Sheet 28. 1/10.000 U.26.c.7.5. Means 75 U.26.c.8½.2) " 75	O.O.1.>2 > 3
"	"	"	relieved by 6 guns of 10th M.M.G. Battery	
"	"	"	10 guns of 124 M.G. Coy relieved 10 guns of 122 M.G. Coy in Front & Support Trenches Positions as follows:— U.15.b.a.t.(us) U.15.d.6.0.7½.(us) U.15.d.(us) U.15.c.7.4. Leinster Avenue U.21.a.2½.9½. Dead Horse Corner U.21.a.9½.7½. Fort Paget U.21.c.3.2. Fort Everett 2 guns U.21.d.3¾.4½. S.2.116 U.27.a.8½.7½. Reading Fort U.27.a.9½.13. Border Barns U.27.d.2¾.8. Cheshire Avenue U.28.d.½.7. T.66	Ref. as above Map

L.H.Dann Capt. M.G.C.
....
124, MACHINE GUN COY.
M. G. C.

Army Form C. 2118.

WAR DIARY
or
INTELLIGENCE SUMMARY
(Erase heading not required.)

Place	Date	Hour	Summary of Events and Information	Remarks and references to Appendices
PAPOT	2/7/16	—	30163/'Flo Clarke T. evacuated to No.6 C.C.S	
	3/7/16	10 or 12 P.M.	Indirect Night Firing from emplacement at U.14.c.8½.1.	
			Targets: Troos Tideouts from U.17.c.1.2 2600 yds	
			U.23.a.1.7 2250 "	
			Dump at 2500 "	
			Increase at	
			Junction of Rd &	
			Trench Tramway at U.10.c.5½.3½ 2150 "	
			U.10.c.5½.3½	
	3/7/16 to 5/7/16	1.30	Extension of Divisional (41st Division) front Northward to include T's from Anton's Ferm to R.Douve. Redistribution of Brigade Sectors 124th Infantry Bde take over Centre Sector from T.11 to T.124 (inclusive) with 123rd Inf Bde on R & 122nd Inf Bde on L	OO.O. 3a.
	3/7/16	10.30 P.M.	124 M.G. Coy take over 5 guns from 10th M.M.G. Battery in introductory line in positions U.14.c.6½.½ U.26.c.7.5	
			U.20.a.3.3 U.26.c.8½.2	
			U.20.c.6½.2½	

LM Davis Capt OC
124, MACHINE GUN COY.
M.G.C.

Army Form C. 2118.

WAR DIARY
or
~~INTELLIGENCE SUMMARY~~
(Erase heading not required.)

Instructions regarding War Diaries and Intelligence Summaries are contained in F. S. Regs., Part II. and the Staff Manual respectively. Title Pages will be prepared in manuscript.

Place	Date	Hour	Summary of Events and Information	Remarks and references to Appendices
	3/7/16	10.30 pm	124 MG Coy hand over 3 Gun Positions to 123 MG Coy at U 27 a 9½ 1¾, U " d 2¾ 8, U 28 d 1½ 7	
		11.45 pm	124 MG Coy take over 3 Gun Positions from 122 MG Coy at U 15 b 0 1, U 15 d 0 7¾, U 15 d 4¾ 4	
	4/7/16		Distribution of Guns in Trenches as follows:-	
			U 15 b 0 1, U 15 d 0 7¾, U 15 c 7 4 } Sec: 1 under 2/Lt W.C. Kibert	
			U 15 d 4¾ 4, U 21 a 9½ 7½, U 21 a 2¼ 9½ } Sec: 3 under 2/Lt F.A. Singleton	
			U 21 a 3 2 (2 Guns), U 21 d 3¾ 4½, U 27 a 8½ 7½ } Sec: 1 under 2/Lt A.L. Carte	

W.H. Davis Capt. O.C.
124, Machine Gun Coy.
M. G. C.

2449 Wt. W14957/M90 750,000 1/16 J.B.C. & A. Forms/C.2118/12.

WAR DIARY or INTELLIGENCE SUMMARY

Army Form C. 2118.

(Erase heading not required.)

Place	Date	Hour	Summary of Events and Information	Remarks and references to Appendices
			Operations	
			Position of Gun · Rounds Expended · Target · Remks · O/C fire	
		10.15 p.m.	T.119 · 100 · Lewis Posts at U.21.6.5.5. · Gun Posn sprayed by every M.G. · 2/Lt F.N. Snifton	under 2/Lt C.B. Woolly under 2/Lt A.S. Litson
		10.45 p.m.	T.116 · 500 · Lewis Posts between U.22.c.3.4 & U.22.c.3.7 · 50 Rds/Min · 2/Lt A Gra...	
Poperinghe	5/7/16	0.35 p.m.	No. 35281 Pte Jones R · Roolards R.b.S joined Coy for Base for better Coast Duties	

1/5th Delhi Coy M.G.C

124, MACHINE GUN COY
M.G.C.

WAR DIARY
or
INTELLIGENCE SUMMARY

Army Form C. 2118.

(Erase heading not required.)

124, MACHINE GUN COY.
M. G. O.

Place	Date	Hour	Summary of Events and Information						Remarks and references to Appendices
			Operations						
			Officer i/c Corps	Posen & Gun	Rounds Expended	Target	Results	Remarks	
	5/7/16	12.30 a.m.	2/Lt A.W. CARLE	ST 116	250	Enemy Support Trenches between U21 C69 U22 C6/7	Unknown	Enemy M.G.'s very active in that sector.	
		1.30 a.m.	2/Lt F.N. SINGLETON	T 122	500	U21 b 90	Unknown	Enemy very active with M.G.'s, Trench Mortars & Rifle Grenades in this Sector.	
		6 p.m.	2/Lt CARLE	T 116	250	Enemy Snipers in trees between U22 R 3/4 T U22 C5.7	Sniping Ceased		
	Night 5/6 July	10.15 pm 6 a.m.	2/Lt CARLE	MUD LANE	750	Dump at U18 b 9 Transverse at U18 b 8/9	Unknown	Indirect Fire Gun Position being heavily shelled	
	6/7/16	2.30 a.m.	2/Lt F.N. SINGLETON	T 122	250	Working Party at	Party Dispersed		
		3.50 a.m.	2/Lt F.N. SINGLETON	T 119	500	U 21 b C.5	Unknown	Two battle emplacements constructed during night (T 119 & T 116)	

Army Form C. 2118.

WAR DIARY or INTELLIGENCE SUMMARY

(Erase heading not required.)

Instructions regarding War Diaries and Intelligence Summaries are contained in F. S. Regs., Part II. and the Staff Manual respectively. Title Pages will be prepared in manuscript.

Place	Date	Hour	Summary of Events and Information					Remarks and references to Appendices
			Operations					
			Officer in Charge	Position of Gun	Rounds Expended	Target	Result	Remarks
	6/7/16 Night	12.30 a.m. to 3.0 a.m.	2/LT W.C. VIBERT	T 124	300	U 15 b 3 6	Unknown	—
	7/7/16	12.50 a.m.	2/LT A.W. EARLE	T 124	300	U 15 b 8 8	Unknown	—
		1.30 a.m.		T 124	400	U 15 a 7 h 6	Unknown	—
				T 116	600	Traverse from U 22 e 3 3 to U 22 b 3 7 at working parties	Work ceased	Fire from enemy M.G's very active during this period
		1 a.m.	2/LT. F.N SINGLETON	T 120	750	Working Party	Work ceased	Enemy Trench Mortars active
		12 M.N to 1 a.m.	2/LT. W.C. VIBERT	U 26 d 4 7 ½	1000	U 22 c 9 4, U 22 c 8 7, U 22 b 6 7	Unknown	Indirect Fire
		1.30 a.m.	2/LT. W.R. VIBERT	U 15	500	U 16 a 7 h 1, U 15 a 8 6 ½	Unknown	New Emplacement begun at U 15 b 1
		2 a.m. to 3.15 a.m.	2/LT F.N SINGLETON	T 122	500	Working Party	Work ceased	

124, MACHINE GUN COY.
M. G. C.

Army Form C. 2118.

WAR DIARY
or
INTELLIGENCE SUMMARY

(Erase heading not required.)

Instructions regarding War Diaries and Intelligence Summaries are contained in F. S. Regs., Part II. and the Staff Manual respectively. Title Pages will be prepared in manuscript.

Place	Date	Hour	Summary of Events and Information					Remarks and references to Appendices
			Operations					
			Officer in Charge	Position of Gun	Rounds Expended	Target	Result	Remarks
	Night 18 July	10.15 to 1.00 a.m.	Capt W.H. Davis	Mud Lane	750	Tram tramway & junction L 23 d 1.7 (tramway from) Dump at W 16 d 4.1	Unknown	
		12.30 a.m	2/Lt F.N. Singleton	T 122	500	Working Party between U 15 d 85 & U 15 d 90	Work ceased.	
		12.30 a.m	2/Lt A.W. Earle	T 116	250	Working Party between U 22 a 31 & U 22 a 51	Satisfactory	Gun Emplacement subjected to very heavy & concentrated m.g. fire
		1 a.m	2/Lt W.E. Vibert	T 124	1000	U 15 b 90 k / U 16 a 24 1/2	Unknown	Enemy M.G. emplacement discovered at U 15 b 50 1/2
		7.15 p.m	2/Lt W.E. Vibert	T 124	250	Hostile Aeroplane	Nil	

W. Devir Capt. O.C.
124, Machine Gun Coy.
M. G. C.

Army Form C. 2118.

WAR DIARY
or
INTELLIGENCE SUMMARY
(Erase heading not required.)

Instructions regarding War Diaries and Intelligence Summaries are contained in F. S. Regs., Part II. and the Staff Manual respectively. Title Pages will be prepared in manuscript.

Place	Date	Hour	Summary of Events and Information					Remarks and references to Appendices
			Operations					
			Officer in Charge	Position of Gun	Rounds Expended	Target	Result	Remarks
	8/9 July 1916	10 P.m to 1 A.m.	2 Lt BROWNRIGG-JAY	U26d 4 6½	1000	U22c94 U22c87 U28667	Unknown	Indirect Fire
		1.30 a.m.	2/Lt BROWNRIGG-JAY	T.124	800	Enemy M.G. & Snipers	Satisfactory	
		10.30 p.m to 3.30 a.m	2/Lt A.W.EARLE	T.116	2,500	Enemy Working Parties	Parties were all dispersed	Guns were heavily shelled during action, retaliation by Enemy's M.G's
		1.30 a.m.	2 Lt F.N.SINGLETON	T.120	750	Working Party Traversed Enemy Parapets	Satisfactory Work ceased	

[signature], O.C.
124, MACHINE GUN COY.
M. G. C.

2449 Wt. W14957/M90 750,000 1/16 J.B.C. & A. Forms/C.2118/12.

Army Form C. 2118.

Instructions regarding War Diaries and Intelligence Summaries are contained in F. S. Regs., Part II. and the Staff Manual respectively. Title Pages will be prepared in manuscript.

WAR DIARY
or
INTELLIGENCE SUMMARY
(Erase heading not required.)

Place	Date	Hour	Summary of Events and Information	Remarks and references to Appendices
	9/7/16 to 10" July/16		5 Vickers Guns Co-operated in Raid on German Trenches at pt U.15 d 9¼.4 by furnishing Platoons fire & Indirect Overhead Fire. Time of Assault by Raiding Party 11.30 p.m.	O.O. No. 5
			Operations	
			Officer in Charge — Position of Gun — Rounds Expended — Targets — Result	
		11.30 p.m.	2/Lt F.N. SINGLETON — T 123 — 4000 570 4HD — 2 Enemy MS — Effective	Reports
		10.30 p.m. –3.30 a.m.	" A CARLE — T 116 — 2000 — Enemy Wire (gap) U.22.c.3.6 to U.22.c.4.2 — Sat'sfactory	Enemy MG's active
		10.15 p.m. –4 p.m. a.m.	" C.B. WOODLEY — U 27 c 3 1½ — 1000 — Road U.23.c.9.6 Dump U.23.c.9.3 Cross Rds U.29.b.2.7 Bridge U.29.b.5.3 — Unknown	
		1 a.m.	" E.H. BROWNRIGG-JAY — Westminster Avenue — 750 — Enemy M.G. — Gun Silenced	
		12.30 to 1.30	" W C Vibert — U'15 d 4/t 7½ — 500	

W Dew C.A. ..........O.C.
124. MACHINE GUN COY.
M. G. C.

2449 Wt. W14957/M90 750,000 1/16 J.B.C. & A. Forms/C.2118/12.

Army Form C. 2118.

WAR DIARY
or
INTELLIGENCE SUMMARY

(Erase heading not required.)

Instructions regarding War Diaries and Intelligence Summaries are contained in F. S. Regs., Part II. and the Staff Manual respectively. Title Pages will be prepared in manuscript.

Place	Date	Hour	Summary of Events and Information	Remarks and references to Appendices
	10th July 1916	10.30 p.m. to 1 a.m.	3 Vickers Guns co-operated in Raid on hostile trenches by party of 21st K.R.R. 1 Gun in Sector of 123rd Bde assisted by Stokes fire from T.106. Time of Assault 1 a.m. Officers in Charge. Gun Position. Target. Rounds. No. of Rds expended. 2/Lt A Goff. T.112. Set 11 Enemy wire from U.22.c.3.6 to U.22.c.4.2 & Standing fire. 1500. Unknown. Enemy Silent. 2/Lt F.N. Singleton. T.122. 2 Enemy M.Guns. 1500. M.Gs. Silenced. Flashing fire 16 bullet Mc Caulth wounded by bullet. 2/Lt S.H. Brownings Jay. T.124. Enemy M.G. at U.15.b.4.6½. 1250. M.G. Silenced. Flashing fire.	
	11/12 July 1916	10.0 p.m. to 1.30 a.m.	2/Lt H. ROSTRON. T.116. Traversing fire from U.22.a.31 to U.22.a.35. 500. satisfactory	
		10.0 p.m. to 1 a.m.	CAPT. W.H. DAVIS. Mud Lane. Dust U.22.C.9.4.9 Trench Taromozay U.28.b.55 Loophole Farm U.22.a.13. 1000. Unknown. Indirect fire.	

W. Smith Capt. O.C.
124, MACHINE GUN COY.
M1. G. G.

2449 Wt. W14957/M90 750,000 1/16 J.B.C. & A. Forms/C.2118/12.

Army Form C. 2118.

WAR DIARY
or
INTELLIGENCE SUMMARY

(Erase heading not required.)

Instructions regarding War Diaries and Intelligence Summaries are contained in F.S. Regs., Part II. and the Staff Manual respectively. Title Pages will be prepared in manuscript.

Place	Date	Hour	Summary of Events and Information	Remarks and references to Appendices
			Operations	
			Officer in Charge — Gun Position — Rounds Expended — Target — Result — Remarks	
	11/12 July 1916	1.30 a.m.	2/Lt G.H. BROWNRIGG-FAY — T.1.24 — 1000 — Working Parties in Unknown — Unknown	
	12/13 July 1916	10.45 p.m. to 1.0 a.m.	2/Lt H. ROSTRON — T.1.6 — 500 — Enemy Parapet U 22 a 31 to U 22 c 35 — Unknown	
			2 Vickers Guns were in co-operation with minor operations of the 122nd Brigade	O.O. No.6
			Operations	
		1.30 a.m.	2/Lt F.N. SINGLETON — T.1.22 — 1000 — U.15 d 8 6 also fired overhead searchlight on enemy communication trench — Unknown	
		1.30 a.m.	2/Lt VIGERT — T.1.24 — 500 — U.15 b 5½ 4 2 — Unknown	The barrel casing of gun was punctured by steel splinter thereupon a prolonged stoppage. 2/Lt BROWNRIGG-FAY was slightly wounded in face & hands by steel splinter.

L. Devens Capt.
O.O
124, MACHINE GUN COY.
M.G.O.

Army Form C. 2118.

WAR DIARY
or
INTELLIGENCE SUMMARY
(Erase heading not required.)

Instructions regarding War Diaries and Intelligence Summaries are contained in F. S. Regs., Part II. and the Staff Manual respectively. Title Pages will be prepared in manuscript.

Place	Date	Hour	Summary of Events and Information					Remarks and references to Appendices
			Operations					
			Officer in Charge	Position of Gun	Rounds Expended	Target	Result	Remarks
	13/1/17 July 1917	10.45 p.m to 12.15 a.m	2/Lt H. ROSTRON	T 11 b	500	U22a3, r U22c8, Enemy Support Trenches	Satisfactory	
		10.30 p.m to 1 a.m	2/Lt F.N. SINGLETON	MUD LANE	1000	Cross Roads at U24627 Dump U29a93 Leaf Hole Gum Trench Tramway r Junction U23c96	Unknown	Indirect fire
		12.30 a.m	2/Lt F.N. SINGLETON	T 12.2	500	Working Party	Satisfactory	
		1.30 a.m & 2.30 a.m	2/Lt W.C. VIBERT	T 12 4	750	M.G. at U15b7x1	Gun Silenced	30166 Pte Dyson J.H. Shrapnel Wound thigh

O.C. "D" Coy
124, MACHINE GUN COY,
M. G. C.

Army Form C. 2118.

WAR DIARY
or
INTELLIGENCE SUMMARY
(Erase heading not required.)

Place	Date	Hour	Summary of Events and Information					Remarks and references to Appendices
			Operations					
			Officer in Charge	Position of Gun	Rounds Expended	Target	Results	Remarks
	14/15 July 1916	10.30 p.m to 12.30 a.m	2/Lt A.S. WILSON	U14c8741	1000	1. TROIS TILLEUL FARM U17C12 2. TRENCH TRAMWAY U23.a17 3. DUMP U16d41 4. From THATCHED COTTAGE to FLATTENED FARM U16a7b7 to U16a914	Unknown	3015 Sgt McKeown bullet wound hand.
		11.30 p.m	2/Lt F.N. SINGLETON	T122	250	Enemy Wire Parapet	Unknown	Very little firing could be seen owing to our own working parties being out
		11.30 p.m to 1 a.m	2/Lt A.W. CARLE	T116	500	M.G. at U635h	Enemy wireparapet gun silenced	
		11.45 p.m to 2.30 a.m	2/Lt W.C. VIBERT	T124	750	Search belt Traversed from U15b27 to U15b80		No repairs were done to enemy wire.

Army Form C. 2118.

WAR DIARY
or
INTELLIGENCE SUMMARY
(Erase heading not required.)

Place	Date	Hour	Summary of Events and Information					Remarks and references to Appendices
			Operations Officer in Charge	Position of Gun	Rounds fired	Target	Result	Remarks
	15/16 July 1916	10.30 p.m. to 12.30 a.m.	2/Lt WOODLEY	Nr LAWRENCE FARM U17 a 9½ 1½	1000	1) U 23 Central 2) Traversing from U29 b 27 (Traversed from U29 c 74 to U29 d 17) 3) Junction Tramway U 23 o 5"x 3½	Unknown	Indirect Fire
		10.50 p.m. to 1 a.m.	2/Lt CARLE	T 115	1000	U 22 a 12½ 6 U 21 b 93 & FACTORY FARM	Unknown	
		10.45 p.m. to 11 p.m.	2/Lt H. ROSTRON	T 123	500	U15 d 89 traversed to U 15 d 93	Unknown	Co-operation with Lewis Guns
		10.45 p.m. to 2.30 a.m.	2/Lt W.G. VIBERT	T 124	1750	Traversed between U15 b 35¼ & U15 b 78¼ Enemy communication trenches searched during bombardment	Unknown	Supporting raiding party of 26th R.F

Army Form C. 2118.

WAR DIARY
or
INTELLIGENCE SUMMARY
(Erase heading not required.)

Instructions regarding War Diaries and Intelligence Summaries are contained in F. S. Regs., Part II. and the Staff Manual respectively. Title Pages will be prepared in manuscript.

Place	Date	Hour	Summary of Events and Information					Remarks and references to Appendices
			Our Offensive Operations					
			Officer in Charge	Position of Gun	Rds Fired	Target	Result	Remarks
	16/17 July 1916	12.0 m to 3. a.m	2/Lt H ROSTRON	T 12.2	500	U 15 d 9.2	Unknown	—
			Remaining guns did not fire owing to new emplacement being built.					

W. Rew. C/.1. O.C.
124, MACHINE GUN COY.
M. G. C.

WAR DIARY or INTELLIGENCE SUMMARY

Army Form C. 2118.

(Erase heading not required.)

Instructions regarding War Diaries and Intelligence Summaries are contained in F. S. Regs., Part II. and the Staff Manual respectively. Title Pages will be prepared in manuscript.

Place	Date	Hour	Summary of Events and Information					Remarks and references to Appendices
			Operations Officer in charge	Gun Position	Rounds expended	Target	Result	Remarks
	17/18 July /16	12 pm to 2 am	2/Lt. H. ROSTRON	T.12.c.	500	V.15.D.9.2.	Unknown	Unknown
	"	10.30 to 3 am	2/Lt. A.W. CARLE	T.11.b.	1500	Enemy Outpost U.22.A.2.1 U.21.c.3½.2.	Very Satisfactory	Enemy M.G. very active red S.O.S. from N. of Bridges?
	"	12 pm	2/Lt. W.C. VIBERT	T.12.d.	1000	Enemy Working Parties in Trenches U.15.A.9.5 + U.15.A.9½.5¼ also U.9.c.5¾.4¾ + V.15.G.2¼.8¾	Party dispersed	
	"	"	"	LeanHouse GUN	1250	Sugar Refinery U.17.d.4/2.0.5 also Cross Roads V.12.c.3½.4. also Bridge U.18.a.6.3 U.18.a.0.6.		Issued List

W.Dons Capt. O.C.
124, MACHINE GUN COY.
M. G. C.

2449 Wt. W14957/M90 750,000 1/16 J.B.C. & A. Forms/C.2118/12.

Army Form C. 2118.

WAR DIARY
or
INTELLIGENCE SUMMARY

(Erase heading not required.)

Place	Date	Hour	Summary of Events and Information	Remarks and references to Appendices

Operations.

			Officer in charge	Gun Position	Rounds Expended	Target	Result Remarks	
	18/19 July 16	11½ pm to 2 am	2/LT H. ROSTRON	T 122.	500	U 15 d 9.2 & Enemy Working party	Very satisfactory.	
		1.15 am to 3 am	2/LT A W CARLE	T 116.	750.	Traversed U 22 a 5.4. U 22 c 7.3.	Unknown.	

W. Dow Capt. O.C.
124. MACHINE GUN COY.
M. G. C.

Army Form C. 2118.

WAR DIARY
or
INTELLIGENCE SUMMARY
(Erase heading not required.)

Instructions regarding War Diaries and Intelligence Summaries are contained in F.S. Regs., Part II. and the Staff Manual respectively. Title Pages will be prepared in manuscript.

Place	Date	Hour	Summary of Events and Information					Remarks and references to Appendices
			Operation	Officer in charge	Gun Position	Rounds expended	Target	Remarks
	10/20 July.16.	10h.m to 3am		2/Lt. F.N SINGLETON.	T.122.	750.	Factory Farm V.15.c. 8.5. to V.16.c. 4.9.	Unknown. Verbal Searching
	"	11pm to 2.30am		2/Lt. H. ROSTRON.	T.113.	750	Enemy enemy unit Intention V.28a. 4.½ to V.28.a. 4.4.	Satisfactory.
	"	2/am		2/Lt W.C VIBERT	Gun 124.	80.	Enemy aeroplane	Aeroplane turned back
				"	T.124	500.	Square V.15a. V.15c.	Scarcely traversed
		12m.N.		"	Westminster Gun	750	Cross Roads at V.12.c. 3.4. Sugar Refinery V.17.d. 4.3.½ LATRUIE. FARM. U.17.a. 5.½. 0.	Indirect fire

The following change and distribution of guns took place. Relief completed by 4pm.
2/Lt A.S WILSON took over Gun positions in T.122. Dead Horse Corner & Fort Royal
8/Lt. F.N SINGLETON " " " " " at REDFIELD. Oxford Circus & 1 at Thorn 75.
and took charge of the whole intercharing line.

[signature] 124. MACHINE GUN COY. M.G.C.

O.O No: 7

Army Form C. 2118.

WAR DIARY
or
INTELLIGENCE SUMMARY

(Erase heading not required.)

Instructions regarding War Diaries and Intelligence Summaries are contained in F. S. Regs., Part II. and the Staff Manual respectively. Title Pages will be prepared in manuscript.

Place	Date	Hour	Summary of Events and Information	Remarks and references to Appendices
	20/21st June 16	12 P.M. to 3 A.M.	Operations. Officer in charge. Gun Position. Rounds Expended. TARGET. Result & Remarks.	
			2/Lt A.W. CARLE T113. 750. Enemy Wire from V22c51 to V28a65. Satisfactory	
	"	"	2/Lt A.S. WILSON T123 1000. Enemy Road Z.12 V15d.8½.6 Silenced two snipers & Hostile Infantry Party	
	"	"	2/Lt W.C. VIBERT Gun 124 500. Working Party V15a.8½.6 Dispersed	
			Lookout Gun 750. Cross Roads at V12c3½. Sugar Refinery V17d4½.5 Bridge V18a.6.3 Bridge V18c.0.6 Satisfactory	
			Strength:- Officers 10. Other Ranks 136. R. Horses 11. Mules 43.	

W. Devir Capt. O.C.
124, MACHINE GUN COY.
M. G. C.

Army Form C. 2118.

WAR DIARY
or
INTELLIGENCE SUMMARY
(Erase heading not required.)

Instructions regarding War Diaries and Intelligence Summaries are contained in F. S. Regs., Part II. and the Staff Manual respectively. Title Pages will be prepared in manuscript.

Place	Date	Hour	Summary of Events and Information	Remarks and references to Appendices
	2/22 July 1916	10 p.m. to 12.1 a.m. July 1916	Operations: Officer in charge. Gun Position. Rounds Expended. TARGET. RESULT REMARKS 2/LT. A.S. WILSON. V26d 4.7½. 750. ① Ford Rouge Gun Pos. at V29 b.2,7 ② From Pont Rouge Gun Pos V29 b.2,7) to Petite Douve Farm (V23c 9½.9) ③ Junction Trench Tramway (V23.c. 6½.3½) Satisfactory Fired on	
			2/LT W.C. VIBERT. Gun 124 520 Enemy Working Party V15a 7.6½. Gun also traversed returned Enemy Support Communication trenches. Party dispersed	
		10.30 p.m. to 2.30 a.m.	2/LT A.W. CARLE. T113. 500. Enemy wire from V28A Wilson A6.5	

W. Devitt Capt O.C.
124, MACHINE GUN COY.
M. G. C.

Army Form C. 2118.

WAR DIARY
or
INTELLIGENCE SUMMARY
(Erase heading not required.)

Instructions regarding War Diaries and Intelligence Summaries are contained in F. S. Regs., Part II. and the Staff Manual respectively. Title Pages will be prepared in manuscript.

Place	Date	Hour	Summary of Events and Information	Remarks and references to Appendices
	22/23rd July 1916.	10.30pm to 2.30am	**Operations**	
			Officer in charge. Gun Position. Rounds expended. TARGET. RESULT. REMARKS	
			2/LT A.W. EARLE T113 750. Enemy Working party between U28.A.14.9 & U28.A.6.5 Unknown.	
			12.45am	2/LT A.S. WILSON T122 230. Enemy Working Party at U.15.B.8½.5. Seen.	
			"	2/LT Brownrigg-JAY T124 500 Enemy machine Gun U.17.d.5.5½. U.12.0.3½; Unknown	
				Lanyard Gun 750 U.18.a.6.3½	
			New emplacement at FORT. BOYD & on T.122 completed by 2/Lt. A.S WILSON	

W. Dew C/M.o.a.
124, MACHINE GUN COY.
M. G. C.

Army Form C. 2118.

WAR DIARY
or
INTELLIGENCE SUMMARY
(Erase heading not required.)

Place	Date	Hour	Summary of Events and Information					Remarks and references to Appendices
			Operations					
			Officer in charge	Gun Position	Rounds Expended	TARGET	RESULT	REMARKS
	23/24 July 16.	10.30pm to 12.30am	2/LT BROWNRIGG-JAY.	U.17d.8±.±	1000	U.17.c.1.2 U.16a.±.± & U.16a.9±.± U.10.c.5.6	Unknown.	Indirect Traversing Fire.
		12.45 to 2.30 am	"	"	750.	Enemy Snipers & machine guns	Satisfactory.	
		12.15 pm to 3am	2/LT A.W. CARLE.	T.11.3.	500	Enemy Wire & sample between U.28.A.4.9 & U.28.A.6.5.	Unknown.	
		1.30 am to 2.30 am	2/LT A.E. PRESCOTT	T.12.2.	500.	Enemy Working Party at U.21.B.8±.8	Party dispersed.	
		"	"	T.12.2		Enemy Supports between U.21.a.3.8 to U.22.a.3±.6	Unknown.	Traversing Fire.

An instructional class under 2/LT A.W. Woolly was found today of 8 men each from 2/o. K.R.R. & 3/o. not Fusiliers for one month's instruction on the machine gun, Sgt Lilley was detailed to assist in the instruction.

O/c Divisional Train, Adjutant, Staff Captain & B.M. transport officer inspected the transport today, & the Divisional Train expressed his satisfaction on the smartness of the Drivers and the good turn out in general.

W. Davis C.M. O.C.
124, MACHINE GUN COY.
M.G.C.

2449 Wt. W14957/M90 750,000 1/16 J.B.C. & A. Forms/C.2118/12.

Army Form C. 2118.

WAR DIARY
or
INTELLIGENCE SUMMARY
(Erase heading not required.)

Instructions regarding War Diaries and Intelligence Summaries are contained in F. S. Regs., Part II. and the Staff Manual respectively. Title Pages will be prepared in manuscript.

Place	Date	Hour	Summary of Events and Information						Remarks and references to Appendices
			Operations						
			Officer in charge	Gun Position	Rounds Expended	TARGET		RESULT	REMARKS
	24/25 July 1916	10.45a to 12.30	2/LT. BROWNWRIGG-JAY.	U16.c.9.3.	750	U17d. 4£.5. U23A 4.12 U18A 6.3.		Unknown.	Overhead fire.
		11 pm to 3 am	2/LT. A.W. CARLE.	T11b.	500	Enemy wire between U28a 4.9. & U28a 6.5.		Satisfactory. Z	
		1.30 am	2/LT. A.F.E. PRESCOTT	T1.2.2.	500	U15D 9.4 to U21 B 8£.8.		Unknown	Overhead fire.

8 men from 32nd The Bordirs. } under instruction in machine
6 "   "   "   210¹ K.R.R.R. } Gun aspire Summary closed
                                 23/24th July 1916

W. Davis Capt. O.C.
124. MACHINE GUN COY.
M. G. C.

Army Form C. 2118.

WAR DIARY
or
INTELLIGENCE SUMMARY
(Erase heading not required.)

Instructions regarding War Diaries and Intelligence Summaries are contained in F. S. Regs, Part II. and the Staff Manual respectively. Title Pages will be prepared in manuscript.

Place	Date	Hour	Summary of Events and Information	Remarks and references to Appendices
	25/26 July 16.		Operations:- Officer in charge. Gun Position. Rounds Expended. Target. Result. Remarks	
		10.30pm to 11pm	2/Lt. A.F. PRESCOTT. T.123. 250 Enemy Parapet between U15d 8.6 Unknown. & U15d 9½.2½.	
		11.15pm to 3am	2/LT. A.W.CARLE. T.113. 750 Enemy Wire & parapet from U28a 4.9 & Satisfactory U28a 6.3.-	
			" Gun from Supports 1000 Leyport FARM.U12.d.1.2½ DUMP U28 C.6.7 Unknown Fire. TRENCH.TRAMWAY U28 b.5.5.	
		10.30pm	2/LT. G.BROWNWRIGHT T.124 J.A.Y. Gun did not fire owing to a gun from 122 M.G. Coy. firing all night from that section.	

.................O.C.
124, MACHINE GUN COY.
M. G. C.

WAR DIARY
or
INTELLIGENCE SUMMARY

Army Form C. 2118.

Place	Date	Hour	Summary of Events and Information				Remarks and references to Appendices
			Operations.				
			Officer in charge.	Enemy Position.	Rounds Expended.	Target.	Result.	Remarks
	26/27 July 1916.	10.30pm to 2am	2/Lt. W.C. Vibert.	T.124.	1500	Wiring Party U.15a.8½.6. Party dispersed		Searching & Traversing fire
	"	11pm to 11.30pm	" A.S. Wilson. T.122.		750	U.15a & U.15b.	Enemy Front Line at U.15a.8¼.5	Co-operated with infantry
	"	10.30 to 2am	" A.F. Prescott. T.116.		1000	Traversed Enemy Parapet from U.21A.0.2 to U.21c.3½.9. Traversed Enemy Support Line from U.21A.3½.5½ to U.21c.6½.6½	Unknown	M.S. in Barrage which all (?) were night

Machine Guns co-operated with the infantry in the raid of 26/27 July during the hrs of 11 pm to 11.30 pm. Smoke Bombs were discharged from T.124. T.123. T.122.

Casualty:- Pte. Cole. No.4. Section.

[signed] W. Vibert. Lt. O.C.
124. Machine Gun Coy.
M.G.C.

WAR DIARY or INTELLIGENCE SUMMARY

Army Form C. 2118.

(Erase heading not required.)

Place	Date	Hour	Summary of Events and Information					Remarks and references to Appendices
			Operations.					
			Officer in charge	Gun Position	Rounds Expended	Target	Result	Remarks
	27/28 July 1916	10.30 pm to 12.15 am	2/Lt. W.C. Vibert.	Gun 124.	300	T15b 2.5.0 & Working Party	Unknown	Owing to necessary patrols no more Rounds could be fired
	"	10.30 pm to 2.15 am	2/Lt. H. Rostron	T113.	—	Searched square T15a & T15b for working parties.		Gun could not fire owing to search parties being out in front
	"	10 pm to 11 pm	2/Lt. A.S. Wilson.	T1x3.	500	T Lines all night.		Enemy machine gun emplacements at T15 A.4.5
	"	10 pm to 12 mn	2/Lt. F.M. Singleton.	T14.c.9.t.1.	1000	Indirect Fire from Two J. Meuletons T12.c.1.2 harassed from thatched cottage to Flatiron Farm. T16 a 7t. 7 to T16a 9.1t. Dump at T10 c. 5.6.		Enemy moved his position away from fire

Intelligence Reports from 12 pm 27/7/16 to 6 am 28/7/16

M. Devit, Capt.
O.C. M.G.C.

Army Form C. 2118.

WAR DIARY
or
INTELLIGENCE SUMMARY
(Erase heading not required.)

Instructions regarding War Diaries and Intelligence Summaries are contained in F. S. Regs., Part II. and the Staff Manual respectively. Title Pages will be prepared in manuscript.

Place	Date	Hour	Summary of Events and Information					Remarks and references to Appendices
			Operations					
			Officer in charge	Gun Position	Rounds Expended	Target	Result	Remarks
	28/29 July 1916.	10.15 pm to 2.30 am	2/Lt. H. Rostron.	T.16.	1250	Enemy Ioupes & dugouts at L22.c.3.3 to L22.c.3.7.	Unknown.	Changed every twenty mins.
	"	6 pm to 8.30 am	2/Lt. N.O. Nibert.	T124.		Sun continuous firing to patrols working parties.		
	"	10.30 10.45 11-30 1-30	2/Lt. A.S. Wilson.	T123.	750	Enemy working party. Enemy machine gun at L15-d.2.4.	win Success.	Silenced the machine gun.
	"		"					
	29th July 1916	6 a.m. to 12 noon	The following reliefs & changes in M.G. dispositions took place. 122 M.G. Company took over the following positions:— T124 T122 Lone House Avenue Westminster Avenue Dead Horse Corner New Cheshire Fort					O.O. No. Vide App 8

R.N. Devis. Capt.
124. MACHINE GUN COY.
M. G. C.

2449 Wt. W14957/M90 750,000 1/16 J.B.C. & A. Forms/C.2118/12.

Army Form C. 2118.

WAR DIARY
or
INTELLIGENCE SUMMARY
(Erase heading not required.)

Place	Date	Hour	Summary of Events and Information	Remarks and references to Appendices
	29th Feb 1916		124 M.G. Company took over from 123 M.G. Coy the position at BORDER AVENUE + CHESHIRE AVENUE.	Vide App 8.
			The following interchange took place within the Company	
			Sec 1 landed over Reading Post to Sec 2.	
			Sec 2 " " Fort Bogol to Sec. 1.	
			Sec 3. occupied the other position at Maison 73 thus two making	
			a total of 4 guns in subsidiary line. viz.	
			Gloucester House. 1 gun	
			Oxford Circus. 1 gun	
			Maison 73 2 guns	

L.W.Dent Capt. O.C.
124, MACHINE GUN COY.
M. G. C.

Army Form C. 2118.

WAR DIARY
or
INTELLIGENCE SUMMARY

(Erase heading not required.)

Instructions regarding War Diaries and Intelligence Summaries are contained in F. S. Regs., Part II. and the Staff Manual respectively. Title Pages will be prepared in manuscript.

Place	Date	Hour	Summary of Events and Information	Remarks and references to Appendices
			Operations.	
			Officer in charge. Gun Position. Rounds expended.	
			2/LT. H. ROSTRON. T.16 1000	
			TARGET. RESULT. REMARKS.	
	29/30th July 16.	10.15 p.m. to 2.30 a.m.	Enemy Parapet & Supports from U.22.c.3.3 to U.22.c.3.7. Unknown.	
		10.30 p.m to 12 M.N.	750. Indirect fire at U.22.D.1.3. Loophole form. U.22.D.3.3 & traverse. to U.22.D.5.8. U.22.C.9.2. & Dumps	

W. Davis 2/Lt.
124. MACHINE GUN COY.
M. G. C.

Army Form C. 2118.

WAR DIARY
or
INTELLIGENCE SUMMARY

(Erase heading not required.)

Place	Date	Hour	Summary of Events and Information	Remarks and references to Appendices
			Observation Officer in charge & Gun Position. Rounds expended. TARGET RESULT REMARKS	
	30/31st July 16.	10.30 to 2.30 a.m.	2/Lt. A.W. CARLE T115 750 Enemy wire Parapet & Supports from 27.22.c.3.9 to 27.22.c.4.2. Enemy Working Party cleared out by our fire at 27.22.c.3.6 Satisfactory.	

Company Headquarters & Transport moved from Camp at PAPOT to
(M A.P. REFERENCE. 36 N.W. Edition 6.B BM 2.G).
38 Attached men moved to Bombing School Map Ref 36 N.W. Edition 6.B.
A2.D.6.8. For Instruction under 27th I.A.F Division. F.N. Singleton, A.W. Woolley
Section 4 moved into Billets at Bombing School under 2/Lt. W.C. Ward & S.H. Brockway.   J. 7.

Army Form C. 2118.

WAR DIARY
or
INTELLIGENCE SUMMARY
(Erase heading not required.)

Instructions regarding War Diaries and Intelligence Summaries are contained in F. S. Regs., Part II. and the Staff Manual respectively. Title Pages will be prepared in manuscript.

124th Inf Bgde Machine Gun Coy

Vol 3

Place	Date	Hour	Summary of Events and Information					Remarks and references to Appendices
			Operations.					
			Officer in charge.	Gun Position.	Rounds Expended.	TARGET.	RESULT.	REMARKS
	3/9/16	10.30 pm to 12.15 a	2/LT. A.S. WILSON	T106 Dug Emplacement	500.	Enemy's front line.	Owing to mist, fire could not be observed.	Damage to emplacement is extensive, aurora now repaired. V. wiring 7 Bootiful now employed.
"	1/9/16	10.30 pm to 2.30 a.m	2/LT. A.W. CARLE.	T115.	500.	Enemy's Wire, parapet & supports between U22.c.35 & U22.c.4½.12.	Satisfactory.	
		10.30 pm to 12 m.n		From Stafford Inclined Trie.	1000	Traversed following Targets. PETITE. HAIE Fn U23 Central CROSS RD U24 b 27. DUMP U23.a.93.	Unknown Unknown	

2449 Wt. W14957/M90 750,000 1/16 J.B.C. & A. Forms/C.2118/12.

WAR DIARY
or
INTELLIGENCE SUMMARY

(Erase heading not required.)

Army Form C. 2118.

Place	Date	Hour	Summary of Events and Information			Remarks and references to Appendices
			Operations. Gun Ordering. Rounds expended. TARGET.		RESULTS.	REMARKS
			Officer in charge.			
	1/9/16 to 2/9/16	11pm to 2.30am	2/LT. A.N.CARLE T115 & T116 1000	Enemy Working Party at T22.C.3.6 & 2F 22.C.4.2 Enemy machine Gun at 27.22.C.88.35	Enemy yell was heard. Machine silenced. Gun silenced.	
		12.45 to 1.45am	2/LT. A.S. WILSON Gun Emplacement 300 T10.C.	Enemy front Line & emplacements 28.C.8.82 & T28.d. O.82.		Working party from N.W. Germans on 4 in front 7 Sep E. tool night under 12.30 am

Army Form C. 2118.

WAR DIARY
or
INTELLIGENCE SUMMARY

(Erase heading not required.)

Summary of Events and Information

Place	Date	Hour						
			Operations.					
			Officer in charge.	Gun Position.	Rounds expended.	TARGET.	RESULTS.	REMARKS
	2/3rd Aug 1916	11.30 am to 1 am	2/LT. A.S. WILSON.	Open emplacement T10.6	3500.	Enemy trench line supports U 28. c. 8½. 8½		Observation obtained on enemy's wire.
	"	11.30 pm to 2.30 am	2/LT. A.W. CARLE.	T11.5.	1500	Enemy wire & trench parapet from U 22. c. 4. 1½. to U 22. 0. 3. 5. Intersect. fire at Dun P. U 22. c. 8. 7½. Trench Tramway from U 22. c. 8. 7½ to U 22. c. 5. 4. Dump U 28. b. 5. 5.	Satisfactory.	Trial bursts at short intervals. Enemy artillery very active.
		10 pm to 11.45		Support.				

WAR DIARY
or
INTELLIGENCE SUMMARY

(Erase heading not required.)

Army Form C. 2118.

Place	Date	Hour	Observations Officer in charge.	Gun Position	Rounds Expended	Target.	Results.	Remarks.
	3/4 Aug 1916.	12.45 am to 10.	2/Lt. A.S. Wilson.	T106.	500	Enemy Front Line.		Observation obtained on enemy wire.
		2am to 10.45 to 12.15am		L.27.c 6.4. 3.4.	750.	Bridge at U.29.d. 7.2.3.4. Bridge at U.29.b. 6.3. Pont-Rouge U.29. 6.2.7. Cross. Rds.		Telephone communications twice been interfered between T106 (4th Artillery) T105 Observation Gun Emplacement.
		2am to 3am	2/Lt. A.W. Carle	T116.	500	Enemy wire opposite from L.22.C.32.6 to Schafsberg. L.22.C.35.		

Army Form C. 2118.

WAR DIARY
or
INTELLIGENCE SUMMARY
(Erase heading not required.)

Instructions regarding War Diaries and Intelligence Summaries are contained in F. S. Regs., Part II. and the Staff Manual respectively. Title Pages will be prepared in manuscript.

Place	Date	Hour	Summary of Events and Information					Remarks and references to Appendices
			Operations					
			Officer in charge.	Gun Position.	Rounds expended.	TARGET.	RESULTS. REMARKS.	
	4/5th Aug 15/16	12.15 a to 1.30 a.	2/LT. A. S. WILSON	T.106.	500	Enemy's Front Supports Trs.	Satisfactory. Scratch sunk of this attached.	
		12.30 a to 2.30 a.	2/LT. A. W. CARLE.	T.115 & T.116	500.	Enemy Ramparts from U.22.d. 2.1 to U.22.c. 3.3		
				Support Lie Indirect Firs.	1000	CROSS-RDS at PONT-ROUGE U.29.b.2.7. Traverses from PONT ROUGE to PETITE. HAIE. Fm. U.23.Central HALT. U.23.a.8.9t.	Unknown.	

Further progress has been made in re Vicinity of Electric Avenue. The trench running in Border Avenue has been retired and improved. Steps have been placed on the mounting. The steps on the trench mounting in Electric Avenue emplacement have also been retired and adjusted accurately. A new & accurate range-card has been made for Electric Avenue and the other Range cards are being made out afresh as they were inaccurate.
Section 4 will return to the trenches on the 5th August 1916 and will take over from Section 1 Gun position at FORT.EVEREST (1). REDDING. FORT (2) STI16 (1). Section 4 will arrive at FORT. EVEREST by 3.30 p.m. 4 Lenders will arrive at the Bombing School at 1 p.m.; 2/Lt Valiel & Bank will make mutually detailed arrangements. Tripods & field Boxes need not be exchanged. On completion of relief Section 4 will proceed to the Bombing School. Rations if required relieving party. i.e the unexpended portion of the days Rations will be carried by all ranks.

Relief Order No. 1.

2449 Wt. W14957/M90 750,000 1/16 J.B.C. & A. Forms/C.2118/12.

Army Form C. 2118.

WAR DIARY
or
INTELLIGENCE SUMMARY.
(Erase heading not required.)

Instructions regarding War Diaries and Intelligence Summaries are contained in F.S. Regs., Part II. and the Staff Manual respectively. Title pages will be prepared in manuscript.

Place	Date	Hour	Summary of Events and Information					Remarks and references to Appendices
			Operations. Officer in charge.	Enemy Position.	Rounds Expended.	Target.	Result. Remarks.	
	August 1916							
	5/6/16	12pm to 2am	2/Lt. W.C. VIBERT.	116.	500.	Enemy Parapet at U.22.c.3¾.4.	Unknown.	
						U.22.d.1.3 (LOOPHOLE FARM)		
	"	10.55pm to 12.10am	2/Lt. A.S. WILSON.	U.27.c.6¾.5¼.	750.	BRIDGE at U.29.6.7¼.3½.	Located.	
						BRIDGE at U.29.b.6.3.	Unknown. Fire.	
						BROKEN CHY U.29.d.9.8.		

New wire boards have been placed in Border Avenue, Cheshire Avenue & T.106.
A tank emplacement has been constructed in R.T.10.5. L.T.10.4.
V wing of Cheshire Avenue continues.
Wooden platforms are being constructed wrecked in the new emplacements.
No casualties.

Army Form C. 2118.

WAR DIARY
or
INTELLIGENCE SUMMARY.
(Erase heading not required.)

Instructions regarding War Diaries and Intelligence Summaries are contained in F. S. Regs., Part II. and the Staff Manual respectively. Title pages will be prepared in manuscript.

Place	Date	Hour	Summary of Events and Information	Remarks and references to Appendices
	Augt. 1916		Operations: Officer in charge. Gun Position. Rounds expended. Target. Result. REMARKS	
	6th to 7th	6pm 6/8/16 to 6pm 7/8/16 August 1916	2/LT. A.S. WILSON T106 — — Owing to extensive infantry patrols the Machine Gun was unable to fire upon the enemy's wire. Work was accordingly done upon emplacements	
			Casualties Nil. Total strength of No2 Section in Line. 1 Officer & 22 other Ranks.	
	"		2/LT. W.C. HÜBERT. 116. Indirect fire. 250. Indirect fire owing to wiring parties	
			" 250. LOOPHOLE FARM. U.22.d.12½. Unknown.	
			" 250. Search to top of G.T. at U.23.a.5½.1.	
			" DUMP at U.28.b.6.7.	
			Strength 2 Officers. 21 NCO's & men.	

WAR DIARY
or
INTELLIGENCE SUMMARY.
(Erase heading not required.)

Army Form C. 2118.

Place	Date	Hour	Summary of Events and Information				Remarks and references to Appendices
				TARGET.	RESULT.	REMARKS	
	7th to 8th August 1916	10pm to 1.45am	Operations. Officer in charge. Evan Perkins. Rounds Expended. 2/Lt. W.C. VIBERT. 116.	750.	Enemy Trench Parapet from U.22.a.3.d. to U.22.c.3.4.5. also at TROIS TILLEULS FARM (U.17.c.12)		
		3am to 3.20am	Strength of Section 1 Officer 2 NCOs 7 men. 2/Lt. A.S. WILSON. "T705" Boxenflammerwerfer.	250.	Enemy Support Line at U.28.a.0.8½.		
		10.55pm to 12.10am	U.27.b.2.2½. Inclined Fire.	500.	C.T. from U.23.c.2.8 to U.23.a.7.3. & C.T. from U.23.c.6.8. 9/4/6 to 23.a.9.1.	Unknown. Indirect Fire.	
			Strength of Section in Line 1 Officer & 22 Other Ranks. 2/Lt. E.W. Browning-Jay & No. 114426 Cpl. T. Briaris proceeded to Divisional Gas School Steenwerke at 5pm for a Course in Anti-Gas measures				

WAR DIARY
or
INTELLIGENCE SUMMARY.

(Erase heading not required.)

Army Form C. 2118.

Place	Date	Hour	Summary of Events and Information				Remarks and references to Appendices
			Operations Officer in charge.	Gun Position. Rounds Expended.	TARGET	RESULT	REMARKS
	8th to 9th Aug. 14/16	9.45 pm to 10.30 pm	2/LT. W.C. VIBERT.	S.T.116. 350.	Enemy Rampart. U22c.3.6. aloof. U22d.1.3.(LOOP-HOLE FARM).		Fire caused. various potato's moving karis.
	11	11.45 pm to 12.30 am	2/LT. A.S. WILSON.	✱ T108	Enemy front line U28a.1½.2½ to U28a.7.3½	Enemy	Veryggod observation was obtained
		1 am to 3.45 am	"	✱ T106 1200.	Enemy front Lis.	harassed enemy bridging the Rampart.	

✱ Above gun cooperated with M.gun J.12 4 T.M.B. in firing on enemy's front line
Enemy retaliated with machine gunfire.
Strength J 2/Lt A.S. WILSON's section in line 1 Officer & 22 other ranks.

Army Form C. 2118.

WAR DIARY
or
INTELLIGENCE SUMMARY.
(Erase heading not required.)

Instructions regarding War Diaries and Intelligence Summaries are contained in F.S. Regs., Part II. and the Staff Manual respectively. Title pages will be prepared in manuscript.

Place	Date	Hour	Summary of Events and Information	Remarks and references to Appendices
			Operations.	
			Officer in charge. Gun Position. Rounds Expended. TARGET. RESULT. REMARKS.	
	9 & 10 Aug. 1916.	11-m to 11.30 am	2/Lt. A.S. WILSON. T.106. Working Party at 27.8.c.88. Part dispersed.	
		10 am to 11.30 am	" T.106. Working Party at 27.8.c.88.	
		1 am to 1.30 am	" T.106 750 Enemy's parapet from 27.8.c.88 to 27.8.c.6.9. Observation obstructed in enemy's wire.	
		11.20 pm to 12.57 pm	" 27.26.2.&.2. 750. GRAND HAIE FARM. 27.23.6.±.7.2. ROAD from 27.17.6.9.0. to 27.17.a.2.3. Unknown. Probable hit.	
			Section officer reports a hostile working party was observed behind the enemy's wires by our 7 m^ howr in T.106 Metres. It was impossible to get fire to bear on them from any of our positions. He informed the M.G. officer of 7/13 M.G. Co. who might otherwise observe enabled to open very effective fire with great success. Time 9-1.5^m	
		11-10 pm to 1-10 am	2/Lt. W.C. VIBERT. S.T.116. 500. Enemy Working Party at 27.22.c.3.5. Party dispersed.	
			Listened Posts on:— TROISTILLE · VIJSFARM. (1) PONT · ROUGE. V.26. B.23. " " Traversed & Searched. (2) V.26.6. (3) PETIT·HAIE FARM V.23 central.	

Army Form C. 2118.

WAR DIARY
or
INTELLIGENCE SUMMARY.
(Erase heading not required.)

Instructions regarding War Diaries and Intelligence Summaries are contained in F. S. Regs., Part II. and the Staff Manual respectively. Title pages will be prepared in manuscript.

Place	Date	Hour	Summary of Events and Information				Remarks and references to Appendices
			Operations.				
			Officer in charge.	Rounds Expended.	TARGET.	RESULT. REMARKS.	
	10th to 11th Aug. 1916.	12.30 am to 4.35 am	2/Lt. W.G. VIBERT.	S.T. 116. 750	Enemy Parapet U.22.d.3.4. O.t.6 U.22.c.3.4. Also at LOOPHOLE FARM U.22.d.1.3.	Unknown	
		2am to 4am		Indirect Fire	C.T. at U.22.d.3½. DUNP at U.22.d.5.6 DUN P at U.22.E.6.6.7 LOOP. HOLE FARM. U.22.d.12½.	Unknown. Indirect Fire.	
	"	1.30 am to 1 am	2/Lt. A.S. WILSON.	T.106. 750	Enemy Working Party at : Parker. U.28.a.7.2.		
	"	1.30 am to 2.30 am			Working Party at U.28.a.4.7.	destroyed "	

Another French mounting has been erected in concrete emplacement in T106 for the left loophole.

Army Form C. 2118.

WAR DIARY
or
INTELLIGENCE SUMMARY.
(Erase heading not required.)

Place	Date	Hour	Summary of Events and Information					Remarks and references to Appendices
			Operations	Officer in charge	Gun Position	Rounds Expended	Target	Result	Remarks
	11th to 12th August 1916	10.45 am to 12.40 am		2/Lt A.S. Wilson	U.27.c.2.2.	1000.	GRANDE·HAIE·FARM. U.23.6.2.7½. ROAD. FROM. U.17.a.6.9.0 to. U.17.a.2.5. ROAD. TO. TROIS. TILLEULS FARM. U.17.c.4.0 to U.17.c.3.2.	Unknown	Indirect Fire " " "
		9.57 to 11.55 pm		"	U.27.a.3.7½	1000.	CROSSRDS nr BROKEN CHIMNEY U.30.c.1½.7½. BRIDGE U.24.6.7½.3½. U.25.d.6.5. PONT. ROUGE from U.25.6.2.6½ to U.29.6.6.3½.	Unknown	Indirect Fire
		12.50 am to 2.10 am		"	T.106.	750.	Enemy Working Party. A.R. U.28.a.8.1.	Unable to verify no results observed	
			2/Lt S.H. Browning Jnr. returned 2/Lt N. Roxton in Subsidiary Line. Section 1 returned to the hands Stock one gun from Section 2 the position at T106. CHESHIRE. AVE. BORDER. AVE. Section 1 Took 4 guns with them. Section 1 Arrived at BORDER·AVE at 3.30pm. + relief completed by 3.30pm. 2/LT A.W. CARLE relieved 2/Lt. A.S. WILSON 2/LT. A.S. WILSON + Section 2 proceeded to BOMBIN & School into Billets referring Section 1.						Relief Order No. 2.

Army Form C. 2118.

WAR DIARY
or
INTELLIGENCE SUMMARY.
(Erase heading not required.)

Instructions regarding War Diaries and Intelligence Summaries are contained in F. S. Regs., Part II. and the Staff Manual respectively. Title pages will be prepared in manuscript.

Place	Date	Hour	Summary of Events and Information				Remarks and references to Appendices
			OPERATIONS.		TARGET.	RESULT. REMARKS	
			Officer in charge	Gun Position. Rounds Expended			
			2/LT. W.C. VIBERT.	S.T.16 500	Enemy Parapet from L22a.3.0 to L22c.5.0 about LOOPHOLE FARM L22d.12½	Unknown. Firing Fair.	
	11th to 12th August 1916	9.30 to 1am					
			Strength 1 Officer & 2 I.N.C.Os & Men.				

T.2134. Wt. W708—776. 500000. 4/15. Sir J. C. & S.

Army Form C. 2118.

WAR DIARY
or
INTELLIGENCE SUMMARY.
(Erase heading not required.)

Instructions regarding War Diaries and Intelligence Summaries are contained in F. S. Regs., Part II. and the Staff Manual respectively. Title pages will be prepared in manuscript.

Place	Date	Hour	Summary of Events and Information	Remarks and references to Appendices

Operations.

			Officer in Charge.	Gun Position	Rounds Expended.	TARGET.	RESULT: REMARKS
	12 N to 13 N August 1916.	9.30 pm	2/LT. A.W. CARLE.	T106	750.	Enemy Machine Gun situated at T.28.a.7.2 T.28.c.8.6	Success, Gun silenced
	"	9.30 to 10.10	2/LT. W.G. VIBERT.	ST116		Traverse enemy parapet from V.22.a.30 to V.22.c.50 about TROIS TILLEULS FARM V.17.c.1.2.	Unknown.

T2134. Wt. W708—776. 500000. 4/15. Sir J. C. & S.

Army Form C. 2118.

WAR DIARY
or
INTELLIGENCE SUMMARY.
(Erase heading not required.)

Place	Date	Hour	Summary of Events and Information					Remarks and references to Appendices
			Operations.					
			Officer in charge.	Gun Position. Rounds & expended.	TARGET.	RESULT.	REMARKS.	
	13th to 14th August 1916.	9.30 pm to 1.30 am	2/LT W.C VIBERT.	ST.116.	500	Enemy Parapet. from V.22.a.3.0.b. V.22.c.5.0.a.b.c.d LOOPHOLE FARM V.22.a.1.3.	Unknown	Harassed Enemy Parapet
	"	10 pm to 12 MN	2/LT. J. TROWNWRIGHT JAY.	V.26.d.4.7.L MAISON.787s.	750	28.b.6.7; V.29.c.S7.9. V.22.a.1.3.	Unknown	Overhead Fire.
		9.30 pm to 1 am	2/LT. A.W.CARLE	T.106.	750.	Enemy Machine Gun. Salisbury. V.28.a.7.2 from prompts ravine between V.28.a.7.1.1 + V.28.c.6.6.		

1 MULE No.2 evacuated to MOBILE COLUMN

Army Form C. 2118.

WAR DIARY
or
INTELLIGENCE SUMMARY.
(Erase heading not required.)

Instructions regarding War Diaries and Intelligence Summaries are contained in F. S. Regs., Part II. and the Staff Manual respectively. Title pages will be prepared in manuscript.

Place	Date	Hour	Summary of Events and Information					Remarks and references to Appendices
			Operations.					
			Officer in charge.	Gun Position.	Rounds Expended.	TARGET.	RESULT. REMARKS.	
	14th to 15th August 1916.	9.30 a.m to 1.30 a.m	2/Lt. W.G.VIBERT.	S.T.116	1000	Enemy Chapel & trench. Enemy from V.22.a.30 to V wiring party 22a.5.0 also fired at dispersed. LOOPHOLE FARM at V.22.d.1.3.		
	"	12 pm to 1.30 am	2/Lt. A.W.EARLE	T.106	250.	Enemy Machine Gun Gun located at V.28.h.7.6.6. silenced		
	"	10.15 am to 11.45 pm	2/Lt. J.R.-Jay.	V.26d.H.7.2.	500.	V.28.c.6.7. V.22d.13. Unknown.		
			The Staff personnel of Section 2 left the Bombing School at 6 pm on the 14th Aug 16 and returned to Billets at Transfeld Line (B.16.c.25). Instruction was carried on at the Transfeld Line on the 15th Aug 1916 at 9 am. The Bombing School closed on Monday evening the 14/8/16.					Relief Order No.3.

W Jones
Capt.

T.2134. Wt. W708—776. 500000. 4/15. Sir J.C. & S.

WAR DIARY or INTELLIGENCE SUMMARY

Army Form C. 2118.

Place	Date	Hour	Summary of Events and Information	Remarks and references to Appendices
Morcehnio	15/16 Aug 1916.	10 pm	Officer in charge: Gnr. Nevilini. Rounds Expended. TARGET. RESULT. REMARKS. Gun at T106 without fire owing to barrels hog out.	
			2/Lt. A.W. CARLE T106	
	"	11.45 pm	No 1 Section was relieved by No 1 Section of 70 M.G.Coy at 6 am on the 16th. 2/Lt. B. JAY. 500. 17260¼75. Inland fire. No 3 Section was relieved by No 3 Section of 70 M.G.Coy at 6 am on the 16th. v728¢.6.7.v.22.d.5.t. Whrown.	Relief orders No. 4
			No 70 M.G.Coy will relieve 104 M.G.Coy over the Trenches however Tuesday the 14th Aug 1916. Relief will commence at 5.30am. 1 Guide from each of the following positions will lead the end of the STRAND at 5.30am. FORT EVEREST: READING FORT: GLOSTER HOUSE: OXFORD CIRCUS. 1 Guide from each of the following positions will lead Nailhead of HIGHLAND RLY. at Same hour. MAISON. 1875: CHESHIRE AVE: BORDER. AVE. T106. Two lists of french Stores that are to be handed over will be prepared and signed by outgoing & incoming Section commanders. the other will be left with incoming Section Commander. outgoing Section Commanders Thomas will be left with incoming Section Commander on completion of relief Sections will return to Billets at M.C.25. & Limbers will be at the Strand Dump to remove at 7.30 am & 2 A.M.M.Highland RLY. at Same Time.	WM. G. "H" Capt.

Army Form C. 2118.

WAR DIARY
or
INTELLIGENCE SUMMARY.
(Erase heading not required.)

Place	Date	Hour	Summary of Events and Information				Remarks and references to Appendices
			OPERATIONS.				
			Officer in chge.	Gun Position.	Rounds Expended.		
			2/Lt. W.G. VIBERT	S.T. 116.	500		
			TARGET.	RESULT.	REMARKS.		
	15/16 August 1916	9.30 to 12.30	Enemy trenches from 25.20.3.0 to 25.26.50.	Unknown.	General harassing.		

Army Form C. 2118.

Instructions regarding War Diaries and Intelligence Summaries are contained in F. S. Regs., Part II. and the Staff Manual respectively. Title pages will be prepared in manuscript.

WAR DIARY
or
INTELLIGENCE SUMMARY.
(Erase heading not required.)

Place	Date	Hour	Summary of Events and Information	Remarks and references to Appendices
		10 a.m. to 17th Aug 1916.	7am	The 124th M.G. Coy. will parade at 7am and march to F.12.a.6.5 by the following route: B.1.6.2.5.: STEENWERK. STN. A.11.D.5.5.: A.10.a.08. CABARET DU SAULE. A.8.a.5.4. - F.12.a.6.5. (Sheet 36)	
	23rd Aug.	9.20 a.m.	The Company Billeted at F.12.a.6.5. Entrained at BAILLEUL WEST. STN.	
	"	10 p.m.	Arrived at PONT REMY (Nr. ABBERVILLE)	
	24th August 1916.	4 am	Went into Billets at MONTFLIERS in 4TH. Divisional Training area.	
	25th to 31st		Training carried on.	

Secret

Relief No 1. df 5/8/16

Section 4 will return to the trenches on Saturday the 5th August 1916 and will take over from Section 1 Gun positions at
FORT. EVEREST ②
REDDING FORT ⓑ
ST. 116 ①

Section 4 will arrive at FORT EVEREST by 3:30 pm.

4 Limbers will arrive at the Bombing School at 1 pm.

2/Lts Vibert & Carr will make mutually detailed arrangements.

Tripods & Belt Boxes need not be exchanged.

On completion of Relief Section 4 will proceed to the Bombing School.

Rations of relieved & relieving parties i.e. the unexpended portion of days rations will be carried by all ranks.

M Schonfeld Lt
14 ... Coy

Secret

Relief No 2. Ap. 10/8/16
─────────────────────────

Section 1 will return to the
trenches on Saturday the
12th August 1916 & will take
over from Section 2 the positions
at T.106, Cheshire Avenue
& Border Avenue. Section 1 will
take their Lewis gun with them.
Section 1 will arrive at
BORDER AVENUE by 3.30 p.m. &
relief will proceed forthwith.
On completion section 2 will
proceed to Bombing School.
2/Lt A.N. Gale will proceed to
the trenches on Saturday morning
& return will arriving at the RITZ at
11 a.m. to settle verbal
arrangement with 2/Lt H.B. Jones
for details of relief.

Lispods & Mill Bombs will not be
exchanged.

Your Lewis gun will arrive at the
Bombing School at 4 p.m.

The independent posts of the boys
salient will be relieved by the allotted
relieving parties.

A.W. Winfield Thomas
2/Lt 9th R.W.F.

Relief No 3 d/ 14/8/16

1. The 9inch Heavy Bell Trench mortar Working & machine Gun School will close on Monday evening the 14/8/16.

2. [blank], The staff, personnel, and Section 2 will leave the Bombing School at 6pm on the 14/8/16 and proceed to the Transport Lines (pt of Ref B1 6 c.a.b.).

3. Limbers will be at the School at 6pm to convey Officers Kits, Sivar, Bed Boxes, etc. C.S. to Transport Lines.

4. You will please inform O/C No 2 Section.

5. Instructions will be carried on at the Transport Lines at 9am on the 15/8/16.

6. The Returns will be sent to the School to-day.

7. No men will be left behind unless you think it necessary to contribute to the guard which is left behind.

8. You will hand to the Adjutant on arrival at Transport Lines a Marching in State.

A W Schonfeld Lt Adjt
161 M. G. Coy

<u>Secret</u>

<u>Relief Order No 4 of 15/8/16</u>

[Stamp: 124 MACHINE GUN COY. MACHINE GUN CORPS.]

① 70 M.G. Coy will relieve 124 M.G. Coy in the Trenches tomorrow Tuesday the 16th inst.

② Relief will commence at 5.30 am

③ 1 Guide from each of the following positions will be at the exit of the Strand at 5-30 am
   FORT EVEREST
   ST. 116
   READING. FORT
   GLOSTER. HOUSE
   OXFORD. CIRCUS.

1 Guide from each of the following positions will be at railhead of HIGHLAN. R<u>l</u>y at the same hour.
   MAISON. 75.
   CHESHIRE-AVE
   BORDER. AVE.
   T. 106.

④ O/C Sections will arrange for trolleys to be at the railheads.

⑤ Two lists of Trench Stores that are to be handed over will be prepared & signed by outgoing & incoming Section commanders, the other will be left

— 2 —

one will be retained by outgoing Section Commander, the other will be left with incoming Section Commander.

⑥ All emplacements and dug outs will be handed over in a clean & tidy condition.

⑦ On completion of relief. Sections will return to Billets at B.1.c.2.5.

⑧ Completion of relief will be notified to O/C Coy by Section Officers on arrival at billets at same time copies of Trench Stores transferred will be handed to the Adjutant

⑨ 4 Limbers will be at the Strand Dump tomorrow at 7.30 am and 2 at the Highland Rly at the same time

M Schonfeld Lt. Adjt
124 M. G. Coy.

Coy Hdqrs.
15. 8. 16.
6.30 pm

WAR DIARY or INTELLIGENCE SUMMARY

Army Form C. 2118.

Vol 4

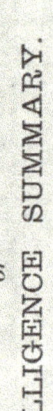

Place	Date	Hour	Summary of Events and Information	Remarks and references to Appendices
	1st to 9th Sept 1916		Training in attack in ABBEVILLE – MONFLIERS area. Section attached to Battalions as follows:— Section 1 = 21st K.R.R.C. " 2 = 26th Bn R.F. " 3 = 10th Queens. " 4 = 32nd R.F.	
	9th Sept		Entrained at LONGPRÉ-LES-CORPS-SAINS (Abbeville 100,000 6L) Detrained at MÉRICOURT, marched to RIVIONAC (Map Ref sheet 62 O 40,000 E m D 8.6.	
	10th Sept		Moved to camp at E12A. Sheet 62D 40,000	
	11th		4 Company In Command visited trenches with Brigade Staff & Bn Units	
	12th to 13th		Company Training at E12A & preparing for Line	
	15th		Operations of 15th, 16th, 17th Sept 1916 (French maps 24000 57c S.W.)	

Army Form C. 2118.

WAR DIARY
or
INTELLIGENCE SUMMARY.
(Erase heading not required.)

Instructions regarding War Diaries and Intelligence Summaries are contained in F. S. Regs., Part II. and the Staff Manual respectively. Title pages will be prepared in manuscript.

Place	Date	Hour	Summary of Events and Information	Remarks and references to Appendices
	13/9/16		The Company took part in operations of above date on front extending from line HARE LANE—FLERS-LONGUEVAL RD. to Line of 41st Divisional Boundary S22D central — S12 D 8:0. This being no front allotted to 124th Infantry Bde. Sect. 2 left Camp at E.Bc. Sheet 62D 40,000 & took over 3 gun positions from 123 Bde M.G. Coy. 2 in INNER TRENCH & 1 in Strong point in front line. Coy transport proceeded to camp at F26 (m.r. of above) Sect 4 left Camp as above, bivouaced on night of 13/14th MONTAUBAN.	
		14h	Sect 1, 3 & 4 proceeded to Trenches & All sections joined up with Infantry units to which they were attached for operations, see following sheet.	

Trench Strength of Company = 4 Officers + 131 Other Ranks

WAR DIARY or INTELLIGENCE SUMMARY

Army Form C. 2118.

Place	Date	Hour	Summary of Events and Information	Remarks and references to Appendices
In the Field	15th Sept 1916		The 4 Sections of the Company were detailed to cooperate with Infantry Units	Batteries
			Sect 1 with 21st K.R.R. (Left Centre Batt.) O/C Section: 2/Lt A W Earle	See Appendices I & 2
			" 2 " 26th R.F. (Left supporting Batt.) " : 2/Lt G.H. B-Jay	
			" 3 " 10th Zealand (Right Leading Batt.) " : F.N. Singleton	Were firing
	16th		" 4 " 32nd R.F. (Right supporting Batt.) " : W.C. Vizent.	9 trench from 12am 9.15th
	17th		and were moved the command of the respective O.C. Battalions.	D.O. No 6.
			O.C. Sect 1. (2/Lt A.W Earle) reports as follows:-	
			The Section under my command crossed the parapet at 6.20am on the 15th	
			inst. and proceeded towards the first objective. On arriving there I	
			received instructions from O/c 21st K.R.R. not to advance further until	
			strong emplacements had been constructed. These were completed about	
			9am. I then moved my guns up to 2nd objective where 3 emplacements	
			were similarly constructed. At this point FLERS TRENCH. I took	
			command of an additional gun from Section 3 and 3 men belonging	
			to 122 M.G.C.	
			As no information came through from our Infantry in front, I left	

M H Denis
Capt.

WAR DIARY or INTELLIGENCE SUMMARY

Army Form C. 2118.

(2)

2 guns to defend 2nd objective & at moved one gun forward to a NE of FLERS near two trees (approx map reference Sheet 57c. S.W. 1/20,000 B1 central) this gun retired twice with Infantry. About 6 p.m. 2 guns ordered by G.O.C. 124th Brigade to take up two guns N of FLERS VILLAGE. I disposed these guns in shell holes about 30 yds apart — both guns 7" fire outwards — the left covering ground N of FLERS the right covering our right front. No enemy target presented itself. About 3 a.m. on the 16th inst. thought took new guns about 500 yds and built emplacements for them in a trench which was in process of being dug. I then proceeded back to FLERS Zone to bring to gun retired that left there (Serjt's gun) but this gun was not performing. In a heavy bombardment on Saturday morning the 16th inst my left gun was knocked of action by a shell which killed the gunner and wounded the Serjeant in charge. We remained in this position until 4 p.m. of the 16th. At this hour guns from 123 M.G. Coy arrived & took over the Section. On the return journey 1 man was killed & th support which he carried blown up. Casualties in this Section 2 killed & 6 wounded.

WDColl
Capt

WAR DIARY
or
INTELLIGENCE SUMMARY.

Army Form C. 2118.

(3)

Ofc Section 2 (2/Lt E.H. Browning's Say) were nominated within 5 minutes of the commencement of the engagement. The Section Sergeant reports arrivement. "The Section under the command of 2/Lt E.H. Browning's Say attacked itself to 26th Royal Fusiliers in front and moved to parapet with the leading wave of this Battalion. Before reaching the first objective 2/Lt Gay was wounded. Both guns were carried by the gun teams forward to Switch trench. There were a good number of actual Germans in this trench. Moving forward with the Infantry FLERS TRENCH was reached. The guns were mounted in a C.T. running Northwards + facing E of FLERS in order to protect our line in case of Counter attack. At 6am on the 16th inst having shot off 26 R.F. had been relieved and machine guns of 123rd Infantry Brigade arriving, the Section was withdrawn. Casualties in this Section = 1 Officer wounded 2/Lt Browning's Gay

1 O.R. Killed
3 O.Rs Wounded.

WAR DIARY
or
INTELLIGENCE SUMMARY.
(Erase heading not required.)

Army Form C. 2118.

Place	Date	Hour	Summary of Events and Information	Remarks and references to Appendices
			(4) O/C Section 3 (2/Lt F.N. SINGLETON) reported as follows:- The Section under my command moved up at 6.30 am with 2 guns. On arrival at the first objective, a strong sandbagged emplacement was built. One gun was sent forward under the Section Sergeant. I was unable to find this gun and Team afternoon but after the action, I teamed the 2/Lt A.N. Earle (commanding Section 1) found them & took them under his command. He team and my command remained in occupation of strong point in Switch Trench, receiving the information of 2/Lt Earle the Section Sergeant moved his gun forward to a point N. of FLERS. The Sergeant contested look gave through shell shock. The Lance Corporal in charge withdrew his team when infantry returned & took up position in Sunken road E of FLERS at about 2-30 pm on the 15th inst. In the evening the gun was withdrawn to FLERS Trench where 2 emplacements were built. At 6 am on the 16th inst on arrival of M. guns of 123rd Brigade the gunners left the trenches. Casualties 3 wounded.	(sd) ov Capt

WAR DIARY or INTELLIGENCE SUMMARY.

Army Form C. 2118.

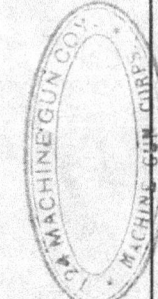

Place	Date	Hour	Summary of Events and Information	Remarks and references to Appendices
	17/9/16 to 30/9/16		O/c No 4 Section (2/Lt W.C. VIBERT) was wounded early in the engagement & 3 of the N.C.Os in command of the guns were killed or wounded. It is difficult therefore to obtain a clear account of what happened. From information gathered from representatives of the 4 teams engaged I find that the Section joined up with the that to which it was attached in Front Trench & crossed the parapet about 6.30 a.m. on the 16th inst. The teams arrived at SWITCH TRENCH & the remaining one at FLERS - TRENCH. The Section was unable to proceed further owing to heavy casualties. Casualties: 1 Officer Wounded (2/Lt VIBERT.M.C.) 4 O.R's Killed 13 O.Rs Wounded The Company proceeded to Bivouacs at [Mont. Rel. Chart 62.D 1/40,000. 14 & E.6.] to reorganise & carry out further training.	

Lintons
Capt

Total casualties during operations 15th 16th & 17th September 1916.

KILLED	WOUNDED	MISSING
Officers O.Rs	Officers O.Rs	Officers O.Rs
Nil. 7.	2. 28.	Nil —

Total reinforcements received during month.

Date	O.R
8/9/16	1
9/9/16	1
15/9/16	3
18/9/16	2
19/9/16	3
20/9/16	34 + 2 Officers

30/9/16 Total strength of Company
10 Officers 1st O.R and ranks including 36 attached men from Infantry Units.

Appendix I.

"124th Machine Gun Coy. will be disposed of as under:—

Section 1 at disposal of O.C. 21st Bn. K.R.R.Corps
Section 3 "   "   " O.C. 10th Bn. "Queens"
Section 4 attached to   26th Bn. R. Fusiliers
Section 2. Two guns in INNER TRENCH for overhead fire.
           Two guns attached to 32nd Bn. R.Fus.

Appendix II

Strong Points will be constructed as under with assistance of R.E.

(a) By 32nd Bn R. Fusiliers
of trenches T 7 a 2.6
T 1 c 95.25
N 26 a 5.8

(b) By 26th Bn R. Fusiliers
S 6 d 72.67
T 1 a 2.5
N 31 b 19.50
N 26 a 5.8

— — — — — O.C. 26th Bn R. Fusiliers will detail 1 Vickers from No 4 Section 124th M.G. Coy. to each of his strong points.
O.C. 32nd R. Fusiliers will detail — — — 1 Vickers Gun from No 2 Section 124 M.G. Coy to T 1 C 95.25 & N 31 b 5.3.
If Vickers Guns are not available Lewis Guns will be detailed.

Army Form C. 2118.

Vol 5

WAR DIARY
or
INTELLIGENCE SUMMARY.
(Erase heading not required.)

Instructions regarding War Diaries and Intelligence Summaries are contained in F.S. Regs., Part II. and the Staff Manual respectively. Title pages will be prepared in manuscript.

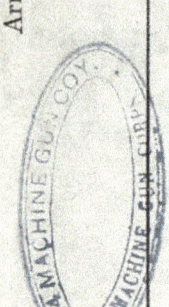

Place	Date	Hour	Summary of Events and Information	Remarks and references to Appendices
In the Field	1.10.16		124th M.G. Company in Bivouac at hop Reference Sheet 62D/N.W.0 14.D.8.6.	
	2.10.16		Company proceeded to Bivouac near Brauner Keuplt arriving at 8 p.m.	Reference Trenches
	3.10.16		Carried out factory. Shoot reported at met with no success. Company proceeded to find took over the following gun positions in support trenches of the 18th Brigade. N. Zealand Sap. Flers Trench (2 guns) Col Trench (4 guns) Sea Lane (2 guns) for anti aircraft work. (8 guns) remaining in reserve at Turtle Lump.	62C.S.W. 150. 59.
	4.10.16		Gp. G.H. attempted proceeded to England to U.P.A. Leave for 9 days. Second half of above Platoons and nothing to report.	
	5.10.16		124th Company relieved 122nd Inf. Brigade in the sub sector of front line from Langny - Tolly - Flers road to Gued Trench at point T.14.M24 as above and the Gued Trench and two Vickers guns taking over positions two in Gued Trench and two near Factory Farm and 130.60.	Map Ref: as above
	6.10.16		B.H.S. 14 Vickers guns attached to 8rds 26th and 32nd Royal Fusiliers under command of Lt. A. Wilson and 2nd Lt. C.B. Woodley and forwarded.	

John Lowery Lieut. For O.C. 124 M.G. Coy.

Army Form C. 2118.

WAR DIARY
or
INTELLIGENCE SUMMARY.
(Erase heading not required.)

Instructions regarding War Diaries and Intelligence Summaries are contained in F. S. Regs., Part II. and the Staff Manual respectively. Title pages will be prepared in manuscript.

Place	Date	Hour	Summary of Events and Information	Remarks and references to Appendices
	6-10-16		with respect to units to assembly reached in the evening the remaining guns of the company were disposed of as follows. 2 Guns under 2nd Lt. A.F.L. Moseli to Tenth Lane for the purpose of indirect fire. 1 Gun in reserve in Fat Alley. 1 Gun for Anti Aircraft work in Fla Trench. 2 Guns in Black Watch Trench. During night of the 6th and 7th ground behind enemy line in neighbourhood of Le-Bargue Longny - Hilly searched by indirect fire 1000 rounds expended. Company of 32nd moved from Black Watch Trench to Tenth Lane near junction with Gird Trench.	Map Ref. 57c.S.W.
	7/10/16		Operations detailed in B.O. no 60 and 61 and warning Order no. 104 carried out. 11 reserve guns moved forward from Fat Alley to Gird trench most done by guns in operations of the 7th as summarised as follows. 1. 3 Guns on Right att to 32nd Roy Fusiliers advanced with Infantry	

John W Kanon Ravi for OC 12th M.G. Coy.

T/131. Wt. W708-776. 500000. 4/15. Sir J. C. & S.

WAR DIARY or INTELLIGENCE SUMMARY.

Army Form C. 2118.

(Erase heading not required.)

Instructions regarding War Diaries and Intelligence Summaries are contained in F. S. Regs., Part II. and the Staff Manual respectively. Title pages will be prepared in manuscript.

Place	Date	Hour	Summary of Events and Information	Remarks and references to Appendices
	Ypres		2nd Lt. C.B. Woolley was killed almost immediately. Infantry advance was held up by very heavy M.G. fire and did not proceed for more than 100 yards. Section Sergeant gave orders to dig in further advance made by supporting Infantry guns proceeding with them again. Progress was stopped by heavy M.G. fire and guns were dug in. 3 Guns on Left at 26th Royal Fusiliers went forward with 1st wave of Infantry. Lt. A.B. Wilson was wounded early in the engagement. Section Sergeants report that Munitions were well kept but at one stage found themselves in front of Infantry. Gave M.G. fire and endeavoured to work from the rocket and guns were dug in 3. 3 Guns under 2nd Lt. A.F.E. Prescott carried out overhead fire from 1-11.5 p.m. to 11 p.m. in support of the attack 3,500 rounds of ammunition expended, given at rear of enemies line being thoroughly swept. 4. 14 Reserve Guns under command of O.C. Company assisted by 2nd Lt. A.F.E. Prescott moved up to Line via road in square L.4.b. 	

John Lawson Reid for O.C. 124 M.G. Coy.

WAR DIARY
or
INTELLIGENCE SUMMARY.
(Erase heading not required.)

Place	Date	Hour	Summary of Events and Information	Remarks and references to Appendices
	4.10.16		N13C which constituted a checking line between units of the Brigade leaving the L fire close range was encountered after emerging about 400 yards. Guns withdrawn for a short distance and first established with detachment of 21st K.R.R. Corps in Strong Point OC Company being informed that this was the next advanced infantry post, all Lloyd N. Guns a shell hole linking up this Strong Point with another on the left occupied by another detachment of 2nd K.R.R. Corps. During the night of Oct 4st the Gun positions were linked up and a continuous line established along the front trench was also effected with 4 Vickers guns that at one forward earlier in the Advance and these were powered up with the new line. While advising O.C. Company to Right gun 2nd Lt. A.F. Prescott was killed by rifle or M.G. bullet, 2nd Lt. 4th M.G.I. Henry was sent for to take his place he arrived at the Right Gun about emplacements were constructed during the night 2-30 am GOC 124 Inf Brigade visited the line and gave instructions that M.G. fire was to be reserved in case of	

J. Hubb Lawrence Lieut. for O.C. 124 M.G. Coy.

Instructions regarding War Diaries and Intelligence Summaries are contained in F. S. Regs., Part II. and the Staff Manual respectively. Title pages will be prepared in manuscript.

WAR DIARY
or
INTELLIGENCE SUMMARY.
(Erase heading not required.)

Army Form C. 2118.

124 MACHINE GUN COY. MACHINE GUN CORPS

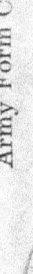

Place	Date	Hour	Summary of Events and Information	Remarks and references to Appendices
	8-10-16		of counter attack.	
	8-10-16 to 10-10-16		New line consolidated and strengthened, no counter attack by enemy nor was line subjected to any severe Bombardment. Chief feature of this period was the extraordinary activity of enemy snipers who met with a good deal of success. While reserving fire in the main several bursts were levelled at the snipers some being certainly accounted for. On the early morning of the 8th. a large party of the enemy was seen filing into trenches about 1200 yards away on the right these were fired upon by 2 Guns result unknown except that they quickly dispersed. Casualties during period 7th to 10th inst.	
			Officers: Killed 2, Wounded 1, S Shock 1, Missing –	
			Other Ranks: Killed 6, Wounded 12, S Shock 4, Missing 6.	
	10-10-16		Brigade relieved by 90th Infantry Brigade M. G. Coy relief completed by 1 am 11-10-16.	

John W Lawson Lieut. for O.C. 124 M. G. Coy.

T2134. Wt. W708-776. 500000. 4/15. Sir J. C. & S.

Army Form C. 2118.

WAR DIARY
or
INTELLIGENCE SUMMARY.
(Erase heading not required.)

Instructions regarding War Diaries and Intelligence Summaries are contained in F. S. Regs., Part II. and the Staff Manual respectively. Title pages will be prepared in manuscript.

Place	Date	Hour	Summary of Events and Information	Remarks and references to Appendices
	12.10.16		Company proceeded to camp B.20.A.0.5.	Map Ref 57D SE
	13.10.16		Billets with full transport to Bruie	57C SW
	14.10.16		Reorganising of sections	
	15.10.16	10 AM	Company attended Church Parade attended by C.O.C. Hist Gp who addresses those concerned	62 g LE
	16.10.16	9 PM	Company minus transport entrained at Mericourt	
	17.10.16	1 PM	Company retained at Amiens transport arrived at Amiens 6 PM	62 c AW Albert
			and the whole company were Billeted in the same.	MAP REF
	18.10.16		Training was carried on	
	19.10.16	12.45	Company with full transport entrained at Longpre for 2nd Army Gen.	
	20.10.16	1 am	Company detrained at Caestre and proceeded to Billets in Meteren	
	21.10.16	9.30	Company with full transport proceeded to Billets in Victoria	Map Ref M3 C.5.5.
			Camp YMCA Hut	
	22.10.16	noon	Headquarters, transport and sections 2 & 3 proceeded to	
			L 6 (trench map ref French map 28 pr N.Y.A.8.6. Sections	
			1 & 4 took over positions in Brigade Sector that is L.E.	

John W Lewson Lieut for O.C. 124 M.G. Coy.

WAR DIARY
or
INTELLIGENCE SUMMARY

Army Form C. 2118.

night. Left of 41st Divisional front taken over on this date from 4th Australian Division.

Divisional Boundaries VIERSTRAAT - WYSCHAETE road to YPRES COMINES canal.

Brigade boundaries VIERSTRAAT - WYSCHAETE road to junction of trenches O99 and O11 to Snipers Barn thence to Lock 8 and thence a line through Lead Dog Farm and IN DE WANDELING CABT. Map Ref. French map 28 SW 1/20,000.

Gun positions taken over:-

Section I. Fort Grantham N11 B 5.17, Majors Copse N5 D 5.7.3. N 11 A 9.9. Captains Post Fort Toronto N11 A.3.3. Officers in command 2nd Lt. Henry & 2nd Lt. No hile

John Rawson Lieut. for O.C. 124 M.G. Coy.

WAR DIARY
or
INTELLIGENCE SUMMARY.

(Erase heading not required.)

Army Form C. 2118.

Place	Date	Hour	Summary of Events and Information	Remarks and references to Appendices
			Section IV. S.B.Y.O.Y.A.2.8. Eastern Breastwork N6c.5.1. McDonalds Post N12.A.2.8. Beggars Post N6.D.1½.6¾.	At 12H 9/30
			These positions were taken over from the 12th Australian Machine Gun Section	Jobs Y trench map Sheet 28 SW
			Company, relief completed by mid-day.	1/20,000.
	23.10.16		Indirect fire carried out as follows.	
			Officer i/c Gun Pos. Nos. & per gun. Target. Results.	Remarks. Boy Pot
			O.C. Coy. N11 A 7½.9. 250 rds. X Roads at O13.C.2.8. Unknown	French map Sheet 29 SW
			" N11 A 7½.9. 500 Rds O13 A.6½.6¾ v.s. to O13 A.8½.5¾. Unknown	1/20,000
			" N11 A 7½.9. 250 Rds O14 D.5.4. Unknown	
	24.10.16		Lt. Jas Lawson arrived at Coy Headquarters and was taken on the strength of the Coy. as 2nd i/c.	
			John W Lawson Lieut For O.C. 12H M.S. Coy.	

WAR DIARY or INTELLIGENCE SUMMARY.

Army Form C. 2118.

Place	Date	Hour	Summary of Events and Information	Remarks and references to Appendices
	24.10.16		Weather fine	
			Indirect fire carried out as follows	
			Officer i/c Lieut Ing.	
			O.C. Coy	
				Rds expended	Target	Results	Remarks
			N11 A 7½ 9	250 Rds	X Roads at O13.c.28.	Unknown	Map Ref. Trench Map Sheet 28 SW 1/20,000
			"	500 Rds	O.13 A.6½.6½ V.S. to O.13.A.8½.5½	Unknown	
			"	250 Rds	O.14.D.5.4	Unknown	
	25.10.16		Indirect fire was carried out as follows				
			Officer i/c Lieut Fox 2nd Lt Henry	Rds expended	Target	Results	Remarks Map Ref. Trench Map Sheet 28 SW 1/20,000
			N11 A 7½ 9	250 Rds	O.7.a.5.4	Unknown	
			"	250 Rds	O.13.C.3.9	Unknown	
			"	450 Rds	O.13 A 6½.6½ V.S. to O.13 A 8½.5½	Unknown	
			Work done				
			A new alternative indirect line emplacement has been started in at				Litt —
			N.5.D.1¾.2¾				

John W. Lawson Lieut for O.C. 124 M.G. Coy.

WAR DIARY
or
INTELLIGENCE SUMMARY.

(Erase heading not required.)

Army Form C. 2118.

Instructions regarding War Diaries and Intelligence Summaries are contained in F. S. Regs., Part II. and the Staff Manual respectively. Title pages will be prepared in manuscript.

Place	Date	Hour	Summary of Events and Information				Remarks and references to Appendices
	26.10.16	8-3.a.m to 10.30a.m	Indirect fire was carried out to verify—				
			Officer i/c	Gun Pos.	Rds fired	Target	Results	Remarks
			2nd Lt Henry	N.11.A.7½.9	250 Rds	0.13.A.9¼.4	Unknown	Supp Ref
			"	"	250 Rds	0.7.D.3½.1	"	Sen. at Rest
			"	"	250 Rds	0.13.C.3.9	"	Feb 28th
			"	"	250 Rds	0.7.D.5.4	"	1/29,000
			2nd Lt Barton	N.6.D.2¾.4	500 Rds	0.14.C.1.8	"	
			"	"	500 Rds	0.8.C.8.4½	"	
			2nd Lt Henry	N.11.A.7½.9	125 Rds	0.7.D.3½.1	"	
			"	"	125 Rds	0.7.D.5.4	"	
			"	"	250 Rds	0.13.A.9¼.4	"	
			"	"	250 Rds	0.13.C.3.9	"	
		1.30p	2nd Lt Thompson	N.6.C.5¼.4	500 Rds	0.13.C.6.3½	"	
		1.30p	" "	" "	500 Rds	0.13.G.9.4½	"	
		10.12	2nd Lt N. Hull	L.11.A.3.3	500 Rds	0.13.A.4½.5	"	
			"	"	500 Rds	0.7.D.3½.1	"	

John Lumsey Lieut. for O.C. 24 M.G. Coy.

WAR DIARY
or
INTELLIGENCE SUMMARY.
(Erase heading not required.)

Army Form C. 2118.

Place	Date	Hour	Summary of Events and Information	Remarks and references to Appendices
	28/12/16	8 am	B Company proceeds on Leave to U.K. Lieut J M Rawson takes over command of Company	
		11 am	Nos 2 and 3 sections relieved Nos 1 and 4 sections in Brigade Sector	Misty
			No 2 section relieves No 1 section — No 3 section relieving No 4 relieved at Riley south	Tmp 28°F
			relieved 2nd Lt Crowder at Eastern Bracken	1/20,000
		9 am to 10.30	Indirect fire was carried out as follows	
			Gun No. Pos.	Target	Results	
			Nos 1 & 4 M.G. A.3.3	500 Rds	C.13. C.C. 2	Unknown
			2nd Lt White M.G. A.3.3	250 Rds	C.14 C.1.8	"
			2nd Lt Barker M.6 D.21.y	250 Rds	C.8 D.8.11.2	"
			"	500 Rds	D.13 & 62.2	"
			"	500 Rds	C.13 D.9 y½	"
					X Roads &c	"
		10.10 to 10.20	One map 2nd Lt White M.H A.3.3	1000 Rds	C.13.A y½ 5	"
		9 pm to 11 pm	2nd Lt Barker M.6 D.21.y	500 Rds	C.14 B.2½.1	"
		"	"	500 Rds	C.14 B.5½.4	"

John Rawson Lieut. for O.C. 124 M.G. Coy.

WAR DIARY
or
INTELLIGENCE SUMMARY.

(Erase heading not required.)

Army Form C. 2118.

Place	Date	Hour	Summary of Events and Information	Remarks and references to Appendices
	29.10.16	8pm to 9pm	Indirect firing was carried out as follows:-	Map Ref Sheet 57cSW
			Officer i/c Lieut Harris. Gun No.	1/20,000
			2nd Lt Henry N.H.A.42.9	
				Target Result
			375 X roads at Unknown
			250 O.13.C.3.9
			X roads at
			O.13.A.9.4.4
			375 O.7.D.H±6 "
			X roads at
			O.13.A.4½.5 "
			500 X roads at
			O.13.C.3.9 v.S.6'
			O.14.B.8½
	30.10.16	9pm	500 O.20.A.3.9 "
		10pm	375 O.8.C.9.5 "
		11pm	395 UNRATTEN
			O.14.A.3.1
			Lewis gun O.8.O.9.5
			250 To O.20.A.3.9
	31.10.16		390 O.7.C.4.3.4.4 "
			Indirect At N.Falls N.11.A.3.3 275 O.7.C.3.H½ "
			250 O.7.C.3.5½ "

John M Lawson Lieut. for O.C. 12th Bn. C.E.F.

WAR DIARY or INTELLIGENCE SUMMARY

Army Form C. 2118.

Place	Date	Hour	Summary of Events and Information	Remarks and references to Appendices
	31/10/16	8 PM	Scheme of Fire corrected as follows.	
		10 P.M.	Officer i/c Gun No. No. of Rounds fired Target Result	Ref
			2nd Lt. 13 m/65 250 X Roads at Unknown	Ref
			O.20.A.3.9	Trench Map
			" 500 on Ract Wood	Sheet 28 SW
			" O.14.C	1/20,000
			" 250 Traversing from O.20.A.3.9	
			to O.8.C.9.5	
			" 250 on Ract Wood	
			O.14.C	"
	1 PM	2nd Lt Riley N.6.C.5½.½		
		To		
		4·5 P.M		
		7·50	250 Cross Roads	
		To	O.20.A.3.9	
		9-10	Traversing from O.20.A.39	
		9-30	500 to O.8.C.9.5.	
		To		
		9.45 P.M		

Note Above.

During Period from 22-10-16 to 31-10-16 Improvements to Drainage and Gun Emplacements were carried out.

John Lawson Lieut. for O.C. 2nd M. G. Coy.

Army Form C. 2118.

WAR DIARY
or
INTELLIGENCE SUMMARY.
(Erase heading not required.)

Instructions regarding War Diaries and Intelligence Summaries are contained in F. S. Regs., Part II. and the Staff Manual respectively. Title pages will be prepared in manuscript.

Place	Date	Hour	Summary of Events and Information	Remarks and references to Appendices
	31/10/16		Casualties for the Month ending 31-10-16 were as follows. Killed Wounded Missing Shell Shock Evacuated Sick	
			Officers 2 1 — 1 —	
			Ranks 6 12 6 4 5.	
			Effective Strength of Coy on the 31st inst.	
			Officers O.Ranks	
			11 143	
			28.	
			Att. from Units	
			Reinforcement arrived at the Above-mentioned dates	
			2nd Lt. J.H.E. Barton 13-10-16 from M.G. Base Depot	
			2nd Lt. C.V. White 15-10-16 "	
			2nd Lt. S.E.S. Bowles 15-10-16 "	
			2nd Lt. A.E. Riley 19-10-16 "	

John W. Lawson Lieut, for O.C. 124 M.G. Coy.

Army Form C. 2118.

WAR DIARY
or
INTELLIGENCE SUMMARY.
(Erase heading not required.)

Instructions regarding War Diaries and Intelligence Summaries are contained in F. S. Regs., Part II. and the Staff Manual respectively. Title pages will be prepared in manuscript.

Place	Date	Hour	Summary of Events and Information	Remarks and references to Appendices
	31.10.16		Reinforcements continued. 3rd C.R. H.Qtrs. Lancs. Bn. 2/ic 24-10-16. 2 other Ranks 3 " 11-10-16	

John Lawson Reid
for O.C. 124 M.G. Coy.

Army Form C. 2118.

WAR DIARY
or
INTELLIGENCE SUMMARY.
(Erase heading not required.)

Instructions regarding War Diaries and Intelligence Summaries are contained in F.S. Regs., Part II. and the Staff Manual respectively. Title pages will be prepared in manuscript.

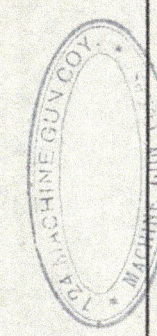

Place	Date	Hour	Summary of Events and Information						Remarks and references to Appendices
			Operations						Map Ref. Cavenchy Sheet 36 S.W. 1/10,000
	3/10/15	6 pm to 6 pm	Practice firing was carried out by Nos 2 and 3 Sections as follows:—						
			Officer i/c	Gun Pos	Rds fired	Target	Results	Remarks	
		9.30 to 10.30 PM	2nd Lt. Riley	N.6.c.5½.½.	500	Junction of trenches & Road at O.13.b.4.7.	Unknown		
	6pm 6/11/15	10.30 to 11.30 PM	"	"	500	Rouly Farm at O.13.b.9½.6.	"		
	1/11/15	10.30 to 12.30 P.M.	2nd Lt. Barton	N.6.d.9½.7	500	O.7.d.3¼.1.	"		
		"	"	"	500	O.7.d.8.4.	"		
		8.30 to 9.15 PM	2nd Lt. Riley	N.6.c.5½.½.	500	Cross Roads at O.20.a.3.9.	"		
	1/11/15 to	9.30 to 10.15 PM	"	"	500	Corrast Farm at O.14.a.3.1.	"		
	6 PM 2/11/15	6 PM to 7 AM	2nd Lt. Barton	N.6.d.9½.7.	500	O.14.a.2½.1.	"		
		"	"	"	500	O.7.d.8.4.	"		
		10 PM to 12 P.M.	2nd Lt. Henry	N.11.a.7½.9.	500	O.13.c.3.9.	"		
		"	"	"	500	O.13.a.3.9.v.s.to O.13.a.7½.5	"		

Army Form C. 2118.

WAR DIARY
or
INTELLIGENCE SUMMARY.
(Erase heading not required.)

Instructions regarding War Diaries and Intelligence Summaries are contained in F. S. Regs., Part II. and the Staff Manual respectively. Title pages will be prepared in manuscript.

[Stamp: 104 MACHINE GUN COY.]

Place	Date	Hour	Summary of Events and Information	Remarks and references to Appendices
			Operations	
			Officer i/c — Gun Pos. — Rds fired — Target — Results — Amounts	
	2/11/16	8.30 to 6 P.M	2nd Lt. White — N.11.a.3.3. — 350 — Neighbourg. trenches O.7.d.8.3 — Unknown	
		6.P.M 10.30	" — " — 360 — O.19.a.8.8. — "	
	3/11/16	P.M.	" — " — 300 — Search unknown Wood in O.13.C. — "	
		6 P.M 8.30 P.M to 3/11/16 9.15 P.M	2nd Lt Riley — N.6.C.5½.½ — 500 — Traverse y.v.s.R.R from O.14.C.6.6½ to O.14.a.6¾.6½ — "	
		to 9.15 6 P.M 10.30 P.M	" — " — 500 — March rear of GRAND BOIS O.13.b.5½.4¾ to O.13.b.10.1. — "	
	4/11/16	8.30 to 10.30 P.M	2nd Lt Henry — N.11.a.7½.9. — 500 — Traverse y.v.s.R from O.8.c.7½.2. to O.14.a.6.3 — "	
			" — " — 500 — Traverse from O.13.b.0.1 to O.13.d.9.5½ — "	

WAR DIARY
or
INTELLIGENCE SUMMARY.

Army Form C. 2118.

Place	Date	Hour	Summary of Events and Information				Remarks and references to Appendices
			Operations				
			Officer i/c	Gun. Pos.	Rounds fired	Target	Results
6 P.M. 3/11/16 to 6 P.M. 4/11/16	8.30	2nd Lt. Barton	N.6.d.2½.Y.	500.	Traversed from O.8.C.9.5 to O.14.a.6½.2.6.	Unknown	Map. Ref. Trench Map. 28.S.W. 1/10,000
4/11/16	9.15 P.M.	"	"	"	Traversed from O.13.b.8.6½ to O.13.b.10.5.	"	
6 P.M. 4/11/16 to 6 P.M. 5/11/16	7 P.M. to 9 P.M.	2nd Lt. Riley	N.6.c.56.04.	1,000.	Traversed from O.7.d.6.4. to O.13.a.8.5.½.	"	
	8 P.M. to 10 P.M.	2nd Lt. Henry.	N.11.a.9½.9.	500.	Traversed junction of tracks at O.7.d.2.½.Y.	"	
5/11/16		"	"	500	Traverse trenches O.7.C and d.	"	
5/11/16		Nos 1 and 4 Sections relieved Nos 2 and 3 Sections in the trenches and took over same Gun positions. The relief was completed by 9 A.M. 5/11/1916. Operator Cpls attached					

L M Don(?)
Capt

Army Form C. 2118.

WAR DIARY
or
INTELLIGENCE SUMMARY.
(Erase heading not required.)

Instructions regarding War Diaries and Intelligence Summaries are contained in F.S. Regs., Part II. and the Staff Manual respectively. Title pages will be prepared in manuscript.

Place	Date	Hour	Summary of Events and Information					Remarks and references to Appendices
		6 P.M.	Operations					Chap. Ref.
	5/11/16	10 P.M. to 10.45 PM	Indirect fire was carried out by C/153 1 and 4 Actions as follows					Sheet Chap. 28 S.W. 1/10,000
			Officer i/c	Gun No	Rds fired	Target	Results	Remarks
			2nd Lt. Riby	N.6.C.5½.½	500	Renty Farm 0.18.6.95.60	Unknown	
	6/11/16	11 P.M. to 12 P.M.	"	"	500	Traversal road at GRAND BOIS from RENTY FARM 0.13.6.95.60 to 0.13.d 3.8	"	
	6/11/16	9 P.M. to 11 P.M.	2nd Lt. Crowder	N.6.9.2½.4	1000	Cross tracks at # O.Y.ol.3¾.1	"	
	6/11/16	9 P.M. to 11 P.M.	2nd Lt. Crowder	N.6.9.2½.7	500	Thornsey Cabinet Cross Quarants Traversed from O.Y.d.35.45 to O.Y.6.95.90	"	
	6 P.M. 7/11/16							

Watson Major

WAR DIARY
or
INTELLIGENCE SUMMARY.
(Erase heading not required.)

Army Form C. 2118.

Place	Date	Hour	Summary of Events and Information						Remarks and references to Appendices
			Operations	Indirect fire was carried out as follows:-					
				Officer i/c	Gun Pos.	Rds. fired	Target	Results	Remarks
	7/11/16	6.P.M to 11.50 P.M		Lieut A. W. Carle	N.11.a.3.3	1,000	GRAND BOIS	Unknown	Map Ref Trench Map 28 S.W. 1/10,000
	8/11/16	6.P.M		"	"		O.13.d.4.3	Unknown	
	8/11/16	6.P.M 8.30 to 11.P.M		2nd Lieut. O.G.Riby	N.6.C.5½.½	250	Dugouts O.7.d.4.0 Howitzer Dump N.18.B.9.3	"	
	8/11/16	6.P.M 8.45 to 11 P.M		"	"	250	"	"	
	9/11/16	6.P.M 7.p to 11 P.M		"	"	250	"	"	
		9-11.P.M		2nd Lt Crowder	N.6.d.9½.4	250	Dugouts G.7.B.4.0 Limber Dump N.18.B.9.3	"	
		6.P.M		2nd Lt Riby	N.6.c.54.04	250	ONRAET FARM O.14.0.3.1	"	
	9/11/16	7 P.M to 8.00 P.M		"	"	250	ZERO HOUSE O.14.a.50.65	"	
	10/11/16	6.P.M to 10 P.M		"	"	250	CATTEAU FARM O.8.C.9.5.	"	

Army Form C. 2118.

WAR DIARY
or
INTELLIGENCE SUMMARY.
(Erase heading not required.)

Instructions regarding War Diaries and Intelligence Summaries are contained in F. S. Regs., Part II. and the Staff Manual respectively. Title pages will be prepared in manuscript.

[Stamp: 124 MACHINE GUN COY.]

Place	Date	Hour	Summary of Events and Information	Remarks and references to Appendices
	10/11/16		Nos. 2 & 3 Sections relieved Nos. 1 & 4 Sections in the trenches and took over same guns. The Relief was completed by 11.45 A.M. Particulars of Relief attached. Indirect fire was carried out as follows:-	May. Ref. Sheet 36cNW 28 S.W. 1/10,000
			Officer i/c Gun no. Rounds fired Target	
		9 P.M.	2nd Lt. Crowder N.6.a.2½.7 500 Croix Trenches	
		"	" " " at 0.13.a.45.50 Unknown	
		11 P.M.	" " 250 Cross Trenches 0.13.a.9.4. "	
		8-10 P.M.	2nd Lt. Henry N.6.c.5½.½ 500 Cross Roads at 0.13.8.3.9. "	
		4-15 "	2nd Lt. Baston N.11.a.3.3. 500 0.13.a.4½.5 "	
		10-15 P.M.	" " 500 0.13.c.3.9 "	

Army Form C. 2118.

WAR DIARY
or
INTELLIGENCE SUMMARY.

(Erase heading not required.)

Instructions regarding War Diaries and Intelligence Summaries are contained in F. S. Regs., Part II. and the Staff Manual respectively. Title pages will be prepared in manuscript.

Place	Date	Hour	Summary of Events and Information					Remarks and references to Appendices
				Officer i/c	Gun Pos.	Rds. fired	Target	Results	Remarks
			Indirect fire was carried out as follows:-						MAP REF-
	11/11/16	6-P.M 10 P.M		2ND LT Henry	N.6.c.5½.½	250	Crow Copse at O.13.c.3.9.	Unknown	Trench map 28 S.W. 1/10,000
	to			"	"	250	Grand Bois O.13.B.0.3 to O.13.B.6.8	"	
	12/11/16	6 P.M 12 P.M		"	"			"	
	13/11/16	9 P.M to 11 P.M		2ND LT. CROWDER	N.6.d. 2½.4.	250	Cottage farm at O.8.C. 9½.4½	"	
				"	"	250	Plenty Farm at O.13.d. 9.5½	"	
				"	"	250	Zero House O.14.a.5½.6½	"	
	13/11/16	6-P.M to 9 P.M		2ND LT. CROWDER	N.6.d. 2½.4.	250	Dugout at O.7.d.4.0.	"	
				"	"	250	RENTY.FARM. O.13.b.9.5½/2	"	
	14/11/16	6-P.M 8 P.M		"	"	250	LOUWAEGE.FARM. O.7.d.8.3.	"	

Army Form C. 2118.

WAR DIARY
or
INTELLIGENCE SUMMARY

(Erase heading not required.)

Place	Date	Hour	Summary of Events and Information					Remarks and references to Appendices
			Indirect fire was carried out as follows :-					
			Officer i/c	Gun Pos	Rds. fired.	Target	Results	Remarks
	13/11/16	6-8 PM to 6 P.M 14/11/16	2nd Lt. Barton	N.11.a.4½.9.	200	O.13.c.3.9	Unknown	Map Ref. French Map 28 S.W. 1/10,000.
			"	"	200	N.18.6.8½.3.	"	
			"	"	200	O.9.d.2.5½	"	
			"	"	200	N.18.6.8.3 to O.13.a.3.8	"	
			"	"	200	O.13.a.45.50.	"	
	13/11/16 to 14/11/16	6-8PM 12 PM to 2 AM	2nd Lt. Henry	N.6.C.5½.½.	250	Junction of Rds & tracks O.13.6.4.4.	"	
			"	"	250	Traverse along track of Grand Bois O.13.6.8.5.	"	
			"	"	250	Search Road from O.13.c.3.9 to O.13.c.8.2.	"	
	14/11/16	6 PM	"	"	250	07677	"	
	14/11/16	12 PM to 2 AM	"	"	250	013 6 35	"	
	15/11/16	6 PM to 2 AM 15/11/16	"	"	250	012 c 83	"	

WAR DIARY
or
INTELLIGENCE SUMMARY

Army Form C. 2118.

(Erase heading not required.)

Place	Date	Hour	Summary of Events and Information	Remarks and references to Appendices
	14/11/16 & 15/11/16	6 P.M. 12-15 a.m. 15/11/16	**Work done**: Several new emplacements were made in the Reserve Trench and behind it. **Aircraft**: Several hostile aeroplanes were heard over, at least of which was dropping signal lights.	MAP REF. Trench Maps 28 S.W. 1/10,000.
	15/11/16 to 6 p.m. 16/11/16	6 P.M.	**Relief.** Nos. 1 & 4 Sections marched up to the trenches but in view of the fact that the whole machine gun line had been re-organised only No. 3 Section was relieved an additional 4 guns being required to hold the new line. The positions taken up by the Guns as shown in copy of Operation Orders No. 18 attached. The relief was completed by 11-45 am on 16/11/16. The new positions in the NEW RESERVE TRENCH are temporarily only pending the construction of permanent ones. **WORKING PARTY** Section 3 along with a working party of Infantry under R.E. supervision commenced the construction of the new permanent emplacements in front of the NEW RESERVE TRENCH.	O. O. No 18 attached.

Army Form C. 2118.

WAR DIARY
or
INTELLIGENCE SUMMARY.
(Erase heading not required.)

Instructions regarding War Diaries and Intelligence Summaries are contained in F. S. Regs., Part II. and the Staff Manual respectively. Title pages will be prepared in manuscript.

Place	Date	Hour	Summary of Events and Information	Remarks and references to Appendices
	15.11.16	6 pm to 6 pm 16.11.16	Our Operations Harassing fire was carried out on the following targets	Sheet Ref Target Ref Sheet 28 SW 1/10,000
			Officer i/c Gun No.	Rds fired	Target	Results
			2nd Lt Stanny M.C. 5½4	250	0.9.D.4.0	Unknown
			"	250	0.13.9.3	"
			"	250	0.13.C.39	"
			"	300	0.13.A.9.6	"
			"	200	0.7.D.8.6	"
			"	100	0.14.A.3.1	"
			Work etc. New emplacement completed at Western Beach short at N.12.A.14.06	
			Weather. The weather has been dark and dry which has made it possible to improve defences in La Boy de Huay Ref N.4.C.8.6 Sheet 28 NW 1/10,000	

Army Form C. 2118.

WAR DIARY
or
INTELLIGENCE SUMMARY.
(Erase heading not required.)

Instructions regarding War Diaries and Intelligence Summaries are contained in F. S. Regs., Part II. and the Staff Manual respectively. Title pages will be prepared in manuscript.

[Stamp: 24 MACHINE GUN CO. / MACHINE GUN CORPS]

Place	Date	Hour	Summary of Events and Information	Remarks and references to Appendices
		4 Pm	Our Operations	Trench Map
	16-1116	4Pm to 5Pm	Indirect fire was carried out on the following targets-	Grandcourt Sheet 57d. 1/40,000
			Officer i/c Section Target Rds fired Results	
			2nd Lt. Barton N.11.A.2.3 Woods nr. 500 Unknown	
		8.30Pm to 10.30Pm	2nd Lt. Riley N.6.d.28.y Grand Bois O.13.B 500	
				Trench del front & Grand Bois S.9.139 Baillescourt Wood	
		6Pm	2nd Lt. Barton N.11.A.3.3 O.13.B.8½.3 250 "	
	7.11.16	8 Pm	" " O.13.A.D.M.4 TRAVERSE TO 250 "	
			" " O.13.A.H.9.	
	8.11.16	6Pm to 10.30Pm	" " O.13.C.3.9. 250 "	
			Intelligence	
			At N.11.A.3.3 noises have been heard reminiscent that position at irregular hours similar to the sound made by moving petrol tins, voices have also be heard at well as muffled thuds, which suggests sapping.	

(Sgd) [signature]

Army Form C. 2118.

WAR DIARY
or
INTELLIGENCE SUMMARY.
(Erase heading not required.)

Instructions regarding War Diaries and Intelligence Summaries are contained in F.S. Regs., Part II. and the Staff Manual respectively. Title pages will be prepared in manuscript.

Place	Date	Hour	Summary of Events and Information	Remarks and references to Appendices
In the Field	19.11.16	6pm to 9pm	Our Operations. Indirect fire was carried out on the following targets:	Map 1/40,000 Trench map Sheet 28 SW. 1/40,000
			Officer i/c Lieut. Riley — Gun Pos. Hols Trench — Target ZERO HOUSE — Rounds 250 — Remarks Artillery on hot pockets slightly active.
			" " " " Higgins Post — N.6.D.12.64 — TRENTY FARM 0.14.A.6.63 — 250 — Unknown
			" " " " " " O.13.B.93.53 — — Unknown
			Considerable amount of rain fell during the last 24 hours and has made roads and trenches very smeshed.
	19.11.16 10.30am		Reconnaissance. Lieut-Colonel Martin Machine Gun Corps attached 10th Corps and Major Grant D.S.O. attached 10th Corps accompanied by O.C. Company visited VERSTRAAT sector line on or abt 15 pg'lt. Replacements in the Corps reserve of machine guns in the 12th Infantry Brigade sector.
	20.11.16	6pm to 6pm	Presentation of Medal Ribbons. G.O.C. 10th Corps presented Medal Ribbons to 12th Infantry Brigade Group. Recipients of this Company, as follows:— Major W.H. Grain — Military Cross Major W. Sgt Harris I. — Military Medal.

Winters Capt.

WAR DIARY or INTELLIGENCE SUMMARY

Army Form C. 2118.

Place	Date	Hour	Summary of Events and Information	Remarks and references to Appendices
	18-7-18	11 A.M.	Congratulatory cards report received by 23rd Lieut. H.R. Lawson Henry or at R.29/4/17 the changeover from 3.O.C. MM-Division	Lawson Henry first Ref. tov 06 Inst. Sheet 28 SW 1/10,000
			Gun Operations	
		6-30 PM	Indirect fire was carried out on the following targets:	
		to		
			Gun Pos.	Rds fired	Target	
			Officer i/c			
		9.30 PM	2nd Lt Clark	N.12.H.29.96.	500	From 0.13.A.9.4 to 0.13.B.2.1.	Unknown
		to			500	Cross Roads at 0.13.C.2.9 R. known	
		11.15 PM		GERMAN NEST. N.6.B.4.65	250	0.13.B.9.6	
				"	250	"	
		9 PM	2nd Lt Barbor	"	250	0.13.B.1.3	
		to				0.13.B.6.8	
		11.15 PM		N.12.A.14.96	250	TIMBER DUMP N.18.B.9.3.	Men to billeting area. Went during the night from 2.45AM to 3.15 AM
		6.30 PM			250	JUNCTION OF TRENCHES A.O.13.E.9.7. 5	
		to					
	1.P.M.	8.15 PM	2nd Lt Barbor	N.6.D.15.6	500	0.8. A. 8.0	
		to					
		11.30 PM	"	"	500	0.8. C. 2.37	

WAR DIARY
or
INTELLIGENCE SUMMARY.

Army Form C. 2118.

Place	Date	Hour	Summary of Events and Information	Remarks and references to Appendices
	21.11.16	11 a.m.	**Conference.** O.C. Company attended conference with O.C. 32nd Battalion Royal Fusiliers and O.C. M.G. machine Gun Company and worked out arrangements for Operations for the 22nd inst. J. Preparation in defence of machine Guns of 12th Infantry Brigade sector and 4 yds. Infantry Brigade sector.	
			Work done. Stationary Gun emplacements constructed in front line for operations on the 22nd inst.	Map Ref. Trench map sheet 36 S.W.
	22.11.16 to 5pm	5am Our Operations	Indirect fire was carried out on the following targets	Remarks. W. Kamer Our artillery and Trench Mortars have been active between 27th and 11th.
	22.11.16		Officer i/c and Duty	Gun Pos.	Target	Rounds	
				Gun Pos. N.C.D.4.4	JUNCTION OF TRENCHES O.8.A.8¾.4. from aeroplane map.	500	
			"	"	LOUWAGE FM O.Y.D.2.3	500	
	22.11.16	8.11am	**Relief.** No 3 Section proceeded to trenches and took over Gun Positions from No 4 Section The relief was completed by 12 noon 22nd inst. See O.O. 19	O.O. 19 attached for Ref.

WAR DIARY or INTELLIGENCE SUMMARY

Army Form C. 2118.

(Erase heading not required.)

Instructions regarding War Diaries and Intelligence Summaries are contained in F. S. Regs., Part II. and the Staff Manual respectively. Title pages will be prepared in manuscript.

12a MACHINE GUN COY. / 12a MACHINE GUN CORPS

Place	Date	Hour	Summary of Events and Information	Remarks and references to Appendices
In the Field	27.11.16	6 P.M. to 6 P.M. 28.11.16	Our Operations — Indirect fire was carried out on the following targets:	Map Ref. Trench Map Sheet 27B SW 1/10,000
			Officer i/c — 2nd Lt. Kemp	
			Gun Pos. — FORT TORONTO N.14.A.3.3.	
			Rds Fired — 250 — Target — N.9.B.8.2 — Result — Unknown	NIERSTRAAT - Wulverghem - between N & SW
			" — 500 — D.18.A.4.8 — Unknown	
			Weather — The weather has been very dull, roads and trenches in a very muddy state.	
	28.11.16	6 P.M. to 6 P.M. 29.11.16	Our Operations — Indirect fire was carried out on the following targets:	
			Officer i/c — 2nd Lt Clark	Remarks — Enemy's trench mortars very active. Artillery slightly active.
			Gun Pos. — EASTERN BRANSTWICK N.12.A.84.96	
			Rds Fired — 500 — Target — Junction of Trenches at O.13.B.1.82 — Result — Unknown	
			" — 250 — Junction of road and trench at O.13.C.3.9	
	29.11.16	6 P.M. to 6 P.M.	2nd Lt Riley — N.B.D.23.1 — 250 — CORNER OF BRAND BROS O.Y.D.3.4.1	
			" — " — 500 — Junction of road and trench O.8.C.8.9½	

WAR DIARY or INTELLIGENCE SUMMARY.

Army Form C. 2118.

(Erase heading not required.)

Instructions regarding War Diaries and Intelligence Summaries are contained in F. S. Regs., Part II. and the Staff Manual respectively. Title pages will be prepared in manuscript.

Place	Date	Hour	Summary of Events and Information	Remarks and references to Appendices
In the Field	24-11-16	10 AM	It below strength Machine Gun. Corps attached 10th Corps accompanied by O.C. Company proceeded to trenches to inspect new retired line and Beggarsrest land.	18th W.S.O.O. 15. 24.11.16
		11-30 AM	Operations arranged for the 24th not cancelled.	
		1 PM	Our Operations.	Morg. Ref.
	24.11.16	3 PM	Indirect fire was carried out on the following targets.	French Map Sheet 28 S.W. 1/40,000.
		3-25PM to 3-35PM	Officer i/c Gun. No 1 Gun No.1 BEGGARSREST. N.6.D.24.y	
		3-35PM	2nd Lt. Kelly	1485 yards Target LOUWAEGH FARM. O.Y.D.8.3. Bingles unknown Remarks.
		3-40PM	"	500 RENTY FARM D.13.B.92.53. "
		3-45PM	"	250 RED CHATEAU. M.18.B.92.± "
		4 PM	2nd Lt. Short	N.B.A.14.96. 250 Junction of tracks at O.Y.D.3.1.
			Work on	M.G.1 continued at BEGGARSREST. on dug outs and store.
			Weather	Dry. M.G.s passed continuously for the last 24 hours consequently the roads and trenches are in a very muddy condition

Army Form C. 2118.

WAR DIARY
or
INTELLIGENCE SUMMARY.
(Erase heading not required.)

1/24 MACHINE GUN COY.

Place	Date	Hour	Summary of Events and Information	Remarks and references to Appendices
In the Field	29.10.16		Our Operations	
			Indirect fire was carried out on the following targets	Map Ref. Sheet-28 SW. 1/10,000
		5 PM to 6 PM	Officer's A	Gun Pos	Range	Target	Result
							Remarks
	10.3	10.30 PM to 11 PM	2nd Lt Halliday	06 D 22 4	1000	Lonwaege Farm and vicinity at 0.7.D.8.3	Unknown
							Hostile trench mortars very active.
		8 PM to 11 PM	2nd Lt Holt	N.4.A.1 9 6	500	Track in filled running through Grandbois to 0.13.C.1.2.	"
			"	"	500	Cross Roads at 0.13.C.3.9	"
	29.10.16	6.30 PM to 9.30 PM	"	N.6.C.5 3½	500	Track in Grandbois traversed from 0.13.B.3.5. to 0.13.B.0.21	"
		4-5 PM to 6 PM	"	"	500	Timber dump N.19.B.9.3.	Aircraft had been in evidence on both sides and several signal rockets flare but no reply could be observed.
	24.10.16	6 PM to 6.30	2nd Lt Peter	N.6.D.5.B. Y.	500	Lonwaege Farm 0.4.D.8.3.	"
		5.30 PM to 6 PM	"	"	500	Buildings at 0.8.A.8.0	"
			Weather	The weather still keeps dull and much rain has fallen the past 24 hours.	

Army Form C. 2118.

WAR DIARY
or
INTELLIGENCE SUMMARY.
(Erase heading not required.)

Place	Date	Hour	Summary of Events and Information	Remarks and references to Appendices
In the Field	27-11-16	6 P.M. 27-11-16 TO 6 P.M. 28-11-16	**Our Operations** —	Map Ref. Trench Map Sheet 28 SW 1/10,000
		9.30 A.M.	Achieved — fire was carried out at the following targets	
			Officer i/c Gun No. Position Target Range Results	
			2nd Lt. Riley N.6.D.17.64. LOW WEG. FARM 500 Unknown O.Y.D.8.3.	
			" " KENTI FARM 580 A.13.B.97.54	
			" " DUG. OUTS AT 500 O.Y.D.4.0	
		5.0 A.M.	**Relief** — No 2 Section proceeded to Ireland and took over Gun positions from No 1 Section. The relief was completed by 11.60 A.M. In relief of relief dic O.O.21.	O.O.21. 25-11-16. attached.
		10.30 A.M.	**Reconn. advance** —	
			No. 6 124 Infantry Brigade accompanied O.C. Company inspected Gun positions and provisionally Vidionate Gun emplacement in the presents daughter in accordance with the near defence scheme.	

Army Form C. 2118.

WAR DIARY
or
INTELLIGENCE SUMMARY.
(Erase heading not required.)

Instructions regarding War Diaries and Intelligence Summaries are contained in F. S. Regs., Part II. and the Staff Manual respectively. Title pages will be prepared in manuscript.

[Stamp: 12th MACHINE GUN COY]

Place	Date	Hour	Summary of Events and Information	Remarks and references to Appendices
In the Field	28.11.16 to 29.11.16		**Our Operations**	Map Ref. Trench Map Sheet 57.D.S.E. 1/10000
	29.11.16		Indirect fire was carried out on the following targets.	
			Officer in charge Gun No. Rds fired Tr. O.H. Results	Remarks Nil
			2nd Lt. Henry N.6 C 5a.1 300 SEARCHED. BRAND BOIS, AND SPRAYED WOOD Unknown	
		2 AM TO 4 AM	2nd Lt Lowndes N.2 A.M 96. 300 SEARCHED TRACK AT O 13.B.5.Y. TO O.13.B.Y.Y. AND SPRAYED WOOD TO THE RIGHT. "	
			" 500 LOU WAE GE. FARM. O.Y.D 8.3	
		6 PM	**Reinforcements** The undermentioned Officers were posted from M. G. Corps. Base Depot. 2nd Lieut. A. H. Whitland. E. Heron.	
			Weather The weather during the last 24 hours has been very cold generally freezing in the morning and turning slightly warmer in the afternoon.	

WAR DIARY
or
INTELLIGENCE SUMMARY.
(Erase heading not required.)

Army Form C. 2118.

Place	Date	Hour	Summary of Events and Information	Remarks and references to Appendices
In the Field	29.11.16 6 P.M. to 6 P.M 30.11.16	7.30 P.M to 10.30 P.M	**Our Operations** Indirect fire was carried out on the following targets. Officer i/c ... Gun No. ... Target ... Result 2nd Lt Henry ... N.12. A.14.96 ... TIMBER DUMP N.18.B.9.3 ... Unknown " ... " ... JUNCTION OF RDS A.0.13.C.22.9 ... " " ... " ... RENTY FARM O.13.B.9.5½ ... " " ... " ... LOUWAEGE FARM O.Y.D.8.3 ... " **Casualties** Casualties during the month ending 30.11.16 ... NIL. through pickness Officers 2. OR 2. NIL. **Strength** Strength of the Company on the 30-11-16 is as follows Officers 11 ORanks. 176 (including 31 attached men.)	Map Ref French Map Hazebrouck Sheet. 28 SW. 1/10,000

Army Form C. 2118.

WAR DIARY
or
INTELLIGENCE SUMMARY.
(Erase heading not required.)

[Stamp: 124 MACHINE GUN COY. MACHINE GUN CORPS]

124 MACHINE GUN COY.

Place	Date	Hour	Summary of Events and Information	Remarks and references to Appendices
In the Field	6 PM 30.11.16 TO 6 PM 1.12.16		**Our Operations.** Indirect fire was carried out on the following targets.	Map Ref. Trench Map 28 SW 1/10,000.
			Officer i/c Gun No. Rds fired Target Results	
		8 PM AND 11 PM	2nd Lt HENRY WESTERN BREASTWORK N.12.A.14.96 50. DUG OUTS AT O.Y.D.4.0 UNKNOWN	Remarks. Enemy Artillery and Trench Mortar Activity Slight.
			" " 500 TIMBER DUMP AT N.18.B.9.3 "	
		9 PM AND 12 PM	2nd Lt CROWDER BEGGARS REST N.6.D.22.4 500 JUNCTION OF TRENCHES AT O.S.A.8¾.4 "	
			" " 500 ROUWAEGE FARM O.Y.D.8.3 "	
			" " 500 JUNCTION OF TRENCHES AT O.Y.D.3.1 "	
			Weather. The weather for the last 24 hours has been very sharp and there was a very sharp frost which has made the roads very hard.	
			Casualties from 6 PM. 30.11.16 TO 6 PM 1-12-16 NIL SICK 2nd Lt A.S. Niby 2 other ranks.	
			Strength. The 32 men attached to the company from Infantry Units since August 1916 were transported to the Company with effect from the 30.11.16. This was owing to the increased establishment of machine gun companies.	

Operation Orders
by
LIEUT J.W. LAWSON CMD G.124 M.G. COY

1) RELIEF.
Nos 1 & 4 Sections will relieve No's 2 & 3 Sections in the line on 5th inst (Sunday).
The distribution of the relief will be as follows.

No 1 team   No 1 Section will take over FORT TORONTO.
No 2   "   "   "   "   "   FORT GRANTHAM
No 3   "   "   "   "   "   MAJORS COPSE
No 4   "   "   "   "   "   CAPTAINS POST

No 1 team   No 4 Section will take over MACDONALD'S POST
No 2   "   "   "   "   "   EASTERN BREASTWORK.
No 3   "   "   "   "   "   BEGGARS REST.
No 4   "   "   "   "   "   S.P.7.

2) COMMAND
2ND LIEUTS WHITE & BARTON will return to Coy H.Q. and their positions will be taken by LIEUT CARLE & 2ND LT CROWDER respectively

3) HANDING OVER.
Relieving teams will take up their own guns but with this exception all other gun equipment and revolver ammunition will

be handed over by the outgoing teams.

4 TIMETABLE.

6″ 45 A.M. Relieving teams & limber leave Coy HQ.
7·30 " Guides from each position will
be at barrier on VIERSTRAAT ROAD

5 INFORMATION

Relieving teams will receive all particulars regarding the positions taken over & the work in hand.

Officers who are relieved will hand over PROGRAMME OF INDIRECT FIRE for the ensuing week.

6 COMPLETION OF RELIEF.

Relief of all positions must be completed by 10 A.M. Each team when relieved will march independently to H.Q. where the N.C.O. in charge will report to the Orderly Room.

7 RATIONS.

Breakfast Rations only will be sent up the line for Sunday. The ingoing teams will take up the unexpired portion of the day's Ration.

In the Field
3/11/16

John M Jawson Lt Ady
124 CMG Coy.

Operation Orders
No 17.
by
MAJOR W. H. DAVIES. Comdg No 124 M.G. Coy.

[Stamp: 124 MACHINE GUN C. MACHINE GUN ...]

1. Relief:

Nos 2 and 3 Sections will relieve No 1 & 4 Sections in the line on 10th inst. (Friday). The distribution of the relief will be as follows:-

No. 1 team No. 2 Section will take over ~~first~~ MACDONALD'S POST
No. 2   "   "   "   "   "   "   "   EASTERN BREAST-WORK.
No. 3   "   "   "   "   "   "   "   BEGGAR'S REST.
No 4   "   "   "   "   "   "   "   S.P. 7.

No. 1 team No 3 Section will take over FORT TORONTO.
No. 2   "   "   "   "   "   "   "   FORT GRANTHAM
No. 3   "   "   "   "   "   "   "   MAJOR'S COPSE
No. 4   "   "   "   "   "   "   "   CAPTAINS POST.

2. COMMAND.

2nd LIEUT RILEY & LIEUT CARLE will return to Company H.Q. & their positions will be taken over by 2nd LIEUT HENRY & 2nd LIEUT BARTON respectively.

3. HANDING OVER

Relieving teams will take up their guns, and with this exception all gun equipment & revolver ammunition will be handed over by the outgoing teams.

4. TIME TABLE
8-45 am   relieving teams & limber leave by H.Q.
9-30 "   guides from each position will be at barrier on VIERSTRAAT ROAD.

5. INFORMATION.
Relieving teams will receive all particulars regarding the positions taken over & the work in hand.
Officers who are relieved will hand over Programme of Indirect Fire and also any orders regarding returns to be made.

6. COMPLETION OF RELIEF.
Relief of all positions must be completed by 12 nn. Each team when relieved will march independently to H.Q. where the N.C.O. in charge will report to the Orderly Room. The limber which takes up the relieving teams' guns will wait and bring back the relieved teams' guns.

7. RATIONS.
Breakfast rations only will be sent up today. The ingoing teams will take the unexpired portion of the day's rations with them.

In the field
9/11/16.

         Major
         Comdr. No. 126 M.G. Coy.

OPERATION ORDER
No 19
by
MAJOR W. H. Davis   CMDG. 124 M. G. COY

1. RELIEF.

No 3 Section will relieve No 2 Section in the trenches tomorrow and take up the following positions:—

No 1 team will go to   MACDONALD'S POST.
No 2   "   "   "   EASTERN BREASTWORK
No 3   "   "   "   S.P. 7.
No 4   "   "   "   BEGGARS REST.

2. COMMAND.

2nd Lt Henry will relieve 2nd Lt Barton at FORT TORONTO and take over same positions.

3. HANDING OVER.

The relieving teams will take guns with them only. All other necessary equipment being handed over by the outgoing section.

4. TIME TABLE.

9.45 a.m. Relieving teams & limbers leave Coy H.Q.
9.30 "   Guides from each team to be relieved to be at Ration barrier on VIERSTRAAT ROAD.

5. INFORMATION.

All necessary information to be given by outgoing teams. Section Officers in particular will see that all orders regarding returns to be made are handed over, especially the return of Ammunition expended during the week which must reach Coy H.Q. not later than 10 A.M. Saturday.

6. COMPLETION OF RELIEF.

The relief of each position must be completed by 12 noon. Each team when relieved will march independently to Coy H.Q. under the senior N.C.O. who will report his arrival to the Orderly Room. The hour of completion must be telephoned from FORT TORONTO using the following code:—
"Post arrives   all." (inserting time).
The limbers will wait at the Barrier & bring back outgoing teams equipment & packs.

7. RATIONS.

Breakfast Rations will only be sent to the outgoing teams (i.e. No 2 Section) The ingoing teams will take with them the unexpired portion of the days rations with them.

8. TRENCH FEET.

Officers will take particular care that all men rub their feet with Oil & change their socks daily, one pair per man to be sent to Coy H.Q. daily for exchange.

OPERATION ORDER
No 21
by
MAJOR W. H. Davies Cmdg Metaphor.

1. RELIEF

No 2 Section will relieve No 1 Section in the trenches on 28th Nov. and take up the following positions:—

No 1 team will go to FORT GRANTHAM
No 2 " " " PRESCOTT POST (No 1/co. NEW. R. TRENCH)
No 3 " " " WOODLEY POST (No 2 " " ")
No 4 " " " SOUTHERN REDOUBT.

As detailed by 2nd Lt Barton.

2. COMMAND. 2nd Lt Henry will relieve 2nd Lt Clark at E. BREASTWORK.
2nd Lt Crowder will relieve 2nd Lt Riley at WESTERN REDOUBT.
2nd Lt Barton will relieve 2nd Lt Henry at FORT TORONTO.
2nd Lt White will relieve 2nd Lt Jacques at MAJOR'S COPSE and will act in the capacity of Sub-Section Officer to 2nd Lt Barton. 2nd Lts Clark, Riley and Jacques will return to Coy HQ.

3. HANDING OVER.

The Relieving teams will take guns with them only. All other necessary equipment being handed over by the outgoing sections.

4. TIME TABLE.

8·45 A.M. Relieving teams & limbers leave Coy H.Qrs.
9·30 Guides from each team to be relieved to be at Ration Barrier.

5. **INFORMATION.**
   All necessary information to be given by outgoing teams. Section Officers in particular will see that all orders regarding returns to be made are handed over especially the return of Ammunition expended during the week which must reach Coy H.Q. not later than 10.a.m. each Saturday.

6. **COMPLETION OF RELIEF.**
   The relief of each position must be complete by 12 NOON. Each team when relieved will march independently to Coy H.Q. under the Senior N.C.O. who will report his arrival to the Orderly Room. The hour of Completion of Relief will be telephoned from FORT TORONTO using the following Code.
   "Tea will be at   A.M. (Inserting time)
   The limbers will wait at the Barrier and bring back outgoing teams Equipment & Packs.

7. **RATIONS.** No 1 Section will bring back with them the unexpired portion of the days rations. Breakfast rations will only be sent to the outgoing teams (i.e. No 1 Section). The ingoing teams will take with them the unexpired portions of the days rations.

8. **TRENCH. FEET.**
   Officers will take particular care that all men rub their feet with Oil & change socks daily one pair per man to be sent to Coy H.Q. for exchange.

   W. Davis   Major

Army Form C. 2118.

WAR DIARY
or
INTELLIGENCE SUMMARY.
(Erase heading not required.)

Instructions regarding War Diaries and Intelligence Summaries are contained in F.S. Regs., Part II. and the Staff Manual respectively. Title pages will be prepared in manuscript.

[Stamp: 12 A MACHINE GUN COY. * MACHINE GUN CORPS *]

Place	Date	Hour	Summary of Events and Information	Remarks and references to Appendices
In the Field	1-12-16 to 2-12-16	6 PM to 6 PM	Our Operations. Indirect fire was carried out on the following targets	Map Ref. Trench Map Sheet 28 SW 1/10,000
	2-12-16	10 PM to 12 MN	**Officer i/c** 2nd Lt Crowder	**Gun Pos** NEW EMP. BEGGARS REST. N.6.D.2½.4. " " "	**Rds fired** 500 500 500	**Target** SUPPOSED L. RAILWAY AT O.8.C.2.3½. BUILDINGS AT D.8.A.8.0 LOUVAGIE FARM O.4.D.8.8	**Result** UNKNOWN " " "	Enemy M.Gs slightly active at irregular periods
		9.30 PM to 11.30 PM	2nd Lt Henry	WESTERN BREASTWORK N.12.A.14.98 " "	250 250 250	RENTY FARM O.13.B.92.5½ O.13.C.9.4½ SEARCH TRACK AT O.13.A.9.4	" " "	
			Work Done. Work was continued on the new dug-outs at Western Breastwork and bivvie line emplacement at N.6.C.5¾.4.					
			Casualties. Casualties from 6PM 1-12-16 to 6PM 2-12-16 NIL Sick 1 other Rank					
			Weather. Weather is still very cold and frosty.					

Army Form C. 2118.

WAR DIARY
or
INTELLIGENCE SUMMARY.

(Erase heading not required.)

Instructions regarding War Diaries and Intelligence Summaries are contained in F. S. Regs., Part II. and the Staff Manual respectively. Title pages will be prepared in manuscript.

[Stamp: 124 MACHINE GUN COY. * MACHINE GUN CORPS *]

Place	Date	Hour	Summary of Events and Information	Remarks and references to Appendices
In the Field	2.12.16 6 PM to 6 PM 3.12.16	12-35 am	**Raid.** The raid by the 32nd Royal Fusiliers on the hostile trenches ordered for the 25-11-16 took place at 12-35 am on 3/12/16. Six Vickers guns were employed. - 3 Co-operating with the Artillery from temporary emplacements in the front line in putting up a barrage round the portion of trenches raided and 3 giving indirect fire on enemy's supports and communications. The right and left guns on the front line each fired 1,000 rds., but the centre gun was evidently spotted by the enemy and subjected to a severe trench mortar fire. The gun was slightly damaged and had to cease firing after firing little over a belt. A copy of Operation Orders is attached. The raid was successful. 3 prisoners being taken and casualties estimated at 50 were inflicted on the enemy.	124 L. 136c. O.O. 45. 124 M.G. Coy O.O. 20.
			Casualties Casualties from 6 PM 2.12.16 to 6 PM 3.12.16 Nil. Sick Nil.	
	3.12.16	6 pm	**Weather.** The weather has not changed during the last 24 hours.	

Army Form C. 2118.

WAR DIARY
or
INTELLIGENCE SUMMARY.

(Erase heading not required.)

Instructions regarding War Diaries and Intelligence Summaries are contained in F.S. Regs., Part II. and the Staff Manual respectively. Title pages will be prepared in manuscript.

Place	Date	Hour	Summary of Events and Information	Remarks and references to Appendices
In the Field	3/12/16	6 PM	Our Operations. Indirect fire was carried out on the following targets.	Map Ref: Trench Map Sheet 28 S.W. 1/10,000.
	3-12-16 to 6PM 4-12-16	1 PM 3 PM 8 PM 0 AM 10 PM 12 PM	Officers. 2nd Lt HENRY. Gun Pos. — Target — Rds fired — Result WESTERN BREASTWORK — SUPPOSED RAILWAY BEHIND GRAND BOIS — 1,000 — UNKNOWN	Remarks. Enemy's trench system slightly active at 11pm.
	4-12-16	9-30 AM	Relief. Owing to extension of Corps Area, the guns at Fort Toronto and Major's Copse under the command of 2nd Lt BARTON took over gun positions from 113 Machine Gun Company at N.11.C.60.35 and N.11.C.40.25 respectively. The relief was completed by 9-30 AM. For further details see operation orders attached.	See M.G. bys A.C. 22.
			Casualties. Casualties from 6pm 3-12-16 to 6pm 4-12-16. NIL. Sick 2 O.Ranks.	
	4-12-16	6 PM	Weather. The weather during last 24 hours has turned rather warmer and the roads are beginning to thaw.	
	4-12-16 12 noon		Transfer. LIEUT A.W. CARLE proceeded to join 112 Machine Gun Company as 2/command.	

Army Form C. 2118.

WAR DIARY
or
INTELLIGENCE SUMMARY.
(Erase heading not required.)

Instructions regarding War Diaries and Intelligence Summaries are contained in F. S. Regs., Part II. and the Staff Manual respectively. Title pages will be prepared in manuscript.

Place	Date	Hour	Summary of Events and Information	Remarks and references to Appendices
In the Field	6 P.M. 11-12-16 to 6 A.M. 5-12-16		Our Operations. Indirect fire was carried out on the following targets.	
		7:30 A.M.	Officer i/c 2nd Lt. HENRY	Gun Pos. WESTERN BREASTWORK N.12.A.14.96.	Target RENTY FARM D.13.B.9.52	Rds. fired 500	Result. Unknown	Normal fixed rifle on tripod battery mounting on short legs. Sheet 28 SW Lindly active. 1/10,000
		8:30 "	"	"	RED CHATEAU D.18.B.9½.4	500	"	
		2:30 A.M.	"	"	TIMBER DUMP N.18.B.9.3	500	"	
		3 "	"	"	DUG-OUT INT. O.Y.D.8.3½	500	"	
		3:30 A.M.	2nd Lt. CROZIER	BEGGARS REST N.6.D.24.7	CATTEAU FARM O.8.C.8.5	500	"	
	6 P.M. 8-12-16	9:30 A.M.	Reconnaissance.				
				Y.O.C. 41st Division, & 830 I., accompanied the O.C. Company and inspected emplacements at N.11.C.60.35 and N.11.C.40.25 respectively and reconnoitred the positions in reference to the VIERSTRAAT Defence Scheme.	

Army Form C. 2118.

WAR DIARY
or
INTELLIGENCE SUMMARY.
(Erase heading not required.)

Instructions regarding War Diaries and Intelligence Summaries are contained in F. S. Regs., Part II. and the Staff Manual respectively. Title pages will be prepared in manuscript.

Place	Date	Hour	Summary of Events and Information	Remarks and references to Appendices
In the Field	5.12.16	4 pm to 6 pm	Our Operations	Map Ref.
			Indirect fire was carried out on the following targets	Remarks/trench map
				Sheet 28 SW
				1/10,000.
		6.12.16	Officer i/c Gun No. Position Rds. fired Target Results
	7.30h		2nd Lt HENRY WESTERN BREASTWORK N.12.A.14.96 500 SEARCH TRACK THROUGH GRAND BOIS 0.13.B.9.2 UNKNOWN
	8.30h		" " " " 500 TRAVERSE TRAMWAY BEHIND GRAND BOIS "
	3 AM	2nd Lt CROWDER BEGGARS REST N.6.D.22.4 1000 SEARCH TRACKS IN GRAND BOIS + TRAMWAY BEHIND 0.13.A.9.4 to 0.Y.D.3.1 "
	4 AM		
6.12.16	6 pm		Casualties during last 48 hours. NIL. SICK NIL
			Weather
			He enters the during the last 48 hours has been very much as and other but very variable during the mornings.
			Work done.
			Work has been carried out on the drainage of WESTERN BREASTWORK and construction of emplacement at N.6.C.5.34.4.

Army Form C. 2118.

WAR DIARY
or
INTELLIGENCE SUMMARY.
(Erase heading not required.)

Instructions regarding War Diaries and Intelligence Summaries are contained in F. S. Regs., Part II. and the Staff Manual respectively. Title pages will be prepared in manuscript.

[Stamp: 124 MACHINE GUN COY. MACHINE GUN CORPS]

Place	Date	Hour	Summary of Events and Information	Remarks and references to Appendices
In the Field	6.12.16 6 PM to 4.12.16 6 PM		Our Operations Nil. Most hostile Artillery emplacements erected at WOODLEYS POST and PRESCOTTS POST. Casualties Nil.	Map Ref. French Map Sheet 28 SW 1/10,000
	4.12.16 to 7.12.16	6 P.M.	Artillery during last 24 hours has been meeker, and much rain has fallen roads nearly. The weather during last 24 hours has been meeker, and much rain has fallen roads in a very muddy state.	
	7.12.16 6 PM to 8.12.16 6 PM	9.30 P.M. to 11.30 P.M.	Our Operations. On shoot fire was carried out on the following targets. Officer i/c 2nd Lieut W.G. INDLITCROWDER.	

	Target	Rds fired	Remarks
	BEGGARS REST. N.6.D.2.1/2.4	500	Hostile M. Guns slightly active
	LOUWAEGE FARM O.4.D.8.3.	250	Instructor
	BUILDINGS AT O.8.A.8.O.	250	
	RENTY FARM O.13.B.9.5½		

Army Form C. 2118.

WAR DIARY
or
INTELLIGENCE SUMMARY.
(Erase heading not required.)

Instructions regarding War Diaries and Intelligence Summaries are contained in F. S. Regs., Part II. and the Staff Manual respectively. Title pages will be prepared in manuscript.

[Stamp: 124 MACHINE GUN COY. / MACHINE GUN CORPS.]

Place	Date	Hour	Summary of Events and Information	Remarks and references to Appendices
In the Field	4-12-16 6PM to 6PM 9-12-16	11 AM	**Relief** — No. 1 Section relieved No. 4 Section in the trenches and took over Gun positions at Jenkins' Post, Kaplan's Post, and Fort Toronto. The relief was completed by 11 am. For further details see O.O. No 23 attached. **Casualties** — Casualties during last 24 hours Nil. Sick Nil. **Weather** — Much rain has fallen during the last 24 hours. **Our Operations** — Indirect fire was carried out on the following targets:-	See O.O. 23.
	6-12-16 to 9-12-16	6:30 PM 6:30 PM 5:30 AM + 5:30 AM	Gun No. LEWIS POLARK WOLF CROWDER " " " Gun Pos. N.12.A.17.96 " N.6.D.25.4 " " " Rds fired 500 500 500 250 250 Target TIMBER DUMP O.13.B.3.1 TIMBER DUMP C.13.C.8.6. CATTEAU FARM O.8.C.8.5. DUG-OUTS O.8.A.4.14 BUILDINGS O.8.A.8.0 Results UNKNOWN " " " " Remarks Hostile Jns. Nightly active

Army Form C. 2118.

WAR DIARY
or
INTELLIGENCE SUMMARY.
(Erase heading not required.)

Instructions regarding War Diaries and Intelligence Summaries are contained in F. S. Regs., Part II. and the Staff Manual respectively. Title pages will be prepared in manuscript.

Place	Date	Hour	Summary of Events and Information	Remarks and references to Appendices
In the Field	8-12-16 to 9-12-16	6 P.M. to 6 P.M.	**Casualties** Casualties during last 24 hours nil. **Weather** Much rain has fallen during last 24 hours, and roads very muddy.	
		6 P.M.	**Strength** The strength of the company at week ending 9-12-16 is as follows:— Officers 10. Other ranks 143. including the undermentioned casuals. 6 to Field Ambulance 4 Leave 1 Course of Instruction (Ch. G. Grenade tannier) 2 Employed away from Company.	

WAR DIARY
or
INTELLIGENCE SUMMARY.
(Erase heading not required.)

Army Form C. 2118.

Place	Date	Hour	Summary of Events and Information				Remarks and references to Appendices
In the Field	9.12.16	6 P.M.	Our Operations				Trench Map
		6 P.M. to 6 P.M. 10.12.16	Indirect fire was carried out on the following targets				Trench Map Sheet 28 SW 1/10,000
				Gun No.	Rds fired	Target	Results
		6 P.M. & 9 P.M.	Officer i/c INDT. CROWDER.	N.6.D.2½.y.	500	LOUVAGE FARM. O.Y.D.8 3/2.	UNKNOWN.
		10.12.16 9 P.M.	"	"	500	O.B.C. 8.9½ JUNCTION OF ROAD AND TRENCH	"
			" CLARK.	N.6.C.5½.2.	500	O.8.C. 8.9½. SEARCH ROAD FROM O.13.C.39.	"
			"	"	500	16.0.13.C.8.2. JUNCTION OF TRACK AT O.13.B.0.22	"
	10.12.16	6 P.M.	Casualties				Our Artillery very active during last 24 hrs.
			Casualties during last 24 hours nil Sick nil				
	10.12.16	6 P.M.	Weather				
			The weather has slightly improved during last 24 hours, but roads are in a very muddy state.				

WAR DIARY
or
INTELLIGENCE SUMMARY.

(Erase heading not required.)

Army Form C. 2118.

Place	Date	Hour	Summary of Events and Information	Remarks and references to Appendices
In the Field	6 PM		Our Operations.	
	10.10.16	1-3.30 PM	Indirect fire was carried out on the following targets.	Map Ref.
		TO	Officers. Gun Pos. Rds Fired. Target. Results.	Trench Map
		6 PM	2nd Lt WHITE MAJORS COPSE 500 N.18.B.8.2 Unknown	Sheet 28 SW.
		3-30 PM	N.11.A.42.9	1/10,000.
		TO		
		6-30 PM	" FORT TORONTO 500 N.18.B.9.24 "	
		11.12.16 9-30 PM	N.14.A.3.3	
		TO	" " 500 N.18.B.9.2 "	
		12-30 AM		
		12-30 AM	2nd Lt CLARK N.12.A.14.96. 500 O.13.A.4½.8 "	
		TO		JUNCTION OF ROADS AT
		1-1½ AM	" " 500 O.13.C.2½.9. "	
				JUNCTION OF TRENCHES AT
			" " 500 O.Y.D.3.1. "	
				SEARCH RECTANGULAR (N.E.) PORTION OF
				GRANDBOIS. CENTRAL POINT OF AREA
				O.13.B.2.6.
	11.12.16 10 PM		Reconnaissance.	
			4 Brigade Major 124 Infantry Brigade accompanied by O.C. Company	
			reconnoitred sites for new Gun Positions in T and O block and BOIS CARRÉ.	
	11.12.16 6 PM		Casualties.	
			Casualties during last 24 hours. Nom ett Other ranks 1. Sec. Lut	
			Weather. The weather during last 24 hours has been very unsettled.	

WAR DIARY
or
INTELLIGENCE SUMMARY.
(Erase heading not required.)

Army Form C. 2118.

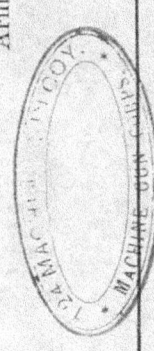

Place	Date	Hour	Summary of Events and Information	Remarks and references to Appendices
In the Field	11.12.16	6 P.M.	Our Operations	Most Ref.
			I attached fire as carried out on the following targets	French Map Sheet 28 S.W. 1/10,000.
	11.12.16 to 12.12.16	8.30 P.M.	Officer i/c Gun No. Rds Fired Target	
			2nd Lt CROWDER N.10.D.2½.7. 500 CATTEAU FARM 0.8.C.2.4.5.	Result
			" " 500 RENTY FARM 0.13.B.9½.5½	UNKNOWN.
	12.12.16	11.30 P.M.	2nd Lt WHITE N.11.A.3.3. 500 0.13.A.4½.8	"
			" " 500 N.18.B.9½.4¾	"
	12.12.16	6 P.M.	Casualties	
			No Casualties during took 24 hours nil Sick nil.	
	12.12.16	7 P.M.	Weather	
			Snow fell heavily during the last 24 hours.	
	11.12.16 to 12.12.16	8.30 P.M. to 7 P.M.	Enemy Operations	
			Hostile Machine Guns were very active at intervals during the evening	
			towards BOIS CARRE and EASTERN BREASTWORK.	

WAR DIARY
or
INTELLIGENCE SUMMARY.

(Erase heading not required.)

Army Form C. 2118.

Place	Date	Hour	Summary of Events and Information	Remarks and references to Appendices
In the field	2.12.16	6 P.M.	**Our Operations**	
		to 6 P.M.	Indirect fire was carried out on the following targets	
			Officer i/c Gun No. Rds. fired Target Results	
		1 P.M. to 7.30 P.M.	2ND LT CLARK. N.6.C.5½.½ 500 CROSS ROADS AT 0.13.C.3.9. Unknown	Map Ref. Sheet 28 SW Sheet 28 SW 1/40,000
		3.30 to 6.30 A.M.	,, ,, 500 JUNCTION OF TRENCHES AT 0.13.C.9.4½. ,,	
		7.30 to 9.30 P.M.	2ND LT. WAITE N.11.A.3.3. 500 N.18.B.9.4½ ,,	
		,,	,, ,, 500 O.Y.C.8.1½ ,,	
		12 M.N. to 3.30 A.M.	2ND LT CROWDER N.6.D.2.4.Y 500 BUILDINGS AT 0.8.A.8.0. ,,	
			500 LOUAGE FARM 0.9.D.8.3½. ,,	
			Enemy Operations	
			Enemy Trench Mortars heavily bombarded our front line nr CHICORY LANE can Stokes Gun retaliated.	
			Conference	
	13.12.16	11 A.M.	O.C. Company attended conference at 41st Division Headquarters with Machine Gun Company commanders of the 41st Division. Arrangements for Gun Positions was discussed and the necessity of training the Gunners in the role of the Howitzer was impressed upon M.G. Company Commanders.	

2353 Wt W2544/1454 700,000 5/15 D.D.&L. A.D.S.S./Forms/C.2118.

Army Form C. 2118.

WAR DIARY
or
INTELLIGENCE SUMMARY.
(Erase heading not required.)

Instructions regarding War Diaries and Intelligence Summaries are contained in F. S. Regs., Part II. and the Staff Manual respectively. Title pages will be prepared in manuscript.

Place	Date	Hour	Summary of Events and Information	Remarks and references to Appendices
In the field	13.12.16	6 PM	Own Operations Indirect fire was carried out on the following targets	Map Ref. Trench Map Sheet 28 SW 1/10,000. See O.O. 25" attached.
		8 PM to 6 PM	Officer i/c Gun Pos. Target Rds. Fired Result 2ND LT CLARK. N.12.A.14.96. TRIANGLE IN GRAND BOIS - BARE 500 UNKNOWN 0.13.A. 64.6. 6.13.C.39. APEX 2. IN BOIS JUNCTION OF TRENCHES AT " " 0.13.B. 1. 8¾. 500	
	14.12.16	11 PM		
	14.12.16	8.30 am	Relief The No 4 Section relieved No 3 Section in the trenches and took over gun positions as shown in the attached Operation Order. The relief was completed by 11 am 14th inst.	
	14.12.16	10 am	Reconnaissance The Brigade Major 144th Infantry Brigade accompanied by O.C. Company reconnoitred sites for new gun positions in Poppy Lane.	
	14.12.16	6 PM	Work Work continued on the draining of trench and dug-outs at DALTON POST.	
	14.12.16	7 PM	Casualties Casualties during last 24 hours. Nil. Sick. Other Ranks 1.	

Army Form C. 2118.

WAR DIARY
or
INTELLIGENCE SUMMARY.
(Erase heading not required.)

24 MACHINE GUN COY. — MACHINE GUN CORPS

Place	Date	Hour	Summary of Events and Information	Remarks and references to Appendices
In the Field	14.12.16	6 pm	**Our Operations**	Map Ref. Trench map Sheet 28 SW 1/10,000
			Indirect fire was carried out on the following targets:—	
			Officer i/c Gun Pos. Rds fired Target Result.	
		to 7.15 pm	2/Lt SUTHERLAND N.11.C.4.2½. JUNCTION OF ROADS AT N.18.B.4.2. UNKNOWN.	
		6 pm	" " " 300 SEARCH ROAD FROM N.18.B.4.2.	"
	15.12.16	11.15 pm	500 TO O.13. C.3.9. RENTY FARM	"
		7 pm to 11 pm	2/Lt SUTHERLAND HERON. N.6.D.2.7.1 500 O.13.B.9½.5½. CATTEAU FARM	"
			500 O.8. C.8½.5.	
			Enemy Operation	
	14.12.16	9 pm	The enemy unsuccessfully raided our trench O.Y.2. The raiders entered our trench at O.Y.A1 they were soon driven out by our garrison leaving one dead. Owing to the nature of the ground Vickers guns were unable to fire.	
	15.12.16	6 pm	**Weather**	
			The weather during last 24 hours has been changeable raining at intervals. Roads very muddy.	
	15.12.16	9 pm	**Casualties**	
			No casualties during last 24 hours. Lt. Sgt. Fil.	

Army Form C. 2118.

WAR DIARY
or
INTELLIGENCE SUMMARY.
(Erase heading not required.)

Instructions regarding War Diaries and Intelligence Summaries are contained in F. S. Regs., Part II. and the Staff Manual respectively. Title pages will be prepared in manuscript.

[Stamp: 124 MACHINE GUN COY. / MACHINE GUN CORPS]

Place	Date	Hour	Summary of Events and Information	Remarks and references to Appendices
In the Field	15.12.16	6 PM	Our Operators	Map Ref trench map Sheet 28 S.W. 1/10,000
		9 PM	Indirect fire was carried out on the following targets	
		To		
		6 PM	Officer i/c	Gun No. Rds Fired Target Results
		9 PM	2ND LT HARLAND	N.11.C.4.2.2. 250 JUNCTION OF ROAD AT N.18.B.Y.2. UNKNOWN
16.12.16		9 PM	" CLARK	N.12.A.Y.96 500 ENFILADE TRENCH THROUGH GRAND BOIS C.13.A.Y.5′ TO O.13.B.15.1 "
		TO		
		12 MN	"	" 500 JUNCTION OF ROAD AT O.13.C.3 "
		9.30 PM	" HERON	N.6. D.2.9.1 500 JUNCTION OF ROAD AND FRENCH AT O.8.C.8.9½ (AEROPLANE PHOTO) "
		TO		
		11.30 PM	" "	" 60 VERTICALLY SEARCHING & TRACK FROM O.13.B.5.9½ TO RENTY FARM "
16.12.16		6 PM	Enemy Activity Normal	
			Casualties Casualties during last 24 hours Nil Sick Ortr Hawks Evac.	
16.12.16		6 PM	Weather The weather during last 24 hours has been changeable raining at intervals, frost during night of 15th inst.	

[Signature]

Army Form C. 2118.

WAR DIARY
or
INTELLIGENCE SUMMARY.
(Erase heading not required.)

Place	Date	Hour	Summary of Events and Information	Remarks and references to Appendices
In the Field	16.12.16	1 pm	**Strength** The strength of the company for week ending 16.12.16 is as follows. Officers 10 Other ranks 142. This total includes the undermentioned totals: 3 On Field Ambulance. 1 Leave 1 At Base (employed) 1 Course of Inst.	
	16.12.16 to 8 pm	6 pm	Our Operations. Indirect fire was carried out on the following targets. (Combined Shoot) Officers Gun Pos. Field Fired Target 2nd Lt. HARLAND N.11.A.74.9. 1000 SEARCHED GRAND BOIS AND " CLARK N.13.A.14.96. 1000 TRAVERSED TRAMWAY " HERON N.6.C.54.2. 1000 BEHIND IT.	Shot No. of [illegible] trench map Sheet 28 SW Scale 1/10,000 UNKNOWN Results
	19.12.16	6 pm	Enemy Activity shown nil.	

Army Form C. 2118.

WAR DIARY
or
INTELLIGENCE SUMMARY.
(Erase heading not required.)

Instructions regarding War Diaries and Intelligence Summaries are contained in F. S. Regs., Part II. and the Staff Manual respectively. Title pages will be prepared in manuscript.

Place	Date	Hour	Summary of Events and Information	Remarks and references to Appendices
In the Field	17.12.16	6 pm	Work — Owing to the large amount of work to be done 2nd Lt Henry has taken charge of all work required at Rugram Lupton in direction of Gun Emplacements, Buildings of dug outs, and drainage. During the last 24 hours work has been in full swing on the above mentioned work.	
	17.12.16	6 pm	Casualties — Casualties during last 24 hours nil — Sick nil	
	17.12.16	6 pm	Weather — The weather during last 24 hours has been fairly, but the roads are in a very muddy state.	

Army Form C. 2118.

WAR DIARY
or
INTELLIGENCE SUMMARY.
(Erase heading not required.)

Instructions regarding War Diaries and Intelligence Summaries are contained in F. S. Regs., Part II. and the Staff Manual respectively. Title pages will be prepared in manuscript.

Place	Date	Hour	Summary of Events and Information	Remarks and references to Appendices
In the field	7/4/16	6 PM	Our Operations	Map Ref.
			Indirect fire was carried out on the following targets	French Map
				Sheet 28 S.W.
			Gun Pos. Rds fired Target	1/10.000
	to	8.25 PM	Officer i/c DUG OUTS AT	Results
			2nd Lt. HARLAND. N 11 C.4.2.2. 500 O.13. A.2.6.	UNKNOWN
	8 PM		" " 500 LARGE DUG OUT IN WOOD	
	7/4/16	to 10 PM		AT O.13.A.8½.5½.	
			" " 500 DUG OUTS AT O.13.A.3½.6. THESE	
	9 PM to 11.30 PM		2nd Lt. CLARK N.6.C.5½.½. 1000 TARGETS ARE TAKEN FROM A.W.J.B. LIST 9 & 43	
				TRAMWAY BEHIND GRAND BOIS	
				TRAVERSED FROM O.13.B.4.3. TO O.13.C.9.2.4.	
	9 PM		Enemy Activity	
	to 11 PM		Enemy Machine Guns slightly active. Artillery normal.	
			Nil.	
	6/4/16	6.7 PM	Much work is in progress under the the supervision of 2/Lt. Henry with regard to	
			dug-outs, Gun Emplacements, and drainage.	
			Casualties	
			Casualties during last 24 hours 1 Nil. Pte Hill 2/4th Riley discharged from the	
			Batt.	
			The weather during the last 24 hours has been very cold & frosty roads very hard.	

2353 Wt. W2544/1454 700,000 5/15 D. D. & L.   A.D.S.S./Forms/C. 2118.

Army Form C. 2118.

WAR DIARY
or
INTELLIGENCE SUMMARY.
(Erase heading not required.)

Instructions regarding War Diaries and Intelligence Summaries are contained in F. S. Regs., Part II. and the Staff Manual respectively. Title pages will be prepared in manuscript.

Place	Date	Hour	Summary of Events and Information	Remarks and references to Appendices
In the field	6 P.M. 18.12.16 to 6 P.M. 19.12.16	6 P.M.	Our Operations. Indirect fire was carried out on the following targets.	
			Gun No. Rds fired Target	
			Officer i/c	
		8 SEP. 2ND LT. HERON.	N.C. 9. 2½ y. 500 LOUWAGE FT FARM O.Y.D.8.3	Map Ref French trench Sheet 28 SW.
		AND	500 BUILDINGS AT O.8.A.8.0 (BRIGADE LIST) RENTY FARM	Unknown 1/10.000.
	19.12.16	12 M.N.	500 O.13.B.9.5½.	
			Enemy Activity Normal.	
			Met. Frost is still in progress and the information of Hobart Henry	
	19.12.16	6 P.M.	Casualties	
			Casualties during last 24 hours Nil. Sick one other rank.	
	19.12.16	6 P.M.	Births Much snow has fallen during the last 24 hours.	
	19.12.16	10 AM	Inspection of Transport J.O.C. 41st Division inspected transport Horses and Mules.	

Army Form C. 2118.

WAR DIARY
or
INTELLIGENCE SUMMARY.
(Erase heading not required.)

Instructions regarding War Diaries and Intelligence Summaries are contained in F. S. Regs., Part II. and the Staff Manual respectively. Title pages will be prepared in manuscript.

[Stamp: 124 MACHINE GUN COY. MACHINE GUN CORPS.]

Place	Date	Hour	Summary of Events and Information	Remarks and references to Appendices
In the field	19-12-16 to 1 PM	6 PM	**Own Operations** Harrass't fire was carried out on the following targets. Officer i/c Gun Pos. Rds Fired Target 2nd Lt Clark N.12.A.14.96 250 Junction of Roads at " " 500 Timber Dump at O.13.C.3.9 " " 250 Timber Dump at O.13.A.8.6 O.13.B.3.1	Results unknown trench map Sheet 28 SW 1/10,000
			Enemy Activity Aircraft slightly active. Artillery, Trench Guns, and Trench Mortars normal.	
	20-12-16	11.15 AM	**Relief** No 3 released No 1 Section in the trenches and took over gun positions as detailed in A.O. 26.	See A.O. 26 Attached.
	20-12-16	1 PM	**Casualties** Casualties during last 24 hours Nil Sick Nil.	
	20-12-16	6 PM	**Weather** The weather during last 24 hours has been very cold and frosty. Roads very hard.	

Army Form C. 2118.

WAR DIARY
or
INTELLIGENCE SUMMARY.
(Erase heading not required.)

Instructions regarding War Diaries and Intelligence Summaries are contained in F. S. Regs., Part II. and the Staff Manual respectively. Title pages will be prepared in manuscript.

Place	Date	Hour	Summary of Events and Information	Remarks and references to Appendices
In the Field	20.12.16	6 P.M.	**Our Operations**	
			Indirect fire was carried out on the following targets	
		9.30 P.M.	Officer i/c Gun No. Rds fired Target	Results. Map Ref.
		TO	2ND LT RILEY. N.11.C.55.25. 500 CROSS ROADS AT 0.13.C.3.9.	UNKNOWN Trench Map Sheet 28 SW
		6 P.M. TO	" " 500 DUG OUTS IMPORTANT POINT 0.13.C.2.6	" 1/10,000.
	21.2.16	11.30 P.M.		
		7.30 P.M.	2ND LT HERON N.6.C.5½.½ 750 ENFILADE TRACK IN GRAND BOIS 0.13. A & B	"
		AND	" " 500. DUG OUTS (MUCH USED) 0.13. A. 3½.6	"
		12 M.N.	" " 500 CROSS ROADS AT 0.13.C.3.9.	"
			Enemy Activity Normal.	
	21.12.16	6 P.M.	**Weather.** The weather during the last 24 hours has been changeable. Heavy rainfall at intervals	
			Casualties. Casualties during last 24 hours. Nil. Sick 1 Other Rank.	
			Work. Much work has been done during last 24 hours in also the supervision of 2/Lt Henry	

Army Form C. 2118.

WAR DIARY
or
INTELLIGENCE SUMMARY.
(Erase heading not required.)

Instructions regarding War Diaries and Intelligence Summaries are contained in F. S. Regs., Part II. and the Staff Manual respectively. Title pages will be prepared in manuscript.

[Stamp: 124 MACHINE GUN COY. MACHINE GUN CORPS]

Place	Date	Hour	Summary of Events and Information	Remarks and references to Appendices
In the field	21.12.16	6 PM to 6 PM	**Our Operations**	
		8 PM	Indirect fire was carried out on the following targets:	Map Ref.
			Officer — Gun no. — Rds fired — Target — Results	Map Ref. Vimeux Trench Map
		6 PM and 2nd Lt Barton — N.6.D.23.4 — 250 — Louvage Farm — Unknown	
	22.12.16 11.15 PM	" — " — 500 — Dump at Cateau Farm / O.Y.D.8.3. — "	
			" — " — 500 — D.8.C.8.5. — "	
			" — " — 250 — Dugouts at O.8.A.14.17. — "	
		9.30 PM 2nd Lt Heron — N.12.A.14.96 — 250 — Dump at O.13.A.1.4. — "	
		and " — 250 — Dump at O.13.C.2.6. — "	
		11.30 PM " — 500 — Dump at O.13.A.4.4. — "	
		7.30 PM 2nd Lt Henry — N.11.A.94.9. — 250 — Red Chateau at Suspected H.Q. N.18.B.9.4. — "	
		and " — 250 — N.18.B.8.2 Timber Dump — "	
		11 PM " — 500 — N.18.B.9.2½ — "	
	22.12.16	6 PM	**Casualties** Casualties during last 24 hours: Nil. Rick 1 Mule Mark	
	23.12.16	6 PM	**Weather** The weather during last 24 hours has been very partly raining at intervals.	

Army Form C. 2118.

WAR DIARY
or
INTELLIGENCE SUMMARY.
(Erase heading not required.)

Place	Date	Hour	Summary of Events and Information	Remarks and references to Appendices
In the field	22/12/16 6.30 P.M. to 6 P.M. 23/12/16 5.0 P.M.		**Our Operations** Indirect fire was carried out by the following targets.	
			Gun Pos. Rounds fired Target	Results
			2ND I. RILEY. 400 TIMBER DUMP O.13.C.2.24	Maj Hy.†
			N.11.C.4.2d. 400 TIMBER DUMP O.13.A.1.4	UNKNOWN TRENCH MORTAR
			" 430 TIMBER DUMP O.13.C.2.6	Shell-28 yds.
				1/10,000
	23/12/16 7 P.M.		**Enemy Activity** Normal.	
			Strength The strength of the Company for week ending 23rd inst. is as follows:-	
			Offrs Other Ranks.	
			10 145 including the undermentioned casuals.	
			" " 1 for field ambulance	
			" " 1 on leave to U Kingdom	
			" " 2 Attached to 21st K.R.R. for testing & locating Xmas mail	
			" " 1 Attached to 299 Coy A.S.C. as loader.	

[stamp: 124 MACHINE GUN COY. MACHINE GUN CORPS]

Army Form C. 2118.

WAR DIARY
or
INTELLIGENCE SUMMARY.
(Erase heading not required.)

[Stamp: No. 24 MACHINE GUN COY. / MACHINE GUN CORPS]

Place	Date	Hour	Summary of Events and Information	Remarks and references to Appendices
In the Field	22-10-16 to 6 pm	6 pm	**Our Operations** No indirect fire was carried out last night 23rd inst. owing to a very high wind.	
	22-10-16	2 pm	**Enemy Operations** Artillery very active, Machine Guns and Trench Mortars normal.	
	22-10-16	6 pm	**Casualties** Casualties during last 24 hours nil. Pak nil.	
	22-10-16	6 pm	**Weather** The weather during last 24 hours has been very bright and much warmer and the roads are drying up. During the evening of the 23rd inst. the wind was too high to allow indirect fire to be carried out.	

Army Form C. 2118.

WAR DIARY
or
INTELLIGENCE SUMMARY.
(Erase heading not required.)

Place	Date	Hour	Summary of Events and Information	Remarks and references to Appendices
In the Field	24.2.6	6 PM	Our Operations	
			Indirect fire was carried out on the following targets	
	6 PM to 6 PM 24.2.16	6.45 PM 9.30 PM 6.30 AM 9.30 PM 7 to 6 6.30 AM 9.30 PM	Officer i/c Gun No. Target Rounds fired	Result
			2nd Lt RILEY No. C.55.25. CROSS ROADS AT 500 UNKNOWN	Trop Map Sheet 28 NW Sheet 28 SW 1/10.000
			O.13.C.3.9
			DUG.OUTS AT 500
			O.13.A.2.6
			DUG.OUTS AT 500
			C.13.C.2.6
			2nd Lt. HERN LOUWAEGE FARM 500
			O.Y.D.8.3
			To DUG.OUTS AT 500
			O.Y.D.3.0
			10.30 PM CATTENU FARM 500
			O.8.C.8.6
			7.30 PM 2nd Lt. BARTON BRACKCOT 500
			C.13.C.0.2
			To DUG.OUTS AT 500
			O.13.C.2.6
			3 AM DUG.OUTS AT 500
			O.13.C.5.4
			Enemy Activity Normal.	
			Casualties	
Field	25.2.16	6 PM	Casualties during last 24 hours 2 Rank & File Sick Nil	

WAR DIARY
or
INTELLIGENCE SUMMARY

Army Form C. 2118.

(Erase heading not required.)

Place	Date	Hour	Summary of Events and Information	Remarks and references to Appendices
In the field	25.12.16	6 pm	Weather. The weather has not changed during last six hours.	
	25.12.16	6 pm	Work done. Much work has been carried out with regards to reconstruction of alternative emplacements and drainage.	
		6 pm	Operations. Indirect fire was carried out on the following targets:	Results High Pct. Source of Inform. Shed 28 SW 1/10,000 UNKNOWN
	25.12.16	6 pm to 9.30 pm	Gun No 8 N.31.c.4.24.	Rds fired: 500, 250, 500. Target: TIMBER DUMP O.13.0.d.24. TIMBER DUMP O.13.A.7.4. TIMBER DUMP O.13.c.2.6.
	26.12.16	6 pm	Enemy Activity. Normal.	
	26.12.16	6 pm	Casualties. Casualties during last 24 hours: Nil.	
	26.12.16	6 pm	Weather. The weather during last 24 hours has been unchanged.	

Army Form C. 2118.

WAR DIARY
or
INTELLIGENCE SUMMARY.
(Erase heading not required.)

[STAMP: 124 MACHINE GUN COY MACHINE GUN CORPS]

Place	Date	Hour	Summary of Events and Information	Remarks and references to Appendices
In the Field	26/12/16	6 P.m.	Our Operations	
	26/12/16 to 6 P.m. 27/12/16	6.30 p.m. to 9.30 p.m.	Indirect fire was carried out on the following targets (Combined Shoot)	Aeroplane French Map Photo 1/8 Set
			Officer i/c Gun No.8 Target Rds fired Target	1.10.00 A
			2nd Lt Riley N.M.C.55.25 1,000 TRAVERSED TRACK THROUGH GRAND BOIS O.13.B.03.TO O.13.B.11 UNKNOWN	
	27/12/16	do	2nd Lt Barton N.8.C.55.½ 1,000 ON RAFT FARM O.14.A.2.1 AND SEARCH TRACK RUNNING SOUTH FROM IT.	
		do	2nd Lt Heron N.12.A.1496 1,000 SEARCH TRAMWAY BEHIND GRAND BOIS.	
		do	2nd Lt Clark N.11.C.1.12 1,000 SEARCH TRACK IN GRAND BOIS FROM O.13.B.03. TO O.13.B.3.5.	
			Enemy Activity	
			Normal.	
	27/12/16	6 P.m.	Casualties	
			Casualties during last 24 hours. 2nd Lieut-A.B.M. Clark wounded. Otherwise nil. Sick nil.	
	27/12/16	6 P.m.	Weather	
			The weather during last 24 hours as slightly improved. No rain.	

WAR DIARY
or
INTELLIGENCE SUMMARY

Army Form C. 2118.

(Erase heading not required.)

Place	Date	Hour	Summary of Events and Information	Remarks and references to Appendices
In the Field	27.12.16	11.30 am	**Relief**. The 4 Section relieved No 3 Section in the trenches and took over gun positions as shown in Operation orders attached.	See A.O. 24.
	27.12.16 6 P.M. to 28.12.16 6 P.M.	6.30 P.M.	**Own Operations**. Indirect fire was carried out on the following targets: Gun No. Officer i/c Rds fired Target N.11.A.3.3. 2ND LT RILEY. 450 ENFILADE SUNKEN ROAD FROM N.18.B.8.2. TO RED CHATEAU. " " 450 TIMBER DUMP N.18.B.9.2.3½	Map Ref French Map Sheet 28SW 1.10.000 Results UNKNOWN
	28.12.16 9.30 P.M		**Enemy Activity**. Artillery slightly active at intervals	
	28.12.16 6 P.M.		**Work done during last 24 hours**. Drainage of trench at FORT GRANTHAM. Reboning revetion & emplacement at HARROWBY POST.	
	28.12.16 6 PM		**Casualties**. Casualties during last 24 hours. Nil Sick 2nd Lieut H.F. St Henry O.R. nil	
	28.12.16 6 PM		**Weather**. Much rain has fallen during last 24 hours, roads very muddy	

Army Form C. 2118.

WAR DIARY
or
INTELLIGENCE SUMMARY.
(Erase heading not required.)

Instructions regarding War Diaries and Intelligence Summaries are contained in F. S. Regs., Part II. and the Staff Manual respectively. Title pages will be prepared in manuscript.

[STAMP: 124 MACHINE GUN COY. MACHINE GUN CORPS]

Place	Date	Hour	Summary of Events and Information	Remarks and references to Appendices
In the field	28.12.16 6pm to 29.12.16 6PM		Own Operations Indirect fire was carried out on the following targets	
			Officer / Gun No / Rounds fired / Target	Results
		7.30pm	2nd Lt WHITE. / A.6.D.2.4. / 500 / LOUVRÈGE FARM O.Y. D.B.3.	Unknown
	29.12.16 to 11.30 PM		" / " / 500 / O.B. Dugouts at A.4.17	Map Ref Sheet 28 SW 1/10,000.
			" / " / 500 / Suspected Signalling Station O.14.A.4.8.	
			Enemy Activity	
			Artillery slightly active. Machine Guns & Trench Mortars normal.	
	29.12.16 10AM		Reconnaissance	
			Lieut Colonel C.V. Martin x Corps Machine Gun Officer accompanied by O.C. Company reconnoitred the 9th Corps area with a view to siting M.G. positions for defence of X Corps front. The position was approved of more suitably for the purpose than COCKATOO TRENCH. (Map Ref N.11.C.6.3) in X Corps area.	
	29.12.16 6PM		Casualties	
			Casualties during last 24 hours 1 Sick hit	
	29.12.16 6PM		Weather Much rain has fallen during the last 24 hours, wind very high	

Army Form C. 2118.

WAR DIARY
or
INTELLIGENCE SUMMARY.
(Erase heading not required.)

Instructions regarding War Diaries and Intelligence Summaries are contained in F. S. Regs., Part II and the Staff Manual respectively. Title pages will be prepared in manuscript.

Place	Date	Hour	Summary of Events and Information	Remarks and references to Appendices
In the field	29.12.16	6 pm	**Own Operations.**	
		to 11.30 pm	Indirect fire was carried out on the following targets	
			Officer i/c Gun No. Rds Fired Target Results.	
	30.12.16	6 pm to 6.30 am	2nd Lt. BARTON M.G.C. 52.2. 950 DUG OUTS MUCHINSED UNKNOWN	Any Ref. trench map Sheet 28 S.W. 1/10.000.
			" " 500 0.13.A.31.6 "	
			" " 250 LARGE DUG OUT 0.13.A.84.53 ENTRANCE TO DUG OUT 0.13.C.5.5 "	
		7.30 pm to 11.30 pm	2nd Lt. WHITE M.G.D.22.9 950 TIMBER DUMP N.18.B.9.3 "	
			" " 250 RENTY FARM 0.13.B.9.53 "	
			" " 500 SEARCH JUNCTION OF TRACKS AT 0.13.A.9.4 "	
			Enemy Activity	
			Aeroplanes very active although a very high wind. Artillery M. Guns, Trench mortars slightly active	
	30.12.16	6 pm	**Casualties**	
			Casualties during last 24 hours hit 6th Bn. nil.	
	30.12.16	6 pm	**Weather**	
			The weather during last 24 hours has been dull, rain at intervals	

Army Form C. 2118.

WAR DIARY
or
INTELLIGENCE SUMMARY.
(Erase heading not required.)

Instructions regarding War Diaries and Intelligence Summaries are contained in F. S. Regs., Part II. and the Staff Manual respectively. Title pages will be prepared in manuscript.

[Stamp: 124 MACHINE GUN COY. MACHINE GUN CORPS.]

Place	Date	Hour	Summary of Events and Information	Remarks and references to Appendices
In the Field	30-12-16	8 P.M.	Strength. The strength of company for week ending 30-12-16 is as follows:-	
			Officers Other Ranks	
			9 144 This total includes the undermention of casuals.	
			1 2 Field Ambulance	
			1 3 Course of Instruction	
			1 1 Leave to England	
			1 1 With 1st Divisional Train	
	30-12-16	1 P.M.	Our Operations.	
			Indirect fire was carried out on the following targets.	Trench Map Belg. sheet 28 S.W. 1/10,000
			Officer Gun Pos. Rds. fired Target	
		8 P.M. 6-30 P.M. TO 9-30 P.M.	2nd Lt. Riley N.11.C.55.25. 1,000 UNNAMED WOOD	UNKNOWN
	31-12-16 10-30 P.M. TO 3 A.M.	" " " " 500 O.13.C.	
			" " " " 500 BLACKCOT	
		9-30 P.M. TO 12 P.M.	Lt. White N.6.D.22.4. 500 O.13.C.O.7.	
			" " " " 500 LOUVAEGE FARM	
			" " " " 500 O.Y.D.8.8.	
			" " " " 500 SUSPECTED SIGNALLING STN.	
			" " " " 500 O.14.A.4.24.8.	
			" " " " 500 SERIES OF DUG OUTS AT	
			" " " " 500 O.Y.D.4.0	

Army Form C. 2118.

WAR DIARY
or
INTELLIGENCE SUMMARY.
(Erase heading not required.)

Place	Date	Hour	Summary of Events and Information	Remarks and references to Appendices
In the Field	31.12.16		Enemy Activity — normal.	
	31.12.16	6 pm	Work — Work as been carried out during the last six hours in the drainage of trenches and dug out, construction of emplacements is still in progress.	
	31.12.16	6 pm	Casualties — Casualties during last six hours nil. Sick 1 other rank.	
	31.12.16	6 pm	Weather — The weather during the last six hours is slightly improved, but the roads and trenches are still very muddy.	

Army Form C. 2118.

WAR DIARY
or
INTELLIGENCE SUMMARY.

(Erase heading not required.)

Place	Date	Hour	Summary of Events and Information	Remarks and references to Appendices
In the field	31.12.16 to 1.1.17	6 pm	**Our Operations.**	
			Indirect fire was carried out on the following targets	
			Officer i/c Gun Pos. Rds fired Target	Results Map Ref
	1.1.17	6 pm 6.30 pm to 10.30 pm	2ND LT RILEY N.H.C.55.25. 300 SUSPECTED COOK HOUSE	unknown 51bNW
			" " 300 O.13.A.1.5½ CROSS ROADS	" 1/10,000
			" " 500 O.13.C.3.9 DUGOUTS	"
	1.1.17	7 pm to 11 pm	LT BARTON N.C.53.4. 150 O.13.C.2.6 TRAVERSE TRACK IN GRAND BOIS	"
			" " 250 O.13.B.3.5 DUG OUTS	"
			" " 300 O.4.D.4.0 TIMBER DUMP N.18.B.9.3	
		6 pm	**Enemy Activity** Artillery very active during the day, Machine Guns & Trench Mortars normal.	
	1.1.17	6 pm	**Casualties** Casualties during last 24 hours Nil Sick 2 other Ranks.	
	1.1.17	6 pm	**Weather** The weather during last 24 hours has slightly improved.	

Army Form C. 2118.

WAR DIARY
or
INTELLIGENCE SUMMARY.
(Erase heading not required.)

Instructions regarding War Diaries and Intelligence Summaries are contained in F. S. Regs., Part II. and the Staff Manual respectively. Title pages will be prepared in manuscript.

Place	Date	Hour	Summary of Events and Information	Remarks and references to Appendices
In the Field	31-12-16		Promotions:- During the past month the undermentioned 2nd Lieutenants were gazetted 1st Lieutenants. 2nd Lieutenants G.H.R. Barton. Gaz. Lieut. 7-12-16. C.V. White. 11-11-16.	

OPERATION ORDER NO.22
by
MAJOR W. H. DAVIS
COMMANDING 124th.MACHINE GUN COMBANY.
****

1. RELIEFS.
   The guns at present in FORT TORONTO and MAJORS COPSE will be moved tomorrow morning to positions at N 11 c 60.35 and N 11 c 40.25 respectively, at present occupied by the 47th.Machine Gun Company.

2. TIME OF RELIEF.
   2nd.Lt.Barton will, accompanied by two men, reconnoitre the best way to the positions. On his return he will bring with him one man of No.47 Machine Gun Coy. from each team who will act as guide to the relieving teams.
   Relief to be completed by 9.30 am.
   The VIERSTRAAT ROAD must not be used.

3. HANDING OVER.
   The relieving teams will take with them guns, tripods, spare parts and 10 belt boxes for each position, and will take over from the outgoing teams the usual trench stores. A list of such stores taken over will be sent to Coy.Headquarters.

4. COMMAND.
   2/Lt.Barton will be in Command of the two new positions.

5. COMPLETION OF RELIEF.
   Completion of relief will be reported to Coy.Headquarters by telephone using the following code:-
   "Mail" left at   am. (insert time).
   A detailed list of teams taking over the new positions should be sent to Coy.Headquarters to facilitate the distribution of rations.

3/12/16.
                                        John Lawson Lieut.& Adjt.
                                        124th.Machine Gun Company.

OPERATION ORDER NO. 23
BY
MAJOR W.H.DAVIS
COMMANDING 124th.MACHINE GUN COMPANY.

1. **RELIEF.**
   No. 1 Section will relieve No. 4 Section in the trenches on 8TH. DECEMBER. and take up the following positions:-

   No. 1 Team will go to ... GORDONS. POST
   No. 2 "   "   "   "   CAPTAINS. POST
   No. 3 "   "   "   " } Report to the Officer at FORT. TORONTO who will allot them
   No. 4 "   "   "   " }   (their positions)

2. **COMMAND.**
   2ND LT. CLARK. will relieve 2ND LT HENRY at E.BREASTWORK.
   "   "   WHITE   "   "   "   " BARTON " FORT TORONTO.
   "   "   HARLAND   "   .   "   " WHITE " MAJORS COPSE.

3. **HANDING OVER.**
   Relieving teams will take guns with them only, all other necessary equipment being handed over by the relieved Section.

4. **TIME TABLE.**
   8.45 am. Relieving teams and limbers leave Company Headquarters.
   9.30 am. Guides from each team to be relieved will be at the RATION BARRIER.

5. **INFORMATION.**
   All necessary information is to be given by outgoing teams.
   Section Officers, in particular, will see that all orders regarding returns to be made are handed over, especially the return of ammunition expended during the week which must reach Company Headquarters not later than 10 am. each Saturday.

6. **COMPLETION OF RELIEF.**
   Relief of each position must be completed by 12 noon.
   Each team when relieved will march independently to Company Headquarters under the Senior N.C.O. who will report his arrival to the Orderly Room.
   Report of completion of relief will be telephoned from FORT TORONTO using the following code :- CEASEDWORK. AT   .AM.
   All limbers will wait at the Barrier and bring back outgoing teams equipment and packs.

7. **RATIONS.**
   Relieved Section will bring back with them the unexpired portion of the day's rations.
   Relieving Sections will take with them the unexpired portion of the day's rations.

8. **TRENCH FEET.**
   Officers will take particular care that all men rub their feet with oil and change their socks daily, one pair of socks per man to be sent to Company Headquarters in exchange.

                                                    Lieut. & Adjt.
                                                    124th.Machine Gun Coy.

OPERATION ORDER NO. 25.
BY
MAJOR W.H.DAVIS
COMMANDING 124th.MACHINE GUN COMPANY.
****

1. **RELIEF.**
   No. 4. Section will relieve No. 3. Section in the trenches on 14TH DECEMBER. and take up the following positions:-

   No. 1 Team will go to EASTERN. BREASTWORK.
   No. 2   "   "   " " CAPTAINS. POST.
   No. 3   "   "   " " MACDONALDS. POST.
   No. 4   "   "   " " BEGGARS. REST.

2. **COMMAND.**
   2ND LT HARLAND. will relieve 2ND LT. WHITE at FORT TORONTO.
   "   " HERON   "   "   " " CROWDER." W. REDOUBT.
   "   " HENRY   "   "   " " HARLAND. MAJORS COPSE.

3. **HANDING OVER.**
   Relieving teams will take guns with them only, all other necessary equipment being handed over by the relieved Section.

4. **TIME TABLE.**
   8.45 am. Relieving teams and limbers leave Company Headquarters.
   9.30 am. Guides from each team to be relieved will be at the RATION BARRIER.

5. **INFORMATION.**
   All necessary information is to be given by outgoing teams. Section Officers, in particular, will see that all orders regarding returns to be made are handed over, especially the return of ammunition expended during the week which must reach Company Headquarters not later than 10 am. each Saturday.

6. **COMPLETION OF RELIEF.**
   Relief of each position must be completed by 12 noon.
   Each team when relieved will march independently to Company Headquarters under the Senior N.C.O. who will report his arrival to the Orderly Room. The VIERSTRAEET ROAD. must not be used.
   Report of completion of relief will be telephoned from FORT TORONTO using the following code :- BOOTS. EXCHANGED.AT.   AM.
   All limbers will wait at the Barrier and bring back outgoing teams equipment and packs.

7. **RATIONS.**
   Relieved Section will bring back with them the unexpired portion of the day's rations.
   Relieving Sections will take with them the unexpired portion of the day's rations.

8. **TRENCH FEET.**
   Officers will take particular care that all men rub their feet with oil and change their socks daily, one pair of socks per man to be sent to Company Headquarters in exchange.

                                          2'Lieut. & Adjt.
                                          124th.Machine Gun Coy.

OPERATION ORDER NO. 26.
BY
MAJOR W.H.DAVIS
COMMANDING 124th.MACHINE GUN COMPANY.
****

1. **RELIEF.**
   NO. 3 Section will relieve NO. 4. Section in the trenches on 20TH DECEMBER. and take up the following positions:-

   No. 1 Team will go to EASTERN BREASTWORK
   No. 2 "   "   " " " CAPTAINS POST
   No. 3 "   "   " " " McDONALDS POST
   No. 4 "   "   " " " BEGGARS REST

2. **COMMAND.**
   LIEUT. BARTON. will relieve 2ND LT. CLARK. at EASTERN BREASTWORK

   2ND LIEUT. RILEY.   "   "   "   " HARLAND " FORT TORONTO.

3. **HANDING OVER.**
   Relieving teams will take guns with them only, all other necessary equipment being handed over by the relieved Section.

4. **TIME TABLE.**
   8.45 am. Relieving teams and limbers leave Company Headquarters.
   9.30 am. Guides from each team to be relieved will be at the RATION BARRIER.

5. **INFORMATION.**
   All necessary information is to be given by outgoing teams.
   Section Officers, in particular, will see that all orders regarding returns to be made are handed over, especially the return of ammunition expended during the week which must reach Company Headquarters not later than 10 am. each Saturday.

6. **COMPLETION OF RELIEF.**
   Relief of each position must be completed by 12 noon.
   Each team when relieved will march independently to Company Headquarters under the Senior N.C.O. who will report his arrival to the Orderly Room.
   Report of completion of relief will be telephoned from FORT TORONTO using the following code :- LIGHTS OUT AT.   AM.
   All limbers will wait at the Barrier and bring back outgoing teams equipment and packs.

7. **RATIONS.**
   Relieved Section will bring back with them the unexpired portion of the day's rations.
   Relieving Sections will take with them the unexpired portion of the day's rations.

8. **TRENCH FEET.**
   Officers will take particular care that all men rub their feet with oil and change their socks daily, one pair of socks per man to be sent to Company Headquarters in exchange.

Lieut. & Adjt.
124th. Machine Gun Coy.

OPERATION ORDER NO. 24
BY
MAJOR W.H. DAVIS
COMMANDING 124th. MACHINE GUN COMPANY.
****

1. **RELIEF.**
   No. 4 Section will relieve No. 3. Section in the trenches on 24TH. DECEMBER. and take up the following positions:-

   No. 1 Team will go to EASTERN BREASTWORK
   No. 2 " " " " CAPTAINS POST.
   No. 3 " " " " McDONALDS POST.
   No. 4 " " " " BEGGARS REST.

2. **COMMAND.**
   LIEUT. WHITE will relieve 2ND LT HERON at WESTERN REDOUBT.

3. **HANDING OVER.**
   Relieving teams will take guns with them only, all other necessary equipment being handed over by the relieved Section.

4. **TIME TABLE.**
   8.45 am. Relieving teams and limbers leave Company Headquarters.
   9.30 am. Guides from each team to be relieved will be at the RATION BARREL.

5. **INFORMATION.**
   All necessary information is to be given by outgoing teams.
   Section Officers, in particular, will see that all orders regarding returns to be made are handed over, especially the return of ammunition expended during the week which <u>must</u> reach Company Headquarters not later than 10 am. each Saturday.

6. **COMPLETION OF RELIEF.**
   Relief of each position must be completed by 12 noon.
   Each team when relieved will march independently to Company Headquarters under the Senior N.C.O. who will report his arrival to the Orderly Room.
   Report of completion of relief will be telephoned from FORT TORONTO using the following code :- BUS LEAVES AT.   AM.
   All limbers will wait at the Barrier and bring back outgoing teams equipment and packs.

7. **RATIONS.**
   Relieved Section will bring back with them the unexpired portion of the day's rations.
   Relieving Sections will take with them the unexpired portion of the day's rations.

8. **TRENCH FEET.**
   Officers will take particular care that all men rub their feet with oil and change their socks daily, one pair of socks per man to be sent to Company Headquarters in exchange.

                                        Lieut. & Adjt.
                                        124th. Machine Gun Coy.

WAR DIARY of 124 Machine Gun Coy.
INTELLIGENCE SUMMARY

Army Form C. 2118.

Place	Date	Hour	Summary of Events and Information	Remarks and references to Appendices
In the Field	1-1-17	6 pm	Our Operations. Indirect fire was carried out on the following targets	Map Ref.
			Officer I/c — Lieut WHITE. Gun Pos. Target Rds fired	Trench Map Sheet 28SW 1:10,000
	1-1-17 to 2-1-17	7-30pm to 6pm	N.6.D.2½.4. O.Y.D.3.11½ to O.Y.B.9.3. 1,500	TRAVERSED SUPPOSED TRAMWAY BEHIND AND TRACK RUNNING PARALLEL TO IT. TARGET TRAVERSED FROM O.Y.D.3.11½ TO O.Y.B.9.3.
	2-1-17	10-30pm	Enemy Activity.	
	2-1-17	6pm	Artillery very active about 5-30pm. Machine Guns & French mortars slightly active.	
		11-30am	Relief. No 3 Section relieved No 2 Section in the trenches and took over gun positions as shown in Operation Orders attached.	See. O.O. 28.
	2-1-17	6pm	Work done. During last 24 hours much work has been done with regard to the wiring round gun positions.	
	2-1-17	6pm	Casualties during last 24 hours Nil. Lot Nil. Weather — the weather during last 24 hours has improved, no rain.	

Army Form C. 2118.

WAR DIARY
or
INTELLIGENCE SUMMARY.
(Erase heading not required.)

Instructions regarding War Diaries and Intelligence Summaries are contained in F.S. Regs., Part II. and the Staff Manual respectively. Title pages will be prepared in manuscript.

[Stamp: 124 MACHINE GUN CO. MACHINE GUN CORPS.]

Place	Date	Hour	Summary of Events and Information	Remarks and references to Appendices
In the field	2.1.17	6 pm	**Operations**	
	to		Indirect fire was carried out on the following targets.	
	6.1.17			
			Officers	Gun Pos.	Target	Reds fired	(Long Range Shoot.)	Map Ref
		6 pm	Lieut WHITE	N.6.D.22.4.	NEW HUTS AT O.14.A.62.42.	450		Sheet 28 S.W. 1:10,000
	5.1.17	10 pm			TRAVERSED DUCK WALKS. FROM O.14.A.13 to O.14.A.62.9. AND TRAVERSED VICINITY.		
	and		2nd Lt. HARLAND	N.12.A.14.96	SEARCH TRAMWAY BEHIND GRAND BOIS FROM O.13.B.0.25 TO O.13.B.6.8.	1000	
	6.1.17	1 am	Lieut. BARTON.	N.6.C.52.z.	SPRAYED ON RAILWAY FARM AND VICINITY	1000	
			Enemy Activity				
			Normal.				
	3.1.17	9.30 am	**Conference**				
			A conference was held at Bgde. Headquarters, attended by Lieut Colonel O.V. Martin, I Corps M.G.O. and Machine Gun Company Commanders of 141st Division. The subject dealt with were as follows:- Anti Aircraft shot, and Promotion of Officers.				
	3.1.17	1.30 pm	**Reinforcements**				
			2nd Lieut E.J. Nicholls joined Company from Machine Gun Corps Base Depot.				

WAR DIARY
or
INTELLIGENCE SUMMARY.
(Erase heading not required.)

Army Form C. 2118.

Place	Date	Hour	Summary of Events and Information	Remarks and references to Appendices
In the Field	3-1-19	6pm	**Casualties** Casualties during last 24 hours Nil Sick 1 Other Rank	
	3-1-19	6pm	**Weather** The weather during last 24 hours has been much colder, frost during night, the roads are drying a little.	
		6pm	**Operations**	
	3-1-19		Indirect fire was carried out on the following targets	Map Ref. French Map Sheet-28 SW 1/10,000
			Gun Position / Rds fired	
	4-3pm	N.11.C.4.22 300	Target: LARGE DUG OUT IN WOOD 0.13.A.82.54. CROSSROADS 0.13.C.3.9. DUGOUTS AT 0.13.A.34.6.
	4-3pm to 11-1-19		" " 300	
	11-1-19		" " 300	
			Officer i/c 2/Lt T. HARLAND.	
			Enemy Activity Artillery slightly active, Machine Guns & Trench Mortars normal.	
	11-1-19	6pm	**Work Done** Drainage of trench at GRANTHAM POST and reconstruction of dug out at BEKTON POST.	

12a MACHINE GUN COY. MACHINE GUN CORPS.

Army Form C. 2118.

WAR DIARY
or
INTELLIGENCE SUMMARY.
(Erase heading not required.)

Instructions regarding War Diaries and Intelligence Summaries are contained in F. S. Regs., Part II and the Staff Manual respectively. Title pages will be prepared in manuscript.

[Stamp: 124 MACHINE GUN CO. MACHINE GUN CORPS]

Place	Date	Hour	Summary of Events and Information	Remarks and references to Appendices
In the field	4.1.17	6 pm	**Casualties** Casualties during last 24 hours Nil. Nil & other ranks.	
	4.1.17	6 pm	**Weather** The weather during last 24 hours has been unchanged.	
		6 pm	**Our Operations**	
	4.1.17		Indirect fire was carried out on the following targets:—	
			Gun Position 1400 feet Target	Map Ref. Trench Map Sheet 28 SW 1/10,000
		6pm 10.45pm TO 5.1.17 4.45am	at BARTON. N.6.C. 32.4. 500 TIMBER DUMP O.13.B.3.1	
			" " 500 TIMBER DUMP O.13.A.8.6.	
			Enemy Activity Artillery active during the morning. Machine Guns & Trench Mortars normal.	
	5.1.17	6 pm	**Casualties** Casualties during last 24 hours Nil. Nil Rek Nil	
	5.1.17	6 pm	**Weather** The weather during last 24 hours has slightly changed, rain at intervals.	

Army Form C. 2118.

WAR DIARY
or
INTELLIGENCE SUMMARY.

(Erase heading not required.)

Instructions regarding War Diaries and Intelligence Summaries are contained in F. S. Regs., Part II. and the Staff Manual respectively. Title pages will be prepared in manuscript.

Place	Date	Hour	Summary of Events and Information	Remarks and references to Appendices
In the field	5.1.14	6 PM	Our Operations	
	to		Indirect fire was carried out on the following targets	Troop Map Trench Map Sheet 28 S.W. 1/10,000
	6.1.14	6 PM	Officer i/c Gun No. From H.B. Rds Fired Target	
		4.30PM	LT. C. WHITE N.6.D.24.7. 500 LOUWAGE FARM O.Y. D.8.3.	
		6 PM to	" " 500 BUILDINGS AT O.8.D. 8.0.	
		10.30 PM	" " 500 RENTY FARM D.13.B.9.54.	
		9.30 PM	2ND LT. HARLAND N.11.C.4.22 250 SEARCHED UNNAMED WOOD O.13.C.	
		10.30 PM	" " ENFILADE TRACK IN GRAND	
		10.15 PM	LT. BARTON N.6.C.52.4. 750 BOIS O.13.A.+B.	
		"	" " 500 DUG OUTS MUCH USED O.13.A.34.6.	
		12.45 PM	" " 500 CROSS ROADS O.13.C.3.9.	
			Enemy Activity	
			Artillery very active during the morning. Machine Guns & Trench Mortars normal.	
	6.1.14	6 PM	Casualties	
			No casualties during last 24 hours but not hit.	
	6.1.14	6 PM	Weather	
			The weather throughout the last 24 hours has been much colder, no rain.	

Army Form C. 2118.

WAR DIARY
or
INTELLIGENCE SUMMARY.
(Erase heading not required.)

Instructions regarding War Diaries and Intelligence Summaries are contained in F. S. Regs., Part II. and the Staff Manual respectively. Title pages will be prepared in manuscript.

[STAMP: 124 MACHINE GUN CORPS / MACHINE GUN CORPS]

Place	Date	Hour	Summary of Events and Information	Remarks and references to Appendices
In the Field	6.1.17	6 PM	Strength. The strength of the Coy for the week ending 6th inst. is as follows.	
			Officers 10	
			Other Ranks 144 Including the undermentioned casuals.	
			6 In Field Ambulance	
			1 House of Correction Rouen	
			2 Employed away from Unit	
			1 With 141st Divisional Train	
	6.1.17	6 PM	Our Casualties. Nil.	
			Indirect fire was carried out on the following targets	
				Trench Map
				Sheet 28 SW
				1:10,000
			Officers i/c Gun Positions Targets Rds Fired	
		10.15 PM to 11.45 PM	Lt H R Barton N.12.A.14.96 DUGOUTS AT 0.13.B.5⅟₂.9¾ 500	
			" " DUGOUTS AT 0.13.A.3.2. 500	
	7.1.17	8 PM to 12.30 AM	2nd Lt W H Harland N.11.C.35.25 SEARCH UNAMED WOOD 0.13.C. 500	
			" " JUNCTION OF ROAD AT 0.13.C.3.9. 250	
			" " BRICKCOT N.18.D.10.1⅟₂. 250	

Army Form C. 2118.

WAR DIARY
or
INTELLIGENCE SUMMARY.

(Erase heading not required.)

Instructions regarding War Diaries and Intelligence Summaries are contained in F. S. Regs., Part II. and the Staff Manual respectively. Title pages will be prepared in manuscript.

Place	Date	Hour	Summary of Events and Information	Remarks and references to Appendices
In the Field	6.11.17	6 PM	Carried on from last page.	Trench Map Sheet 28 SW 1/10,000
			Officer i/c — Lt. C V WHITE	
	6.11.17 to 7.11.17	4-30 PM to 11-30 PM	Gun position N.6.D.22.y.	
		6 PM to 11-30 PM	"	
			Target — RENDY FARM O.13.c.9.5½ CATTEAU FARM O.8.c.8.5	
			Rds fired — 500, 500	
	7.11.17		Enemy Activity	
			Artillery active all day. Machine Guns & Trench Mortars normal.	
	7.11.17	12 PN	Work Done	
			A trench has been dug along the whole of the Breastwork and a new t/m emplacement has been completed at the eastern/right end.	
	7.11.17	6 PM	Casualties	
			Casualties during last 24 hours Nil. Sick 1 other Rank	
	7.11.17	6 PM	Weather	
			Much rain has fell during the last 24 hours.	
	7.11.17	4 AM	Leave	
			Lieut. J.H. Hanson proceeded to England on Special Leave (10 days)	
	7.11.17	7 AM		Lieut. A.G. Kiley proceeded to Atwell for transport course.

Army Form C. 2118.

WAR DIARY
or
INTELLIGENCE SUMMARY.
(Erase heading not required.)

Instructions regarding War Diaries and Intelligence Summaries are contained in F. S. Regs., Part II. and the Staff Manual respectively. Title pages will be prepared in manuscript.

[Stamp: 124 MACHINE GUN COY. — MACHINE GUN CORPS]

Place	Date	Hour	Summary of Events and Information	Remarks and references to Appendices
In the Field	7.1.17	6 PM	**Our Operations** Indirect fire was carried out on the following targets	
				Map Ref. French Map Sheet 28 SW 1.10.000
				Target
		6 PM	Gun position Nr. 6. C. 54. 2.	SAP IN UNNAMED WOOD 500 O. 13. C.
	8.1.17	10 PM	LT. GHR BARTON "	DUGOUTS AT 500 O. 13. A. 4. 3.
		12 MN	"	SEARCHED TRACK IN GRAND BOIS 500 CENTRE OF SEARCH O.13. B.5.5.
			Enemy Activity normal.	
	8.1.17 12 noon		**Relief** No 2 Section relieved No 1 Section in the trenches and took over gun positions as shown in O.O.not.4 attached	See D.O. 29. attached
	8.1.17	6 PM	**Work done** Work done during last 24 hours. Drainage of trench at Gran Rav Rd. was improved and connected to COCKATOO TRENCH.	
	8.1.17	6 PM	**Casualties** Casualties during last 24 hours. Pct. Pot. John Marks 3.	

2353 Wt. W2514/1454 700,000 5/15 D.D. & L. A.D.S.S./Forms/C. 2118.

Army Form C. 2118.

WAR DIARY
or
INTELLIGENCE SUMMARY.
(Erase heading not required.)

Instructions regarding War Diaries and Intelligence Summaries are contained in F. S. Regs., Part II. and the Staff Manual respectively. Title pages will be prepared in manuscript.

[Stamp: 124 MACHINE GUN COY. MACHINE GUN CORPS]

Place	Date	Hour	Summary of Events and Information	Remarks and references to Appendices
In the Field	8.1.17	6 pm	Our Operations	
			Indirect fire was carried out on the following targets from Pos.	Map Ref. trench map Sheet 28 SW 1:10,000
	8.1.17 to 9.1.17 1.15 am	6 pm	Officer I/c	
			10.45 pm 2nd Lt. HARLAND N.11.C.55.25 500	Target
	9.1.17 to 2 am	11.15pm	" N.12.A.17.96 500	TIMBER DUMP N.18.B.9.3
		9.30 pm	2nd Lt. HERON " 500	DUGOUTS AT O.13.C.2.6.
			" 500	DUMP AT O.13.B.3.1
				RED CHATEAU O.18.B.94.2
			Enemy Activity	
			Normal.	
	9.1.17	6 pm	Work Done.	
			Work done during last 24 hours. System of drainage at WESTERN BREASTWORK continued, wiring in front of MANTHORPE POST also continued.	
	9.1.17	6 pm	Casualties	
			Casualties during 24 hours _Nil_. Sick Nil	
	9.1.17	6 pm	Weather	
			Snow fell during night, overcast, and rain at intervals, roads very muddy.	

Army Form C. 2118.

WAR DIARY
or
INTELLIGENCE SUMMARY.
(Erase heading not required.)

Instructions regarding War Diaries and Intelligence Summaries are contained in F. S. Regs., Part II. and the Staff Manual respectively. Title pages will be prepared in manuscript.

[Stamp: 173 MACHINE GUN C?]

Place	Date	Hour	Summary of Events and Information	Remarks and references to Appendices
In the Field	9.1.17	6PM	**Our Operations**	
		to	Indirect fire was carried out on the following targets	
			Gun Position	Rds Fired	
		6PM 6.55PM	2ND LT HARLAND. N.11.C.56.25 1000	Combined Shoot
				Target
		10.1.17 9.15PM	2ND LT HERON N.6.C.5½.½ 1000	E. REC. ANGLE OF GRANDBOIS
				CENTRAL POINT O.13.B.3.6. Trench Map
				W. REC. ANGLE OF GRANDBOIS French Sheet
			LT. WHITE N.6.D.2½.Y 1000	AND ON RAET FM. C. POINT O.13.B.9 Sheet 28 SW
				ON RAET FM. T.N. PART OF ONRETWOOD 1.10.000
				O.14.A.H.2. TO O.14.B.5.9 SEARCH
			The above program was carried out in conjunction with 141st Divisional Artillery and	O.O. 30
			X Korps Heavy Artillery in a dummy raid and wire cutting operation for further	att.
			details see O. Order attached and 141st D. O.O. 26.	
			Enemy Activity	
			Normal during our Operations.	
		10.1.17 6PM	**Casualties**	
			Casualties during last 24 hours nil. Sick nil.	
		10.1.17 6PM	**Weather**	
			The weather during last 24 hours has been overcast, showery at intervals, not at coldest.	

2353 Wt. W2514/1454 700,000 5/15 D. D. & L.   A.D.S.S./Forms/C. 2118.

Army Form C. 2118.

WAR DIARY
or
INTELLIGENCE SUMMARY.

(Erase heading not required.)

Instructions regarding War Diaries and Intelligence Summaries are contained in F. S. Regs., Part II. and the Staff Manual respectively. Title pages will be prepared in manuscript.

Place	Date	Hour	Summary of Events and Information	Remarks and references to Appendices
In the Field	6 P.M.		Our Operations	
	10.1.14 to	6 P.M.	Indirect fire was carried out on the following targets	Map ref. French Map Sheet 28 S W 1/10,000
			Gun Nos. Target. 1,000 rounds	
		6.30 P.M.	2nd Lt. HARLAND N. 11. A. 9. 9. SUSPECTED H.Q. IN N. 19. B. 8. 2. 500	
			" " JUNCTION OF TRACK AT O. 13. A. 4. 8. 500	
	11.1.14	10.15 P.M.	" " DUGOUTS AT O. 13. C. 8½. 6. 500	
		7.30 P.M.	2nd Lt. HERON. N. 6. C. 5½. ½. SEARCH UNAMED WOOD O. 13. C. 500	
		12 Mid.		
			Enemy Activity normal.	
	11.1.14	6 P.M.	Casualties Casualties during last 24 hours Nil. Sick Nil.	
	11.1.14	6 P.M.	Weather The weather during last 24 hours has not altered except for a little snow which fell during the afternoon.	
	11.1.14	6 P.M.	Work done. New dug out completed at BEATON POST.	

Army Form C. 2118.

WAR DIARY
or
INTELLIGENCE SUMMARY.
(Erase heading not required.)

Instructions regarding War Diaries and Intelligence Summaries are contained in F. S. Regs., Part II. and the Staff Manual respectively. Title pages will be prepared in manuscript.

[Stamp: 124 MACHINE GUN COY. MACHINE GUN CORPS.]

Place	Date	Hour	Summary of Events and Information	Remarks and references to Appendices
In the Field	11.1.19 to 12.1.19	6 P.M. to 6 P.M.	**Our Operations**	Map Ref: French Map Sheet 28 SW 1/10,000.
	12.1.19	7.45 A.M.	Indirect fire was carried out on the following targets	
			Officer i/c Gun Pos. Targets Rds fired	
		7.45 A.M.	2ND LT. HARLAND N.11.C.55.25 SEARCH TRENCH SYSTEM ROUND POINT N.18.B.9½.4½. 500	
		10.30 A.M.	" " JUNCTION OF ROADS AT O.13.C.3.9. 500	
		9.30 P.M.	LT. WHITE N.6.D.24.4 LOUWAGE FARM. O.Y.D.8.3. 500	
		12.30 A.M.	" " ENFILADE TRACK ALONG N.E. EDGE OF GRANDBOIS. O.Y.D.4.1 TO O.13.B.9.4. 500	
			Enemy Activity	
			Machine Guns slightly active otherwise normal.	
			Work Done:	
	12.1.19	6 P.M.	Much work has been done during the last 24 hours with regard to the wiring of Gun Positions.	
			Casualties	
	13.1.19	6 P.M.	Casualties during last 24 hours Nil Sick Nil	
			Weather	
	12.1.19	6 P.M.	During last 24 hours much snow has fell turning to rain towards the afternoon.	

Army Form C. 2118.

WAR DIARY
or
INTELLIGENCE SUMMARY.

(Erase heading not required.)

Instructions regarding War Diaries and Intelligence Summaries are contained in F. S. Regs., Part II. and the Staff Manual respectively. Title pages will be prepared in manuscript.

[Stamp: 24 MACHINE GUN COY. MACHINE GUN CORPS]

Place	Date	Hour	Summary of Events and Information	Remarks and references to Appendices
In the Field	12.1.19 to 13.1.19	6 P.M. to 6 P.M.	**Own Operations** — Indirect fire was carried out on the following targets.	Map Ref. Trench Map Sheet 28SW 1/10.000
			Officer i/c Gun Nos. Rds. Fired Target	
		7.30 P.M. & 9.30 P.M.	LT WHITE N.12.A.14.96. 500 Junction of Trenches at O.13.C.9.4.	
			" " 500 Timber Dump O.13.A.8.6.	
			Enemy Operations — Artillery normal machine guns & trench mortars slightly active	
	13.1.19	6 P.M.	**Casualties** — Casualties during last 24 hours nil. See nil.	
	13.1.19	6 P.M.	**Weather** — The weather during last 24 hours has been very frosty. roads very hard.	
	13.1.19	6 P.M.	**Strength** — The strength of the Company for week ending 13th inst. is as follows.	
			Officers Other ranks	
			11 190	
			1 1 Including the undermentioned casuals.	
			2 leave to England	
			6 course of instruction	
			1 2 Field Ambulance	
			With 41st Div Train (Force)	

WAR DIARY
or
INTELLIGENCE SUMMARY.

Army Form C. 2118.

Place	Date	Hour	Summary of Events and Information	Remarks and references to Appendices
In the Field	13.1.19 6PM TO 6PM		**Our Operations**	
	14.1.19	9PM to 10.30PM	Indirect fire was carried out on the following targets.	Map Ref. Trench Map Sheet 28 SW 1/10,000
			Gun No. Rds Fired Target Combined Shoot	
			Lt. WHITE N.6.D.2.4. 500 TRAVERSE ROAD FROM O.2.D.11½. TO O.8.C.4¼.0.	
		10.30PM to 11PM	" " 500 VERTICALLY SEARCH TRENCH FROM O.8.C.Y2.3½ TO O.8.D.24.0.	
		4PM to 11PM	2nd Lt. HERON N.12.A.14.96. 500 HEADQUARTERS AT O.14.A.2.1.	
			" " 500 SEARCHED VICINITY OF O.13.D.Y.9.	
			" " 500 SEARCHED VICINITY OF O.14.A.8.6	
		7PM to 10.30PM	2nd Lt. HARLAND N.11.C.55.25. 500 TRENCH RAILWAY JUNCTION AT O.13.C.5.6½. BRICKSTACK AT O.13.C.Y.0.	
		6PM	**Enemy Activity** Normal.	
			Casualties Casualties during last 24 hrs Sick Nil	
	14.1.19	6PM	**Weather** The weather during last 24 hours has been unchanged. 3 Showers.	
	14.1.19 11.45 AM		**Relief** No.1 Section relieved No.2 Section in the trenches and took over gun positions. See O.O.31 attached. O.O. att.	

Army Form C. 2118.

No. ...
MACHINE GUN
COMPANY.

Date............

WAR DIARY
or
INTELLIGENCE SUMMARY.
(Erase heading not required.)

Instructions regarding War Diaries and Intelligence Summaries are contained in F. S. Regs., Part II. and the Staff Manual respectively. Title pages will be prepared in manuscript.

Place	Date	Hour	Summary of Events and Information	Remarks and references to Appendices
In the Field	14.1.14 to 15.1.14	6 PM to 6 PM	Our Operations. Indirect fire was carried out on the following targets.	Map Ref. Trench Map Dec. 28 PM 1/10,000
			Officer i/c Guns A.C. Rds fired Target	
		6.30 PM to 10.30 PM	LIEUT WHITE N.6.D.2½.4. 500 DUGOUTS AT O.8.D.1½.4½.	
			" " 500 DUG OUTS O.Y.D.4.D.	
		9.30 PM to 11.30 PM	2ND LT. HERON N.12.A.14.96. 500 VERTICALLY SEARCH TRENCH RAILWAY FROM O.13.A.1.2. TO JUNCTION AT O.13.C.5.6½.	
			" " 500 SEARCH TRENCH FROM O.13.A.6.1 TO O.13.C.9.4.	
			Enemy Activity Normal.	
	15.1.14	6 PM	Work done. Much work has been done during the last 24 hours with regard to sandbagging and strengthening of our positions.	
	15.1.14	6 PM	Casualties. No casualties during last 24 hours. 1 Other Rank evacuated sick. Nil	
	15.1.14	6 PM	Weather. The weather during last 24 hours has been much milder, turning colder towards the evening.	

A5831 Wt. W4973/M687 750,000 8/16 D.D. & L. Ltd. Forms/C.2118/13.

Army Form C. 2118.

No. 124
MACHINE GUN COMPANY.

WAR DIARY
or
INTELLIGENCE SUMMARY.
(Erase heading not required.)

Instructions regarding War Diaries and Intelligence Summaries are contained in F. S. Regs., Part II. and the Staff Manual respectively. Title pages will be prepared in manuscript.

Place	Date	Hour	Summary of Events and Information	Remarks and references to Appendices
In the Field	6.1.17 to 16.1.17	6 PM 6 PM	Operations Indirect fire was carried out on the following targets	
			Officer i/c Gun Pos. Rds Fired Target	
		6.30 PM & 9 HOPM	2nd Lt. RIDDLES N.11.C.55.25 500 MACHINE GUN EMPLACEMENT Trench Map Sheet 28 SW 1/10,000	Trench Map Sheet 28 SW 1/10,000
			" N.6.c.6.2. 500 AT O.13.C.3/2. 6/2. DUMP AT O.13.A.5/2. 4/2.	
			2nd Lt. HERON N.6.c.6.2. 500 LINE OF DUGOUTS FROM O.13.C.83.45. TO O.13.C.92.9.	
			" " 500 DUMP AT O.13.B.3/4. 1/4.	
			Enemy Activity J French trenches slightly active otherwise normal.	
	16.1.17	6 PM	Casualties Casualties during last 24 hours Nil Sick Nil	
	16.1.17	6 PM	Weather Weather during last 24 hours has been very dull, snow at intervals	

Army Form C. 2118.

No. 124
MACHINE GUN
COMPANY.

WAR DIARY
or
INTELLIGENCE SUMMARY.
(Erase heading not required.)

Instructions regarding War Diaries and Intelligence Summaries are contained in F. S. Regs., Part II and the Staff Manual respectively. Title pages will be prepared in manuscript.

Place	Date	Hour	Summary of Events and Information	Remarks and references to Appendices
In the Field	16.1.17 to 17.1.17	6 pm	Our Operations	
			Indirect fire was carried out on the following targets	Map Ref
	17.1.17	6 pm		Trench Map Sheet 28 SW 1/10,000
			Gun No. 1 Field Laid Target	
		6.30 pm	2ND LT CROWDER. N.6.D.2½.4 500 VERTICALLY. SEARCH TRENCH RAILWAY FROM O.13.B.4½.8¼ TO O.13.B.6½.4½.	
		10 pm	" " 500 ENFILADE TRENCH FROM O.13.B.4¼.6 TO O.13.B.10.3.	
		9.30 pm	2ND LT HERON N.12.A.14.9b 500 NEW WORK AT O.13.C.6.9	
		12 MN	" " " 500 ENFILADE TRENCH FROM O.13.B.8¾.1. TO O.13.B.5.14¾.	
			Enemy Activity Normal.	
	17.1.17	6 pm	Casualties – Casualties during last 24 hours nil. Seck diel	
	17.1.17	6 pm	Weather The weather during last 24 hours has been much milder. Snow has fell continuously for this period	

Army Form C. 2118.

WAR DIARY
or
INTELLIGENCE SUMMARY.

(Erase heading not required.)

No. 124 MACHINE GUN COMPANY.

Place	Date	Hour	Summary of Events and Information	Remarks and references to Appendices
In the Field	17.1.17 to 18.1.17	6 PM to 6 PM	**Our Operations** Indirect fire was carried out on the following targets.	
			Officer i/c Lens 42. Rds fired **Target**	
		4:30 PM	2ND LT RIDDLES. N.11.C.55.25 500 SEARCH TRENCH TRAMWAY FROM CRATER AT O.Y.C.3½/2.3	Map Ref French map Sheet 28 dw 1/10,000
		to	" " 500 SEARCH TRAMWAY FROM 0.13.A.0.4/M TO 0.13.A.4.3½.	
		2 MN	" " 500 DUG OUTS AT 0.13.C.2.6.	
			Enemy Activity Artillery slightly active. Machine Guns & Trench Mortars normal.	
	18.1.17	5:30 PM	**Conference.** A conference of officers commanding machine gun companies in the 41st Division took place at Div Headquarters. The question of training Machine Gunners in open warfare, and the building of concrete dugouts in view of a possible offensive by the enemy was discussed. It was decided to speed up in both these matters.	
	8.1.17	6 PM	**Casualties** Casualties during last 24 hours 9 nil. Sick nil	

Army Form C. 2118.

No. 124 MACHINE GUN COMPANY.

WAR DIARY
or
INTELLIGENCE SUMMARY.
(Erase heading not required.)

Instructions regarding War Diaries and Intelligence Summaries are contained in F. S. Regs., Part II. and the Staff Manual respectively. Title pages will be prepared in manuscript.

Place	Date	Hour	Summary of Events and Information	Remarks and references to Appendices
In the Field	18.1.19	6 PM TO	Our Operations	Trench Map French Map Sheet 38SW 1/10,000.
	19.1.19	6 PM	Indirect fire was carried out on the following targets	
			Officer i/c Gun Pos. Rds fired Target	
		6 PM	2nd Lt CROWDER N.6.D.2½.4. 500 BUILDINGS AT O.8.A.8.0.	
		9.30 PM	" " 500 JUNCTION OF TRENCHES AND TRACKS IN VICINITY OF O.13.B.7½.6½.	
		9.30 PM	2nd Lt RIDDIAS N.11.C.55.25 500 SEARCH NETWORK OF TRENCHES ROUND POINT N.24.B.4.4.½.	
		11 PM	" " 500 BUILDINGS AT O.13.A.6½.6½.	
			Enemy Activity: Normal.	
	19.1.19	5-30 PM	Lecture. O.C. Company lectured to the Divisional school on the tactical handling of Lewis guns.	
	19.1.19	6 PM	Casualties: Casualties to 6 PM 19.1.19 Nil. Sick Nil	
	19.1.19	6 PM	Weather: The weather during last 24 hours has very cold. Snow at intervals. Roads very muddy.	

WAR DIARY
or
INTELLIGENCE SUMMARY.
(Erase heading not required.)

Army Form C. 2118.

No. 724 MACHINE GUN COMPANY.

Place	Date	Hour	Summary of Events and Information	Remarks and references to Appendices
In the Field	19.1.19 TO 6 PM	6 PM	Our Operations	
	20.1.19		Indirect fire was carried out on the following targets	Map Ref Ypres & Neuve Chapelle Sheet 28 SW 1/10,000
			Officer i/c Gun Pos. Rds fired Target	
		6.30 PM	2ND LT RIDDLES N.11.A.9.9. 500 SEARCH TRENCH TRAMWAY FROM POINT O.13.A.1.2. TO O.13.A.3½.0.	
		4 PM	" " 500 JUNCTION OF TRENCHES AT N.18.B.9¾.H¾. AND SEARCH VICINITY	
		11.15 PM	LT. BARTON N.6.C.5½.½. 500 SEARCH TRAMWAY AND TRENCH FROM POINT O.13.A.H.2¾.H. TO POINT O.13.C.0.8.	
		"	" " 500 GROUP OF DUGOUTS AT O.13.A.5.2.	
		11.45 PM	" " 1100 CATTEAU FARM O.8.C.9¾.4½.	
		11.15 PM	2ND LT CROWDER N.6.D.2½.4. 1100 RENTY FARM O.13.B.9.5¾.	
		"	" " 450 LOUWAEGE FARM O.Y.D.8.3.	
		12.15 PM	At about programme was carried out in cooperation with raid by 143 Brigade at request of officer commanding 123 Machine Gun Company.	See O.O.33 att.
	20.1.19	6 PM	Enemy Activity Artillery active during day. Machine Gun & Trench Mortars normal.	

Army Form C. 2118.

WAR DIARY
or
INTELLIGENCE SUMMARY.
(Erase heading not required.)

No. 124 MACHINE GUN COMPANY.

Instructions regarding War Diaries and Intelligence Summaries are contained in F. S. Regs., Part II. and the Staff Manual respectively. Title pages will be prepared in manuscript.

Place	Date	Hour	Summary of Events and Information	Remarks and references to Appendices
In the Field	20.1.14	6 PM	**Casualties** Casualties during last 24 hours nil. Sch. Pit.	
	20.1.14	6 PM	**Weather** The weather still continues to be very cold, freezing hard, roads very hard. Preparations to made for a thaw.	

	20.1.14	6 PM	**Strength** The Strength of the Company for week ending 20th inst is as follows.
			Officers 10
			          2
			Other Ranks 141
			          1 Including the undermentioned Casuals.
			          3 Leave.
			          3 Sick in Field Ambulance
			          2 Course of Instruction
			          1 Officers & Ors away from Coy.
			           With 148th Bn. L.Inn.	

	20.1.14	11.30 PM	**Relief** No. 2 Section relieved No. 1 Section in the trenches and took over guns & positions as shown in O.O. att.	See O.O. attached. 32.

A5834 Wt.W4973/M687 750,000 8/16 D. D. & L. Ltd. Forms/C.2118/13.

WAR DIARY
or
INTELLIGENCE SUMMARY.

Army Form C. 2118.

NO. 124 MACHINE GUN COMPANY

Place	Date	Hour	Summary of Events and Information	Remarks and references to Appendices
In the Field	20.11.19 6PM to 21.11.19 6PM		Our Operations	
			Indirect fire was carried out on the following of targets	Map Ref. Trench Map Sheet 28SW 1/10,000
		8.45PM	Officer i/c — Lt. BARTON	
		10.15PM	" "	
			2nd Lt. RIDDLES	
			Enemy Activity Normal	
	21.11.19 6PM		Casualties during last 24 hours 1 to Sick list	
	21.11.19 6PM		Weather The weather during the last 24 hours remained unchanged. Still freezing hard.	

Gun Pos.	Target	Rds fired
N.6.D.2½.4.	BUILDINGS AT 0.8.A.8.0.	500
" "	SEARCH TRENCH SYSTEM (TRIANGLE) CENTRE AT 0.14.A.1½.8.	500
N.12.A.2/4.2½	SEARCH TRENCH FROM 0.13.C.5½.½. TO 0.13.D.4.2½.	500
" "	DUMP AT 0.13.B.3.3	250
" "	RENTY FARM. 0.19.B.9½.5½.	250

Army Form C. 2118.

WAR DIARY
or
INTELLIGENCE SUMMARY.

(Erase heading not required.)

No. 124
MACHINE GUN
COMPANY.

Place	Date	Hour	Summary of Events and Information	Remarks and references to Appendices
In the Field	20.1.19 6PM to 22.1.19 6PM		**Our Operations** Indirect fire was carried out on the following targets	

		6PM	Officer i/c Gun Pos Rate Fired Target
			2ND LT RIDDLES N.11.C.6.4 260 DUMP AT O.13.A.3½.1½
			       " " 1000 SEARCHED THOROUGHLY UNAMED WOOD
			       " " 250 SUSPECTED COOKHOUSE AT O.13.A.1.5½
				Map Ref: Trench Map Sheet 26 SW 1/10,000

		8 PM	**Enemy Activity** Normal.	
	22.1.19	6PM	**Casualties** Casualties during last 24 hours 2 Other Ranks Sick. 1 Other Rank.	
	21.1.19	6PM	**Weather** The weather during the last 24 hours has been very bright, but it still continues to freeze hard.	

Army Form C. 2118.

No. 124 MACHINE GUN COMPANY.

WAR DIARY
or
INTELLIGENCE SUMMARY.
(Erase heading not required.)

Place	Date	Hour	Summary of Events and Information	Remarks and references to Appendices
Field	22.1.17 6PM TO 6PM 23.1.17		Our Operations. Indirect fire was carried out on the following targets. (Combined Shoot)	Map Ref Vanschap Sheet 28SW 1/10.000.
			Officer i/c Gun Pos. Rds Fired Target.	
		8.30PM	2ND LT CROWDER. N.6.D.2½.4. 500 TRAVERSE ROAD FROM O.8.A.Y½.0. TO O.8.C.Y½.0.	
		"	" " 250 CATTEEUW FARM O.8.C.8½.5.	
		11.30PM	" " 250 SEARCH TRENCH FROM O.8.C.9.3½ TO O.8.D.2.1.	
		9.30PM	LT BARTON. N.12.A.14.96. 500 TRAVERSE ROAD FROM O.8.C.Y½.0 TO O.14.C.6.1½. MT. ZERO HOUSE ON RAET FARM MT. O.14.A.2/A.3.	
		"	" " 250	
		11.30PM	" " 250	
		8.30PM	2ND LT RIDDLES N.18.A.2/4.2½. 500 TRAVERSE ROAD FROM O.14.A.6.1½. TO CROSS ROADS AT O.20.A.3.9.	
		"	" " 500 SEARCH THOROUGHLY ON RAETWOOD O.14.C.	
		11.30PM		
	23.1.17	6PM	Enemy Activity Normal. Weather Fine to the late P.M.	

Army Form C. 2118.

No. 124
MACHINE GUN COMPANY.
No. ....
Date ....

WAR DIARY
or
INTELLIGENCE SUMMARY.
(Erase heading not required.)

Instructions regarding War Diaries and Intelligence Summaries are contained in F.S. Regs., Part II. and the Staff Manual respectively. Title pages will be prepared in manuscript.

Place	Date	Hour	Summary of Events and Information	Remarks and references to Appendices
In the Field	23.1.19	6 P.M.	Casualties — Casualties during last 24 hours nil. Lick nil	
	6 P.M. 23.1.19 to 6 P.M. 24.1.19		Our Operations — Indirect fire was carried out on the following targets	Map Ref: Fre en Artois Sheet 28sw 1/10,000
			Gun Pos. Rds Fired Target:	
			Officer i/c	
		7.15 P.M.	2ND LT RIDDLES N. 11. C. 6.4 500 DUGOUTS AT O.13.C.2.6.	
		9.30 P.M.	" " 500 TRENCH RAILWAY JUNCTION AT O.13. C.3½. 6.½.	
		10.15 P.M.	2ND LT BARTON N.6.C. 5½. ½. 500 DUGOUTS AT O.13. B. 4½. 4.	
		11.45 P.M.	" " 500 ENFILADE SUNKEN ROAD FROM O.13.C.3.9. TO O.13. C. 4.2. & SEARCH TRENCH SYSTEM ROUND LATER POINT.	
			Enemy Activity — Normal	
	24.1.19	6 P.M.	Casualties — Casualties during last 24 hours nil. Lick nil	
	24.1.19	6 P.M.	Weather — The weather has been unchanged during last 24 hours.	

Army Form C. 2118.

WAR DIARY
or
INTELLIGENCE SUMMARY.

(Erase heading not required.)

No. 124 MACHINE GUN COMPANY.

Place	Date	Hour	Summary of Events and Information	Remarks and references to Appendices
In the Field	6pm 24.1.19 TO 6pm 25.1.19		Our Operations	
			Indirect fire was carried out on the following targets	Map Ref French Map Sheet 28 SW 1/10,000
			Officer i/c — Gun Pos — Rds fired — Target	
		7pm & 12 mn	2nd Lt Crowder — N.6.D.2/3.7 — 500 — Suspected Signalling Stn at O.14.A.43/4.8	
			" — " — 500 — Louvaege Farm O.Y.D.8.3.	
		6pm & 11.15pm	Lt Barton — N.12.A.14.96. — 500 — Search vertically trench railway from O.13.B.14/2.6 to O.13.B.10.2/2.	
			" — " — 500 — Group of Dug outs at O.13.A.5.8.	
			Enemy Activity	
	25.1.19	6pm	Casualties — Normal	
			Troop alties during last 24 hours hit L/Cpl O'Rourke I	
	25.1.19	6pm	Weather	
			The weather has been unchanged during last 24 hours.	

Army Form C. 2118.

WAR DIARY
or
INTELLIGENCE SUMMARY.
(Erase heading not required.)

No. 154
MACHINE GUN COMPANY.

Instructions regarding War Diaries and Intelligence Summaries are contained in F. S. Regs., Part II. and the Staff Manual respectively. Title pages will be prepared in manuscript.

Place	Date	Hour	Summary of Events and Information	Remarks and references to Appendices
In the Field	25.1.17 to 26.1.17	6 PM to 6 PM	Our Operations Indirect fire was carried out on the following targets.	Map Ref. Trench Map Sheet-28 SW 1/10.000.
			Officers i/c Gun Posn. Rds Fired Target	
		8-30 PM & 11-30 PM	2ND LT. CROWDER. N.6.D.2½.9. 500 ZERO HOUSE O.14.A.6.6½.	
			" " 500 SEARCH TRENCH FROM O.Y.D.8.4½. TO O.8.C.1.2½	
		9-15 PM & 11-30 PM	LT. BARTON N.6.C.5½.½. 500 ENFILADE SUNKEN ROAD FROM O.13.C.3.9 TO O.13.C.7.2.	
			" " 500 DUGOUTS AT O.13.A.3½.6.	
		7-15 PM & 10-15 PM	2ND LT HARLAND N.11.C.6.4. 500 TRACK COT N.18.D.10.7 AND SEARCH VICINITY MACHINE GUN EMPLACEMENT AT O.13.C.3½.6½.	
	26.1.17	6 PM	Enemy Activity Slightly active all round.	
			Casualties Casualties during last 24 hours nil sick nil	
	26.1.17	6 PM	Weather. The weather during last 24 hours remains the same as before.	
	26.1.17	11-30 AM	Relief No Section relieved to Section in the trenches and took over gun positions as shown in OO attached	See OO 345 att.

A 5834 Wt. W4973/M687 75,000 8/16 D.D. & L. Ltd. Forms/C.2118/13.

WAR DIARY
or
INTELLIGENCE SUMMARY.
(Erase heading not required.)

Army Form C. 2118.

Instructions regarding War Diaries and Intelligence Summaries are contained in F. S. Regs., Part II. and the Staff Manual respectively. Title pages will be prepared in manuscript.

No. 124 MACHINE GUN COMPANY

Place	Date	Hour	Summary of Events and Information	Remarks and references to Appendices
In the Field	26.1.17 to	6PM	**Our Operations**	Trench Map Sheet 57 Photo 28W. 1/10,000
	27.1.17	6PM	Indirect fire was carried out on the following targets	
		1.15PM	Officer i/c Lieut: BARTON Guns No. Rds fired Target	
			N.6.c.5½.½. 450 ENFILADE TRACK IN GRAND BOIS O.13.A.Y.B.	
			500 DUG OUT S MUCH USED O.13.A.3½.6.	
		10.30PM	500 CROSS ROADS O.13.C.3.9.	
		6.30PM	N.12.A.17.96 1000 TRAVERSE TRAMWAY BEHIND GRAND BOIS AND SPRAY WOOD.	
	27.1.17	6PM	**Enemy Activity** Normal.	
	27.1.17	6PM	**Casualties** Casualties during last 24 hours Nil Sick Nil	
	27.1.17	6PM	**Weather** The weather during last 24 hours has been fine otherwise unchanged.	
	27.1.17	6PM	**Strength** The strength of the Company for week ending 27th inst is as follows: Officers 10 Others 192 including the undermentioned casuals on leave of instruction visit Embattaged, employed away from Company	

Army Form C. 2118.

No. 124
MACHINE GUN
COMPANY.

WAR DIARY
or
INTELLIGENCE SUMMARY.
(Erase heading not required.)

Place	Date	Hour	Summary of Events and Information	Remarks and references to Appendices
In the Field	28.11.14	6 P.M. to 6 P.M.	Our Operations	
			1 Check fire was carried out on the following targets:—	
	28.11.14	9.15PM to 9.30PM	Officer i/c Gun No. Rds fired Target	Map Ref: Trench Map Sheet 28 SW 1/10,000
			2ND LT. HARLAND N.11.C.6.4. 500. SEARCH W. RECTANGLE OF GRAND BOIS.	
			" " 500. SEARCH TRENCH TRAMWAY FROM CRATER AT O.Y.C.5½.3½ TO O.Y.C.10.4.	
			LT. BARTON N.6.D.2½.4. 500. SEARCH E. RECTANGLE OF GRAND BOIS.	
			" " 500. DUG OUT 3 MT. O.B.D.1½.4½.	
	28.1.14		Enemy Activity	
			Artillery very active all day, Trench mortars & machine guns normal.	
	28.1.14	6PM	Casualties	
			Casualties during last 24 hours nil Pts hit	
	28.1.14	6PM	Weather	
			The weather during last 24 hours has been fine otherwise unchanged.	

WAR DIARY
or
INTELLIGENCE SUMMARY.

(Erase heading not required.)

Army Form C. 2118.

No. 124 MACHINE GUN COMPANY.

Place	Date	Hour	Summary of Events and Information	Remarks and references to Appendices
In the Field	28.1.14 6pm to 29.1.14 6pm		**Our Operations** Indirect fire was carried out on the following targets	Map Ref. Trench Map Sheet 28 SW 1/10,000.
			Gun Pos. Rds Fired Target.	
			Officer i/c	
		11:30PM & 2AM	2ND LT HARTLAND N.11.C.6.4. 500 DUMP AT O.13.A.6.2.	
			" 300 DUMP AT O.13.B.1.2.	
		11PM & 1AM	LT. WHITE N.6.D.2½.7. 500 LOUWAGE FARM O.Y.D.8.3.	
			" 250 CATTEAU FARM O.8.C.8½.5.	
			" 250 TRAVERSE TRAMWAY ALONG ROAD IN VICINITY OF CATTEAU FARM.	
	29.1.14	6pm	**Enemy Activity** Normal. **Casualties** Casualties during last 24 hours nil Dick hill	
	29.1.14	6pm	**Weather** Weather during last 24 hours has been fine otherwise unchanged.	

Army Form C. 2118.

WAR DIARY
or
INTELLIGENCE SUMMARY.

(Erase heading not required.)

124 MACHINE GUN COMPANY.

No. ....
Date ....

Place	Date	Hour	Summary of Events and Information	Remarks and references to Appendices
In the Field	29.1.17	6 P.M.	Operations	
	30.1.17	6 P.M.	Indirect fire was carried out on the following targets	Map Ref Trench Map Sheet 28 Sw 1/10,000
			Gun Pos. Target Rds Fired	
			DUG OUTS AT	
	30.1.17	9.45 P.M.	Lt BARTON. N.6.C.5½.½. O.Y.D.4.0. 300	
			RENTY FARM	
		"	O.13.B.9½.5½. 250	
			DUMP AT	
		12.15 P.M.	" " O.13.B.1.2. 250	
			Enemy Activity	
			Artillery slightly active otherwise normal.	
	30.1.17	3 P.M.	Conference	
			O.C. Company attended Conference at 124th S.I.B. Hqrs. The following was discussed. Disposition of Vickers Guns and Lewis Guns in connection with the 41st Division Defence Scheme.	
	30.1.17	6 P.M.	Casualties	
			Casualties during last 24 hours Nil. Rect. 2 O. Ranks	
	30.1.17	6 P.M.	Weather	
			The weather during last 24 hours has been fine generally, snow at intervals	

Army Form C. 2118.

WAR DIARY
or
INTELLIGENCE SUMMARY.
(Erase heading not required.)

Instructions regarding War Diaries and Intelligence Summaries are contained in F.S. Regs., Part II. and the Staff Manual respectively. Title pages will be prepared in manuscript.

[Stamp: 162 MACHINE GUN COMPANY No........ Date........]

Place	Date	Hour	Summary of Events and Information	Remarks and references to Appendices
In Cd	30.1.17	6PM	Own Operations	
Ticket	TO		Indirect fire was carried out on the following targets	
	31.1.17	6PM		
			Officer i/c Gun Pos. Rds Fired LONG RANGE SHOOT Target	Map Ref. Trench map Sheet 28 SW 1/10.000.
		8PM	Lt BARTON N.6.C.5½.1½. 250 ONRAET FARM O.14.A.2½.1½. + SUSPECTED H.2RS.	
		+ 10.30PM	" " 450 SPRAY ONRAET WOOD.	
		4PM	Lt WHITE N.11.A.14.96 500 O.13.C.0.2.	
		+ 11PM	" " 250 O.13.C.2.6.	
			" " 250 O.13.C.5.Y.	
		8PM + 10.45PM	2nd Lt HARLAND N.11.C.6.4. 450 HOSPICE O.19.A.8.4; TRAVERSE TRAMWAY FROM O.13.C.9.4 TO O.13.B.1.O.	
			Enemy Activity	
			Normal	
	31.1.17	6PM	Casualties	
			Casualties during last 24 hours Nil. Sick Nil.	
	31.1.17	6PM	Weather	
			The weather during last 24 hours has been fine. Snow at intervals	

OPERATION ORDER NO. 28.
BY
MAJOR W.H. DAVIS
COMMANDING 124th. MACHINE GUN COMPANY.
****

1. **RELIEF.**
   No. 3. Section will relieve No. 2. Section in the trenches on 2.1.1917 and take up the following positions:-

   No. 1 Team will go to *BELTON POST.*
   No. 2 " " " " *HARROWBY POST.*
   No. 3 " " " " *PRESCOTTS POST*
   No. 4 " " " " *FORT TORONTO*

2. **COMMAND.**
   2ND LT W.H. HARLAND will relieve 2ND LT. A.G. RILEY at FORT TORONTO

3. **HANDING OVER.**
   Relieving teams will take guns with them only, all other necessary equipment being handed over by the relieved Section.

4. **TIME TABLE.**
   8.45 am. Relieving teams and limbers leave Company H.Q.
   9.30 am. Guides from each team to be relieved will be at the ration barrier.

5. **INFORMATION.**
   All necessary information is to be given by outgoing teams
   Section Officers in particular will see that all orders regarding returns to be made are handed over, especially the return of ammunition expended during the week which must reach Company Hqrs. not later than 10 am. each Saturday.

6. **COMPLETION OF RELIEF.**
   Relief of each position must be completed by 12 noon.
   Each team when relieved will march independently to Company Hqrs. under the Senior N.C.O. who will report his arrival to the Orderly Room.
   Report of completion of relief will be telephoned from FORT TORONTO using the following code:- *SERVICE WILL BE AT*   AM.

   All limbers will wait at the barrier and bring back outgoing teams equipment and packs.

7. **RATIONS.**
   Relieved section will bring back with them the unexpired portion of the day's rations.
   Relieving Sections will take with them the unexpired portion of the day's rations.

8. **TRENCH FEET.**
   Officers will take particular care that all men rub their feet with oil and change their socks daily, one pair of socks per man to be sent to Company Headquarters in exchange.

9. **GUM BOOTS.**
   Relieved teams will bring their gum boots out with them and relieving teams will take their gum boots with them.

10. **STRAGGLING.**
    O.C. Company has noticed with much displeasure that the relieved teams when returning to Company Hqrs. straggle all over the roads. This must cease. The N.C.O. of each team will be responsible for the collecting of all his men and marching them down in a proper, soldierlike manner.

                                              [signature]
                                              Lieut. & Adjt.
                                              124th M.Gun Company.

OPERATION ORDER NO. 29.
BY
MAJOR W.H. DAVIS
COMMANDING 124th. MACHINE GUN COMPANY.
****

1. RELIEF.
   No. 2. Section will relieve No. 1 Section in the trenches on 8.1.1917 and take up the following positions:-

   No. 1 Team will go to GORDONS POST
   No. 2 "   "   " " TELFORDS POST
   No. 3 "   "   " " SOUTHERN REDOUBT
   No. 4 "   "   " " WOODLEY POST.

2. COMMAND.
   2ND LT. E HERON will relieve LT G.H.R. BARTON at EASTERN BREASTWORK.

3. HANDING OVER.
   Relieving teams will take guns with them only, all other necessary equipment being handed over by the relieved Section.

4. TIME TABLE.
   8.45 am. Relieving teams and limbers leave Company H.Q.
   9.30 am. Guides from each team to be relieved will be at the ration barrier.

5. INFORMATION.
   All necessary information is to be given by outgoing teams
   Section Officers in particular will see that all orders regarding returns to be made are handed over, especially the return of ammunition expended during the week which must reach Company Hqrs. not later than 10 am. each Saturday.

6. COMPLETION OF RELIEF.
   Relief of each position must be completed by 12 noon.
   Each team when relieved will march independently to Company Hqrs. under the Senior N.C.O. who will report his arrival to the Orderly Room.
   Report of completion of relief will be telephoned from FORT TORONTO using the following code:- DINNERS WILL BE AT   AM.

   All limbers will wait at the barrier and bring back outgoing teams equipment and packs.

7. RATIONS.
   Relieved section will bring back with them the unexpired portion of the day's rations.
   Relieving Sections will take with them the unexpired portion of the day's rations.

8. TRENCH FEET.
   Officers will take particular care that all men rub their feet with oil and change their socks daily, one pair of socks per man to be sent to Company Headquarters in exchange.

9. GUM BOOTS.
   Relieved teams will bring their gum boots out with them and relieving teams will take their gum boots with them.

10. STRAGGLING.
    O.C. Company has noticed with much displeasure that the relieved teams when returning to Company Hqrs. straggle all over the roads. This must cease. The N.C.O. of each team will be responsible for the collecting of all his men and marching them down in a proper, soldierlike manner.

Lieut. & Adjt.
124th .M.Gun Company.

SECRET.

OPERATION ORDER NO.30
by
MAJOR W.H.DAVIS
COMMANDING METAPHOR.
*****

1. The Divisional Artillery and the 10th.CorpsH.A. will carry out wire cutting and dummy raid on the 9th.inst.

2. The front of the operation will extend from:-
   N 18 b 15.60 to O 2 c 9.5.

3. The Right and Left Battalions in the line will co-operate with Rifle and Lewis Gun fire.
   Dummy figures will be issued and smoke bombs will be used if weather conditions permit.

4. Vickers Guns will co-operate generally. The combined shoot as outlined in the Weekly Programme will be carried out. Firing will commence 5 minutes before ZERO HOUR and rate of fire will be quicker than ~~usual~~ normal and will consist of alternate bursts of concentrated and swift traaversing fire through an angle not exceeding 12°.

5. All Machine gunners except sentries and those immediately concerned with the indirect fire will remain in their dugouts as retaliation is to be expected. ZERO HOUR will be 7 pm. on the 9th. inst.

6. 2/Lt.HARLAND will send a runner round to Officers concerned between 2 and 4 pm. on the 9th. inst. to give them the correct time, which will be communicated to him at FORT TORONTO from Coy. H.Q.

W H Davis
Major,
Commanding 124th.M.G.Coy.

OPERATION ORDER NO..3/
BY
MAJOR W.H.DAVIS
COMMANDING 124th.MACHINE GUN COMPANY.
############

> No. 124
> MACHINE GUN
> COMPANY.
>
> No............
> Date............

1. **RELIEF.**
    No. 1 Section will relieve No. 2 Section in the trenches on 14th Dec and take up the following positions:-

    No. 1 Team will go to "PARSONS POST"
    No. 2   "   "   " " "TELFORD POST"
    No. 3   "   "   " " "SOUTHERN REDOUBT"
    No. 4   "   "   " " "WOOLLEY POST"

2. **COMMAND.**
    2nd LT. E.P. RIDDLES will relieve 2nd LT. W.H. HARLAND at FORT TORONTO
    2nd LT. G.C.G. CROWDER will relieve LT C.V. WHITE at WESTERN REDOUBT
    on his return from C of Inst

3. **HANDING OVER.**
    Relieving teams will take guns with them only, all other necessary equipment being handed over by the relieved Section.

4. **TIME TABLE.**
    8.45 am. Relieving teams and limbers leave Company H.Q.
    9.30 am. Guides from each team to be relieved will be at the ration barrier.

5. **INFORMATION.**
    All necessary information is to be given by outgoing teams
    Section Officers in particular will see that all orders regarding returns to be made are handed over, especially the return of ammunition expended during the week which must reach Company Hqrs. not later than 10 am. each Saturday.

6. **COMPLETION OF RELIEF.**
    Relief of each position must be completed by 12 noon.
    Each team when relieved will march independently to Company Hqrs. under the Senior N.C.O. who will report his arrival to the Orderly Room.
    Report of completion of relief will be telephoned from FORT TORONTO using the following code:- BREAKFAST WILL BE AT   A.M

    All limbers will wait at the barrier and bring back outgoing teams equipment and packs.

7. **RATIONS.**
    Relieved section will bring back with them the unexpired portion of the day's rations.
    Relieving Sections will take with them the unexpired portion of the day's rations.

8. **TRENCH FEET.**
    Officers will take particular care that all men rub their feet with oil and change their socks daily, one pair of socks per man to be sent to Company Headquarters in exchange.

9. **GUM BOOTS.**
    Relieved teams will bring their gum boots out with them and relieving teams will take their gum boots with them.

10. **STRAGGLING.**
    O.C. Company has noticed with much displeasure that the relieved teams when returning to Company Hqrs. straggle all over the roads. This must cease. The N.C.O. of each team will be responsible for the collecting of all his men and marching them down in a proper, soldierlike manner.

Lieut. & Adjt.
124th M.Gun Company.

OPERATION ORDER NO. 32.
BY
MAJOR W.H.DAVIS
COMMANDING 124th.MACHINE GUN COMPANY.
****

1. **RELIEF.**
   No. 2 Section will relieve No. 1 Section in the trenches on 20TH JAN. and take up the following positions:-

   No. 1 Team will go to GORDONS POST
   No. 2 "   "   " " TELFORDS POST
   No. 3 "   "   " " SOUTHERN REDOUBT
   No. 4 "   "   " " WOODLEY POST

2. **COMMAND.**
   LIEUT BARTON WILL RELIEVE 2ND LT HERON AT EASTERN BREASTWORK

3. **HANDING OVER.**
   Relieving teams will take guns with them only, all other necessary equipment being handed over by the relieved Section.

4. **TIME TABLE.**
   8.45 am. Relieving teams and limbers leave Company H.Q.
   9.30 am. Guides from each team to be relieved will be at the ration barrier.

5. **INFORMATION.**
   All necessary information is to be given by outgoing teams
   Section Officers in particular will see that all orders regarding returns to be made are handed over, especially the return of ammunition expended during the week which must reach Company Hqrs. not later than 10 am. each Saturday.

6. **COMPLETION OF RELIEF.**
   Relief of each position must be completed by 12 noon.
   Each team when relieved will march independently to Company Hqrs. under the Senior N.C.O. who will report his arrival to the Orderly Room.
   Report of completion of relief will be telephoned from FORT TORONTO using the following code:- POST ARRIVED AT   AM.

   All limbers will wait at the barrier and bring back outgoing teams equipment and packs.

7. **RATIONS.**
   Relieved section will bring back with them the unexpired portion of the day's rations.
   Relieving Sections will take with them the unexpired portion of the day's rations.

8. **TRENCH FEET.**
   Officers will take particular care that all men rub their feet with oil and change their socks daily, one pair of socks per man to be sent to Company Headquarters in exchange.

9. **GUM BOOTS.**
   Relieved teams will bring their gum boots out with them and relieving teams will take their gum boots with them.

10. **STRAGGLING.**
    O.C. Company has noticed with much displeasure that the relieved teams when returning to Company Hqrs. straggle all over the roads. This must cease. The N.C.O. of each team will be responsible for the collecting of all his men and marching them down in a proper, soldierlike manner.

John McLawson
Lieut. & Adjt.
124th.M.Gun Company.

Operation order No.33 by Major W.H.Davis,
Commanding METAPHOR.
****

From:- O.C.
    METAPHOR.

To:- Lieut.Barton,
    2/Lt. Riddles,
    2/Lt. Crowder.

    Brigade Machine Gun Officer of Brigade on our left has requested our co-operation in the raid which will take place tonight.
    Please note:-
    The ordinary Programme of Fire will be adhered to with the following additions:-

Gun Position.	Target	Range	Rounds.
BEGGARS REST.	1. CATTEAU FARM (O 8 c $9\frac{1}{2}.4\frac{1}{2}$)	2100	400
	2. RENTY FARM (O 13 b $9.5\frac{1}{2}$)	2100	400
	3. LOUWAEGE FARM (O 7 d 8.3)	1800	450

1.   All guns will direct an intense fire on their respective targets from 15 minutes before Zero to 15 minutes after Zero and then commence the ordinary rate of fire.

2.   Zero Hour will be notified to Officers by a special runner in the following code :-

    " Working party will arrive at   ".

3.   All, except those on duty, should be kept to their dugouts as there may be retaliation.

                                         Major,
19/1/17.   Commanding METAPHOR.

OPERATION ORDER NO 24.
BY
MAJOR W.H.DAVIS
COMMANDING 124th.MACHINE GUN COMPANY.
****

1. **RELIEF.**
   No. 1 Section will relieve No. 4 Section in the trenches on 26TH. JAN. and take up the following positions:-

   No. 1 Team will go to EASTERN BREASTWORK
   No. 2 "   "   " " MANTHORPE POST
   No. 3 "   "   " " McDONALDS POST
   No. 4 "   "   " " BEGGARS REST

2. **COMMAND.**
   2ND LT HARLAND WILL RELIEVE 2ND LT RIDDLES AT FORT TORONTO
   LT C V WHITE   "   2ND LT CROWDER AT WESTERN REDOUBT.

3. **HANDING OVER.**
   Relieving teams will take guns with them only, all other necessary equipment being handed over by the relieved Section.

4. **TIME TABLE.**
   8.45 am. Relieving teams and limbers leave Company H.Q.
   9.30 am. Guides from each team to be relieved will be at the ration barrier.

5. **INFORMATION.**
   All necessary information is to be given by outgoing teams
   Section Officers in particular will see that all orders regarding returns to be made are handed over, especially the return of ammunition expended during the week which must reach Company Hqrs. not later than 10 am. each Saturday.

6. **COMPLETION OF RELIEF.**
   Relief of each position must be completed by 12 noon.
   Each team when relieved will march independently to Company Hqrs. under the Senior N.C.O. who will report his arrival to the Orderly Room.
   Report of completion of relief will be telephoned from FORT TORONTO using the following code:- KICK OFF AT   AM

   All limbers will wait at the barrier and bring back outgoing teams equipment and packs.

7. **RATIONS.**
   Relieved section will bring back with them the unexpired portion of the day's rations.
   Relieving Sections will take with them the unedpired portion of the day's rations.

8. **TRENCH FEET.**
   Officers will take particular care that all men rub their feet with oil and change their socks daily, one pair of socks per man to be sent to Company Headquarters in exchange.

9. **GUM BOOTS.**
   Relieved teams will bring their gum boots out with them and relieving teams will take their gum boots with them.

10. **STRAGGLING.**
    O.C. Company has noticed with much displeasure that the relieved teams when returning to Company Hqrs. straggle all over the roads. This must cease. The N.C.O. of each team will be responsible for the collecting of all his men and marching them down in a proper, soldierlike manner.

                                            Lieut. & Adjt.
                                            124th.M.Gun Company.

Army Form C. 2118.

WAR DIARY
or
INTELLIGENCE SUMMARY

(Erase heading not required.)

Instructions regarding War Diaries and Intelligence Summaries are contained in F. S. Regs., Part II. and the Staff Manual respectively. Title Pages will be prepared in manuscript.

No. 124. MACHINE GUN COMPANY.

Place	Date	Hour	Summary of Events and Information	Remarks and references to Appendices
IN THE FIELD	31.1.19 6 PM TO 1.2.19 6 PM	6 PM	Our Operations. Indirect fire was carried out on the following targets	
			Officer i/c — Gun Pos. — 1900 Fired. — Target.	MAP REF.
			2ND LT CROWDER. N.C.D.2/2.Y. 500. LOUWAGE FARM.	TRENCH
			" " 500. O.Y.D.8.3. DUGOUTS AT	MAP SHEET
			" " 500. O.8.A.4/1.2.12.	28.S.W.
				SUSPECTED SIGNALLING
				STATION. O.14.A.9/14.8.
				1.10.000
1.2.19		6 PM	Enemy Activity. normal.	
			Casualties. Casualties during last 24 hours NIL Sick NIL	
1.2.19		6 PM	Weather. Weather during last 24 hours has been fine otherwise unchanged.	
1.2.19		10 AM	Relief. No. 4 Section relieved No. 3 Section in the trenches, for distribution of Gun Teams See O.O. attached.	124. MACHINE GUN COY. M.G.C. SEE O.O. N°35 ATT.

Army Form C. 2118.

WAR DIARY
or
INTELLIGENCE SUMMARY
(Erase heading not required.)

No. 124 MACHINE GUN COMPANY.

Instructions regarding War Diaries and Intelligence Summaries are contained in F. S. Regs., Part II. and the Staff Manual respectively. Title Pages will be prepared in manuscript.

Place	Date	Hour	Summary of Events and Information	Remarks and references to Appendices
IN THE FIELD	1.2.17 to 2.2.17	6 PM to 6 PM	Our Operations. Indirect fire was carried out on the following targets.	MAP. REF. TRENCH MAP SHEET 28 SW 1.10.000
			Officer i/c Gun Position Target Rds. fired	
		6-30 PM to 9-30 PM	Lt. BARTON N.6.D.2/2.4. BUILDINGS AT O.8.A.8.0 500	
			RENTY FARM. O.13.B.9.5½. 500	
		6-3 PM	2nd Lt. HARLAND N.11.C.6.4. DUGOUTS O.13.A.3.5. 250	
		"	CROSS ROADS O.13.C.3.9. 250	
		10-15 PM	SPRAY UNNAMED WOOD 500	
	2.2.17	6 PM	Enemy Activity. Normal.	
			Casualties. Casualties during last 24 hours nil. Sick Nil.	
			Weather. The weather during last 24 hours has been fine otherwise unchanged.	
	2.2.17	6 PM	Work Done. The wiring in front of MANTHORPE POST. EMP. continued in the cover of night.	

Army Form C. 2118.

WAR DIARY
or
INTELLIGENCE SUMMARY

(Erase heading not required.)

No. 124 MACHINE GUN COMPANY.

Instructions regarding War Diaries and Intelligence Summaries are contained in F. S. Regs., Part II. and the Staff Manual respectively. Title Pages will be prepared in manuscript.

Place	Date	Hour	Summary of Events and Information	Remarks and references to Appendices
IN THE FIELD	2-3-17 6 PM to 3-3-17 6 PM	6 PM	Our Operations. Indirect fire was carried out on the following targets	MAP. REF. TRENCH MAP SHEET 28. S.W. 1:10,000.
			Officer i/c. Gun No. Rds Fired Target	
		7.15 PM	2ND LT. HERON. N.6.C.5½.½. 500. GROUP OF DUGOUTS O.13.A.5.2.	
		"	" 500. DUMP AT O.13.B.3.1.	
		10 PM	"	
		6 PM	2ND LT HARLAND N.12.A.14.96. 500. JUNCTION OF ROAD AND MAIN TERMINUS OF TRENCH TRAMWAY O.13.C.9.0.
		"	"	
		9.30 PM	" " 500. DUMP AND TRAMWAY TERMINUS O.13.A.5½.½.
			Enemy Activity. Artillery slightly active, M. Guns and Mortars normal.	
	3-3-17	6 PM	Strength. The strength of the Company for week ending 3rd inst is as follows.	
			OFFICERS. O. RANKS.	
			10 168 Including the undermentioned casuals.	
			1 2 Course of Instruction	
			5 Field Ambulance	
			1 With 1st A. Y.M.B.	
			1 1ST DIV TRAM'Y ABBEVILLE ON DUTY	

Army Form C. 2118.

No. 124 MACHINE GUN COMPANY.

No.................
Date...............

WAR DIARY
or
INTELLIGENCE SUMMARY
(Erase heading not required.)

Instructions regarding War Diaries and Intelligence Summaries are contained in F. S. Regs., Part II. and the Staff Manual respectively. Title Pages will be prepared in manuscript.

Place	Date	Hour	Summary of Events and Information	Remarks and references to Appendices
IN THE FIELD.	3.2.17	6 P.M.	**Casualties** Casualties during last 24 hours NIL Sick NIL.	
	6 P.M.		**Our Operations** Indirect fire was carried out on the following targets.	
	3.2.17 to 6 P.M. 4.2.17		Gun Pos. Target Rds Fired	Target
			Officer i/c	
			2ND LT HERON N.12.A.14.9b 250	DUMPON. TRENCH TRAMWAY. O.13.C.3.8½.
			" " 500	LOUWAEGE FARM. O.Y.D.8.3.
			2ND LT HARLAND N.11.C.6.4. 500	DUGOUTS IN GRAND BOIS O.13.C.3.8½.
			" " 500	CROSS ROADS AT. O.13.C.5.2.
	4.2.17	6 P.M.	**Enemy Activity** Normal	MAP REF TRENCH MAP SHEET 28 SV 1.10,000.
	4.2.17	6 P.M.	**Casualties** Casualties during last 24 hours NIL Sick. 3 O RANKS	Weather The weather during last 24 hours has been very fine otherwise unchanged

WAR DIARY or INTELLIGENCE SUMMARY

Army Form C. 2118

No. 124 MACHINE GUN COMPANY.

Place	Date	Hour	Summary of Events and Information	Remarks and references to Appendices
IN THE FIELD	4.2.16 TO 5.2.16	6PM TO 6PM	**Our Operations** Indirect fire was carried out on the following targets	MAP REF. TRENCH MAP SHEET 28 SW 1.10.000
		7. PM	Officer i/c — Gun pos — Target — Rds fired	
			LT WHITE — N.6.D.2½.4. — DUMP NR CATTEAU FARM 0.8.C.8.5. — 500	
		TO	" — " — TRENTY FARM 0.13.B.9½.5½ — 500	
		10 PM	" — " — DUG-OUTS. 0.Y.D.4.0 — 500	
			2ND LT HERON — N.6.C.5½.½. — PROBABLY M.G.ERS. N.19.B.8.2. — 250	
			" — " — CONSTANTLY USED DUGOUT 0.13.B.4.4½ — 250	
			" — " — SEARCH TRACK IN GRANDBOIS 0.13.A.4.8. TO 0.13.B.1.1. — 250	
			Work Done A new dugout completed at FORT GRANTHAM. Framing & dugouts at MARROWBY POST worth for shelter for next amt.	
	5.2.16	6PM	**Enemy Activity** Normal.	
	5.2.16	6PM	**Casualties** Casualties during last 24 hours nil **Weather** The weather has been fine during last 24 hours.	
			SICK NIL	

Army Form C. 2118

WAR DIARY
or
INTELLIGENCE SUMMARY
(Erase heading not required.)

No. 124 MACHINE GUN COMPANY.

No..........
Date..........

Place	Date	Hour	Summary of Events and Information	Remarks and references to Appendices
IN THE FIELD	5.2.17 to 6.2.17	6PM to 6PM	Our Operations. Indirect fine was carried out on the following targets	MAP REF. TRENCH MAP SHEET 28 SW 1.10.000
			Gun Pos. Rds Fired Target	
			SCREENED DUGOUTS	
		6.30 PM	Officer I/c LT. WHITE. N.12.A.2¾.2½. 250 O.13.C.8½.6.	
		&	TIMBER AND WIRE	
		8.45 PM	" " 500 DUMP O.13.B.3.1.	
			TRAVERSE GRANDBOIS	
		6.45 PM	2ND LT HARLAND. N.11.C.6.4. 500 FROM O.13.A.4.8 TO O.13.C.3.9.	
		&		
		11 PM	" " " 250 PLATEAU FARM N.18.B.5.6.	
			Enemy Activity normal.	
	6.2.17	6PM	Casualties. Casualties during last 24 hours Nil. Sick Nil.	
	6.2.17	6PM	Weather. The weather during last 24 hours has been fine, much warmer about mid-day.	

124. MACHINE GUN COY.
M.G.C.
O.O.
124. MACHINE GUN COY.
M.G.C.

Army Form C. 2118

WAR DIARY
or
INTELLIGENCE SUMMARY

(Erase heading not required.)

No. 124 MACHINE GUN COMPANY.

Place	Date	Hour	Summary of Events and Information	Remarks and references to Appendices
IN THE FIELD	6-2-19 6PM TO 6PM 7-2-19		Our Operations	
			Indirect fire was carried out on the following targets LONG RANGE SHOOT	
			Gun Nos. Officer i/c Target Rds Fired	
		6-30PM to 10-15PM	2ND LT HARLAND N.11.C.6.4. ONRAET FARM 500	MAP. REF.
		"	" " SUSPECTION SIGNAL AND WIRELESS STATION 500	TRENCH MAP
		6-30PM to 11-PM	LT WHITE N.6.D.2½.4. BRANCH OF TRAM WAY O.8.D.4.0. 500	SHEET 28 SW
		"	" " DUG OUT JUST OFF TRENCH O.8.D.Y¾/4.Y. 250	1.10.000
		"	" " ZERO HOUSE O.14.A.6.6½. 250	
		6-30PM to 9-30PM	2ND LT HERON. N.6.C.5½.½. SEARCH ROAD O.13.C.6.5 TO O.13.B.½.6½. 500	
		"	" " SPRAY ON RAET WOOD. 500	
	6PM		Enemy Activity Normal.	
			Weather	
			The weather during last 24 hours has been fine otherwise unchanged.	
	7-2-19 6PM		Casualties Casualties during last 24 hours NIL SICK NIL	

(in)
124, MACHINE GUN COY.
M.G.O.O.

Army Form C. 2118

Instructions regarding War Diaries and Intelligence Summaries are contained in F. S. Regs., Part II. and the Staff Manual respectively. Title Pages will be prepared in manuscript.

No. 124 MACHINE GUN COMPANY.

No..............
Date..............

WAR DIARY
or
INTELLIGENCE SUMMARY
(Erase heading not required.)

Place	Date	Hour	Summary of Events and Information	Remarks and references to Appendices
IN THE FIELD.	7.2.17 TO 8.2.17	6 PM TO 6 PM	Our Operations. Indirect fire was carried out on the following targets.	MAP REF TRENCH MAP SHEET 28 SW 1.10.000.
			Officer i/c Gun No. Rds Fired Target	
		7.30 PM TO 10.30 PM	2ND LT. HARLAND N.11.C.6.4.H. 500 DUG-OUTS O.13.A.2.6.	
			" " 250 FORTIFIED CRATER. O.Y.C.6.3½.	
			" " 500 SEARCH TRENCH. O.13.A.6.2½ TO O.13.B.1/3.2.	
	8.2.17		Work Done. Wiring in front of BEGGARS REST Alguin. " in front of MANTHORPE POST. nearly completed.	
			Enemy Activity. Normal.	
	8.2.17	6 PM	Casualties. Casualties during last 24 hours NIL. Sick NIL.	
	8.2.17	6 PM	Weather. The weather during the last 24 hours has been fine much milder.	

Army Form C. 2118.

No. 124 MACHINE GUN COMPANY.
No. ....
Date ....

WAR DIARY
or
INTELLIGENCE SUMMARY.
(Erase heading not required.)

Instructions regarding War Diaries and Intelligence Summaries are contained in F.S. Regs., Part II. and the Staff Manual respectively. Title pages will be prepared in manuscript.

Place	Date	Hour	Summary of Events and Information	Remarks and references to Appendices
IN THE	6 PM 8-2-14 TO 6 PM 9-2-14			
F.L.D.			Our Operations	MAP REF
			Indirect fire was carried out on the following targets	TRENCH MAP SHEET 28 SW 1.10.000
			Officers i/c Gun Pos. Target Rds fired	
		6.30 PM	2ND LT HERON N.12.A.1.4.9.6 DUGOUTS AT O.13.B.1/2.Y 500	
		7 PM	" " DUGOUTS AT O.13.B.6.9. RENTY FARM. 500	
		9 PM	" "	
		4 PM	LT WHITE N.6.D.2/2.Y DUGOUTS AT O.13.B.9/2.5/2. 500	
		10 PM	" " DUGOUTS AT O.8.A.2/2.5/2. 250	
			Work done.	
	8.2.14		A new emplacement dug at GRANTHAM POST.	
			Enemy Activity	
			Normal.	
	9.2.14	6 PM	Casualties	
			Casualties during last 24 hours - NIL. Sick NIL.	
	9.2.14	6 PM	Weather	
			The weather during the last 24 hours has been fine, much milder.	

124, MACHINE GUN Co.
M.G.O.

Army Form C. 2118.

WAR DIARY
or
INTELLIGENCE SUMMARY.

(Erase heading not required.)

No. 124 MACHINE GUN COMPANY.

Instructions regarding War Diaries and Intelligence Summaries are contained in F. S. Regs., Part II. and the Staff Manual respectively. Title pages will be prepared in manuscript.

Place	Date	Hour	Summary of Events and Information	Remarks and references to Appendices
IN THE FIELD	9-2-17 to 10-2-17	6 PM to 6 PM	Our Operations. Indirect fire was carried out on the following targets	MAP. REF. TRENCH MAP SHEET 28 SW 1 : 10,000
				Target
			Rds fired	SEARCH TRENCH O.13.A.5.1. TO O.13.B.2.4.
			Gun 108. 500	SEARCH ROAD O.13.C.3.9. O.13.C.6.3.
			N.6.C.5½.½. 500	GROUP OF DUGOUTS AT O.13.A.3.5.
			″ 250	
			Officer i/c	
			2ND LT HERON	
	10-2-17		Enemy Activity	
			Artillery slightly active	
	10-2-17	11-45 AM	Relief	
			No 3 Section relieved No 2 Section in the trenches	
			For further details of relief see Coy's att.	
			Strength	
			The strength of the Company for week ending 10th inst. was as follows.	
			Officers Other Ranks	
			10. 168.	See E.O.D. 36.
			including the undermentioned casuals.	
			Held up by Rly. 1	ATTACHED
			S.T. Amt. 5	
	10-2-17	6 PM	Casualties	
			No casualties during last 24 hours. Sick Nil.	
			H Comm'd of Inft. 4	
	10-2-17	6 PM	Weather	12 H TM Bd. 1
			The weather during past 24 hours has been fine otherwise unchanged.	DIV Train 1
				Leave.

124, MACHINE GUN CO.
N.G.C.

WAR DIARY
or
INTELLIGENCE SUMMARY.
(Erase heading not required.)

Army Form C. 2118.

No. 124 MACHINE GUN COMPANY.
No.................
Date................

Place	Date	Hour	Summary of Events and Information	Remarks and references to Appendices
IN THE	6PM		Our Operations	MAP REF
F.D.	10.2.17 TO 6PM		Indirect fire was carried out on the following targets	TRENCH MAP SHEET 28 SW 1: 10,000.
			Gun No. Officer i/c Target Rds fired	
	11.2.17	9PM + 11PM	N.11.C.6.4 2ND LT RIDDLES SEARCH TRENCH O.13.A.4.9 to O.13.B.1.2. 500	
			" " DUGOUTS AT O.13.A.4.6. 500	
		10PM	N.6.D.2½.4. 2ND LT CROWDER DUGOUTS AT O.8.A.2½.5½. 250	
		12.30AM	" " CATTEAU FARM O.8.C.8.½.2. 500	
			Enemy Activity	
			Normal.	
			About 5am.	
			Firing still continued in front of	
			BEGGARS REST.	
			Weather	
			The weather during last 24 hours has been	
	11.2.17	6PM	Casualties during last 24 hours	
			Nil Sick Nil.	
	10.2.17	8PM	Reinforcements	
			2ND LIEUT. A. WILLIAMS rejt from M.G.C. Base depot fine, much milder thawing slightly.	

Army Form C. 2118.

WAR DIARY
or
INTELLIGENCE SUMMARY.
(Erase heading not required.)

No. 124 MACHINE GUN COMPANY.

No. .... Date ....

Instructions regarding War Diaries and Intelligence Summaries are contained in F.S. Regs., Part II. and the Staff Manual respectively. Title pages will be prepared in manuscript.

Place	Date	Hour	Summary of Events and Information	Remarks and references to Appendices
IN THE FIELD.	11.2.17 to 12.2.17	6 PM to 6 PM	Our Operations. Indirect fire was carried out on the following targets.	MAP REF. TRENCH MAP SHEET 28 SW 1.10.000
				Target.
			Gun Pos. Rds fired	SEARCH TRENCH IN
	12.2.17		Officer I/C 500	GRAND BOIS 0.13. A.5.2 TO 0.13. C.9.4.
		4 PM	2ND LT HERON N.6.C.5½.½. 250	DUMP AT 0.13. B.9.1
		"	" " 500	SEARCH ROAD 0.13.C.38½ TO 0.13.C.9.3.
		10.15 PM	"	
	12.2.17	6 PM	Enemy Activity. Normal.	
	12.2.17	6 PM	Casualties. Casualties during last 24 hours NIL Sick NIL	
			Weather. The weather during last 24 hours has slightly changed, much milder, thawing slowly.	

Army Form C. 2118.

NO. 124 MACHINE GUN COMPANY.

No..................
Date................

WAR DIARY
or
INTELLIGENCE SUMMARY.
(Erase heading not required.)

Instructions regarding War Diaries and Intelligence Summaries are contained in F. S. Regs., Part II. and the Staff Manual respectively. Title pages will be prepared in manuscript.

Place	Date	Hour	Summary of Events and Information	Remarks and references to Appendices
IN THE FIELD	6 PM 12.2.17 TO 6 PM 13.2.17		Our Operations	
			Indirect fire was carried out on the following targets	MAP REF
			Officer i/c Gun No Rate Fire	TRENCH MAP SHEET 28 SW 1:10,000
		6.30 PM	2ND LT CROWDER. N.E.D.2½.4. 300	SEARCH ON FACET WOOD O.14.C
		TO	" Gun No 3 250	MARTIN'S FARM O.8.D.9½.9½
		9.30 PM	" " 250	NIELE FARM. O.8.D.b.½
		8.30 PM	2ND LT. HERON. N.12.D.14.96. 250	SUSPECTED H.QRS. D.14.A.2.1.
		TO	" " 250	SUSPECTED SIGNAL STATION O.14.A.1¾.8.
		11 PM	" " 500	SEARCH ROAD FROM O.19.A.9.9. TO O.13.C.4½.6.
			2ND LT. RIBBLES N.11.C.6.4. 500	SEARCH TRENCH IN GRAND BOIS FROM O.13.A.6½.3 TO O.13.B.3.8.
			" " 250	DUGOUTS AT O.13.B.4.4½.
			" " 250	DOUBTFUL CONSTRUCTION AT O.13.D.0.8.
	13.2.17		Enemy Activity Artillery slightly active	
			Casualties during past 24 hours NIL	
			Sick Nil.	
			Weather Mild and fine.	

124, MACHINE GUN COY.
M. G. C.

Army Form C. 2118.

No. 124 MACHINE GUN COMPANY.

No..................
Date..................

WAR DIARY
or
INTELLIGENCE SUMMARY.
(Erase heading not required.)

Instructions regarding War Diaries and Intelligence Summaries are contained in F. S. Regs., Part II. and the Staff Manual respectively. Title pages will be prepared in manuscript.

Place	Date	Hour	Summary of Events and Information	Remarks and references to Appendices
IN THE FIELD	13.2.19	6 PM TO	Our Operations	MAP REF
	14.2.19	6 PM	Indirect fire was carried out on the following targets	TRENCH MAP
				SHEET 28
			Gun No.	Target	Rds Fired	SW.1.16.000
			Officer i/c		
		7 PM & 10 PM	2ND LT. HERON	SEARCH TRENCH IN GRAND BOIS FROM O.13.A.5.2 TO O.13.C.9.4.	500
			"	N.6.D.2½.4.	500	SEARCH ROAD FROM O.13.C.3.8½ TO O.13.C.4.3.
	14.2.19	6 PM	Enemy Activity		
			normal.		
			Casualties		
			casualties during last 24 hours NIL		
			sick NIL		
	14.2.19	6 PM	Weather		
			The weather during last 24 hours has been fine, a sharp frost during the night, turning warm towards noon.		
	13.2.19	2 PM	Transport Inspection		
			O.C. 124 Div. R.I.F.X. inspected Company's transport		
	11.2.19		2ND LT. A.F. RILEY. took over command of transport and learned roads.		

124 MACHINE GUN COY.
M. G. C.

Army Form C. 2118.

WAR DIARY
or
INTELLIGENCE SUMMARY.
(Erase heading not required.)

No. 124 MACHINE GUN COMPANY.

No............
Date............

Instructions regarding War Diaries and Intelligence Summaries are contained in F. S. Regs., Part II. and the Staff Manual respectively. Title pages will be prepared in manuscript.

Place	Date	Hour	Summary of Events and Information	Remarks and references to Appendices
IN THE FIELD	6 PM 14.2.17 To 6 PM 15.2.17		Our Operations. Indirect fire was carried out on the following targets	MAP REF. TRENCH MAP SHEET 28 S.W.
			Gun Nos. Rds Fired Target	
			Officer i/c	SUPPLY DUMP O.13.B.6.4.
		6.30 PM	2ND LT CROWDER. N.6.D.2½.7. 260	LOUVAGE FARM AND DISTRICT O.Y.D.8.3. DUMP AT.
		9. PM	" " 500	O.13: B.3.1.
		7. PM	2ND LT E. HERON N.12.A.14.96. 250	SEARCH TRENCH FROM O.13. A.5.2. TO O.13. C.9.7.
		10 PM	" " 500	
			Enemy Activity.	
			Artillery very active during morning. Archway to FORT GRANTAM completely destroyed.	
	15.2.17	6 PM	Casualties during last 24 hours NIL Sick NIL.	
	15.2.17	6 PM	Weather. The weather during last 24 hours has been fine, otherwise unchanged.	

D.C.
124, MACHINE GUN COY.
M. G. C.

Army Form C. 2118.

WAR DIARY
or
INTELLIGENCE SUMMARY.
(Erase heading not required.)

No. 124 MACHINE GUN COMPANY.

Place	Date	Hour	Summary of Events and Information	Remarks and references to Appendices
EN.7.b.E	15.2.17 to 16.2.17	6PM to 6PM	Our Operations	
			Indirect fire was carried out on the following targets	MAP REF.
			Officer i/c Gun No. Rds fired Target	TRENCH MAP.
			DUMP ON TRAMWAY AT. O.13.A.5½.1½.	SHEET 28 S.W.
		7.15PM	2nd Lt RIDDLES N.N.C.6.14. 250 SIGNAL DUGOUT AT O.Y.C.6½.½.	1/10,000.
		"	" " 250 DUGOUTS AT O.13.A.2.6.	
		11.30PM	" " 500 SERIES OF DUGOUTS AT	
		9.PM	2nd Lt HERON N.6.C.3½.½. 250 O.13.A.4.5.	
		11PM	" " 500 SEARCH ROAD FROM O.13.C.3.8½. TO O.13.C.8.0	
	16.2.17 2.20am		2nd Lt RIDDLES reports that on firing first burst on DUMP AT O.13.A.5½.1½. an explosion was heard resembling that of grenades. This was exactly in direction of the fire.	
			Enemy activity	
				Artillery slightly active
	16.2.17	6PM	Casualties during last 24 hours Nil-16th Feb 1917	
	16.2.17	6PM	Weather during last 24 hours has been unchanged.	

Army Form C. 2118.

Instructions regarding War Diaries and Intelligence Summaries are contained in F. S. Regs., Part II. and the Staff Manual respectively. Title pages will be prepared in manuscript.

No. 124 MACHINE GUN COMPANY.

No. ....
Date ....

WAR DIARY
or
INTELLIGENCE SUMMARY.
(Erase heading not required.)

Place	Date	Hour	Summary of Events and Information	Remarks and references to Appendices
IN THE FIELD	16.2.17	11AM	**Relief** The No 2 Section relieved No 1 Section in the trenches. The distribution of Gun teams was as follows:- No 1. Gun team to E. BREASTWORK. No 2 to McDONALDS POST. No 3 to BEGGARS REST. No 4 to MANTHORPE POST. LIEUT G.H.R. BARTON relieved 2ND LTE. HERON. BREASTWORK. The relief was completed by 11am the 16th inst, for further details of relief orders see O.O. 35 attached to page 1.	
			Our Operations	
	16.2.17 TO 17.2.17	6PM 6PM 9.30PM 12MN 7AM 12MN 10PM 12MN	Indirect fire was carried out on the following targets Gun Nos. 1400 rounds fired Officer i/c 2ND LT CROWDER . . . . . Gun No.s N.6.D.2/2.4. 250 ,, ... 430 LIEUT BARTON N.12.A.14.36. 250 ,, ... 500	MAP REF. Target ZERO HOUSE O.14.A.6.6½ TRAVERSE WOOD O.B.B.C.D. RENTY FARM SEARCH OBSTRUCTION LANE FROM O.13.B.9½.5½ TO O.13.A.6½.½ FROM 0.13.C.9½.6½. TRENCH MAP SHEET 28 SW 1.10.000
	17.2.17	6PM	**Enemy Activity** Artillery very active during the afternoon, trench mortars slightly active during enemy's artillery activity a dud shell passed through the front of emplacement.	

124, MACHINE GUN COY.
M. G. C.

O.C.

Army Form C. 2118.

WAR DIARY
or
INTELLIGENCE SUMMARY.
(Erase heading not required.)

No. 124 MACHINE GUN COMPANY.

Place	Date	Hour	Summary of Events and Information	Remarks and references to Appendices
IN THE FIELD	14.2.17		At TELFORDS POST, missing the tripod but managing cradle, little damage was done to the emplacement but the parados needs building up.	
	14.2.17	6 PM	Casualties Casualties during last 24 hours Nil. Sick Nil.	
			Weather The weather during last 24 hours has been mild, rather misty. Wind 35.	
	14.2.17	6 PM	Strength The strength of Company for week ending 14th inst. is as follows.	
			OFFICERS. OTHER RANKS. 11 168 including the undermentioned casuals. 1 Att 16-123 M.G. Coy for duty 3 Field Ambulance. 2 Course of Instruction 1 Leave 1 1st Divisional Train 1 Att 124 Bde T.M. Baty.	

124, MACHINE GUN COY.
M. G. O.

Army Form C. 2118.

WAR DIARY
or
INTELLIGENCE SUMMARY.

(Erase heading not required.)

Instructions regarding War Diaries and Intelligence Summaries are contained in F. S. Regs., Part II. and the Staff Manual respectively. Title pages will be prepared in manuscript.

No. 124 MACHINE GUN COMPANY.

Place	Date	Hour	Summary of Events and Information	Remarks and references to Appendices
IN THE FIELD	17.2.17	6PM TO 6PM	Our Operations	
			Indirect fire was carried out on the following targets	MAP REF
				TRENCH
			Gun No9. Target Rds Fired	MAP SHEET
				1.10.000.
			Officer i/c	
	17.2.17	10PM	LIEUT BARTON N.6.C.5½.½. TIMBER DUMP. 250	
			O.13.A.8.6.8½	
	18.2.17	4	" " SEARCH ROAD O.13.C.3.8½ 500	
			TO O.13.C.8.0.	
		1 AM	" " SEARCH OBSTRUCTION-LANE 500	
			O.13.A.6.2.TO O.13.D.1¼.4½ 28 SW	
	18.2.17		Enemy activity	
			There was a considerably heavy bombardment by enemy artillery on our sector yesterday from 4-10 PM & 6-11.0 PM, during which the gun at TELFORDS POST was put out of action.	
	18.2.17	6PM	Casualties	
			Casualties during last 24 hours 1 OR slightly wounded 1 OR sick 1 O.R.	
	18.2.17	6PM	Weather	
			The weather during last 24 hours has been very dull, thaw continues	

124, MACHINE GUN COY.
M. G. C.

WAR DIARY or INTELLIGENCE SUMMARY

Army Form C. 2118.

No. 124 MACHINE GUN COMPANY.

Place	Date	Hour	Summary of Events and Information	Remarks and references to Appendices
IN THE FIELD	18.2.19	6 PM To	**Our Operations** Indirect fire was carried out on the following targets:	
			Officer i/c Gun Pos.	
	6PM 9PM	2ND LT. MARLAND. N.11.C.6.4.	Target Rds Fired	Map Ref. French Trench
			WORK IN PROGRESS O.Y.C.31.24. 250	Sheet 28 S.W.
	19.2.19	"	JUNCTION OF TRAM WAYS 250	1.10.000
		11.15 PM	O.13.C.53.54. 500	
			SEARCH NEW TRENCH O.13.B.8.95 TO O.13.A.40.90	
	19.2.19	10 PM	One Vickers Gun under the command of 2ND LT RIDDLES was mounted to the left of POPPY LANE last night and worked in conjunction with Infantry listening Patrol. The intention was to stop the enemy from repairing the wire in front of their trenches, which has been cut by our Artillery and French Mortars. At 10 PM the patrol reported that the enemy working party were busy repairing the wire in front of their trenches. The gun opened fire and traversed the enemy wire. On observation this morning no additions had been made by the enemy on his wire.	
	19.2.19	6 PM	**Enemy Activity**	
	19.2.19	6 PM	Normal. Casualties during last 24 hours NIL Sick NIL. Weather during last 24 hours had been chilly. Rain at intervals.	

WAR DIARY or INTELLIGENCE SUMMARY

Army Form C. 2118.

No. 124 MACHINE GUN COMPANY.

Place	Date	Hour	Summary of Events and Information	Remarks and references to Appendices
IN THE FIELD	6TH		Our Operations	MAP REF. TRENCH MAP SHEET 28 SW 1/10,000
	13.2.17		Indirect fire was carried out on the following targets:	
	TO			
			Gun Pos. Target Yds Front	
	6PM	6.30PM	2ND LT CROWDER N.6.D.2/2.4. BOUWAERIE FARM AND VICINITY O.Y.5.B.10.15 TO O.8.C.Y.5.B. TRENCH TRAMWAY 500	
		10.2M	" O.8.D.H.Q. DUMP AT O.8.C.80.50. 250	
		"	" O.8.C. SEARCH TRAMWAY 250	
		10.30PM	2ND LT HARLAND N.11.C.6.4. O.13.B.14.90 TO O.13.B.90.80 SEARCH O.Y.D.60.38 TO D.Y.D.95.34. 500	
		6.30PM 2.30AM	"	
		4.15PM	LIEUT BARTON N.12.A.14.96 SEARCH TRENCH O.Y.D.90.18 TO O.8.C.5.30. 500	
	13.2.17	7.30PM	As stated on the 12th inst. a gun was mounted to the left of POPPY LANE under the command of 2ND LT RIDDLES for the same purpose as before. The enemy working party were dispersed by a few short bursts fired from the gun. On observation this morning no additions had been made on the enemy's wire.	
			Enemy Activity Normal	
	14.2.17	6PM	Weather during last 24 hours had been dull, much rain. Casualties during last 24 hours NIL.	

Army Form C. 2118.

No. 124 MACHINE GUN COMPANY.

WAR DIARY or INTELLIGENCE SUMMARY.
(Erase heading not required.)

Instructions regarding War Diaries and Intelligence Summaries are contained in F. S. Regs., Part II. and the Staff Manual respectively. Title pages will be prepared in manuscript.

Place	Date	Hour	Summary of Events and Information	Remarks and references to Appendices
IN THE		6 PM	Our Operations	
≠ 15.1.D	20.2.14 to		Indirect fire was carried out on the following targets	MAP REF. TRENCH MAP SHEET 28 SW 1.10.000
	6 PM	12.30 PM	Officer i/c	Gun Pos.	Yds fired	Target
	21.2.14	3.30 AM	Lt BARTON	N.6.C.C. 5½.½.	250	DUMP AT O.13.C.9.0
			"	"	450	SEARCH ROAD AND TRAMWAY O.13.C.30.85 TO O.13.A.90.85.
		9 PM	2nd Lt CROWDER	N.12.A.2½.3½	500	DUMP AT. O.13.B. 60.40. JUNCTION OF TRAMWAYS.
		11.30 PM	"	"	300	N.18.B.95.25 TO N.18.B.35.H.
	21.2.14	2.15 AM	A Vickers gun was mounted to the right of POPPY LANE on the front line last night under the command of 2nd Lt RIDDLES for the purpose of preventing the enemy from covering two Infantrymen went out as a listening post and occupied a shell hole 10 yds from the enemy's front line. He was in communication with the gunners by means of a wire at 2-15 AM an enemy party came out and started work on the wire this was reported to the gunners immediately who opened fire causing the working party to retire to their trenches. They came out again several times but were driven off by our fire the listening post reported that casualties were inflicted on the enemy.	
	22.2.14	11 PM to 12 PM	From 11 PM to 12 MN the Belgian 1st was anti-aircraft and the above gun co-operated in sweeping Lines 3 Lines 4 in a combined shoot on the Enemy's Front and Support Line 3	

Army Form C. 2118.

WAR DIARY
or
INTELLIGENCE SUMMARY.
(Erase heading not required.)

No. 124 MACHINE GUN COMPANY.

Place	Date	Hour	Summary of Events and Information	Remarks and references to Appendices
IN THE FIELD	21.2.17	6 PM	Enemy Activity Normal. Work done Conseling of dug out at PRESCOTT POST. Employment water.	
	21.2.17	6 PM	Casualties Casualties during last 24 hours Nil. Sick 2 OR. The weather during last 24 hours has been very dull and sultry, rain at intervals.	

	6 PM
	21.2.17
	TO
	6 PM
	22.2.17
		12 AM
		TO
		3.0 AM
			Our Operations
			Indirect fire was carried out on the following targets
			Officer i/c Gun No. Rds fired Target MAP REF.
			2ND LT HARLAND N.11.C.6.4. 1000 DUGOUTS WORK GOING ON TRENCH MAP
			    " " 500 CROSS ROADS O.13.C.3.9. SHEET 28 SW
			LT. BARTON N.12.A.14.96 250 SEARCH OBLIQUE AVENUE O.13.A.40.85 TO O.13.A.60.65. 1.10.000.
			    " " 250 DUMP AT O.13.B.2.2.
			    " " 500 TRAVERSE TRAMWAY O.13.B.58.45 TO O.13.B.25.10
			A Vickers gun was mounted in the FRONT LINE last night for the purpose of	

124, MACHINE GUN COY.
M. G. C.

Army Form C. 2118.

WAR DIARY
or
INTELLIGENCE SUMMARY.
(Erase heading not required.)

NO. 124 MACHINE GUN COMPANY.

Instructions regarding War Diaries and Intelligence Summaries are contained in F. S. Regs., Part II. and the Staff Manual respectively. Title pages will be prepared in manuscript.

Place	Date	Hour	Summary of Events and Information	Remarks and references to Appendices
IN THE FIELD	21.2.19	9 PM	Preventing the enemy from repairing his wire. An Infantry listening patrol went out an occupied a shell hole about 10 yds from the enemy wire. This patrol were in communication with the gunners by means of a rope and a code of signals was arranged. Only one Enemy party were reported moving near their parapet. The gun opened fire causing them to return. On observation this morning no additions had been made, and the enemy's front line were seems to be sullent.	
	22.2.19	6 PM	Enemy Activity Normal.	
	22.2.19	11.30AM	Relief. No.1 Section relieved No.4 Section in the trenches, and took over gun positions at BELTON POST, HARROWBY POST, PRESCOTTS POST, and FORT TORONTO. No officers were relieved. For further details of relief orders see Appendix.	SEE OO 35" att to SHEET I
	22.2.19	6 PM	Casualties during last 24 hours Nil. Lieut O.R. 2.	
	22.2.19	6 PM	Weather The weather during last 24 hours has been very foggy, rain at intervals	

Army Form C. 2118.

WAR DIARY
or
INTELLIGENCE SUMMARY.
(Erase heading not required.)

No. 124 MACHINE GUN COMPANY.

Instructions regarding War Diaries and Intelligence Summaries are contained in F.S. Regs., Part II. and the Staff Manual respectively. Title pages will be prepared in manuscript.

Place	Date	Hour	Summary of Events and Information	Remarks and references to Appendices
IN THE FIELD	22-2-19	6PM TO 8-30PM	Our Operations. Indirect fire was carried out on the following targets	MAP REF FRENCH MAP SHEET 28 SW 1:10,000
		6PM	LONG RANGE SHOOT.	
			Officer i/c Gun No. Rds fired Target	
	23-2-19	12-30AM	2ND LT THARLAND N.11.C.6.4. 450 TIMBER DUMP AND TRAMWAY JUNCTION O.15.C.9.0.	
		9-30PM TO 11-30PM	" " 450 TRAVERSE ROAD FROM O.13.C.3.9 TO O.13.C.6.5.	
		11-30PM	2ND LT CROWDER N.6.D.2½.4. 1500. CATTERN FARM DUMP O.8.C.8.5.	
		9-30PM TO 11-45PM	LT. BARTON N.6.C.5½.½. 450 TIMBER DUMP, JUNCTION OF ROAD AND MAIN TERMINUS OF RAILWAY AT O.13.C.9.0.	
			" 450 ENFILADE SUNKEN ROAD. O.13.C.5.5 TO O.13.C.6.5.	
	22-2-19	6PM	A Vickers Gun was mounted on the front line trench for the purpose of preventing the enemy from repairing his wire. This was carried out in conjunction with an infantry listening patrol. No enemy party were reported deliberation this morning showed that no additions has been made on the enemy wire.	
			Enemy Activity normal.	
	23-2-19	6PM	Casualties during last 24 hours S/Nk Pte Nk	
	23-2-19	6PM	Weather During last 24 hours has been very chill and misty, roads very muddy.	

124, MACHINE GUN COY.
M.G.O.

WAR DIARY
or
INTELLIGENCE SUMMARY.
(Erase heading not required.)

Army Form C. 2118.

No. 124 MACHINE GUN COMPANY.

Place	Date	Hour	Summary of Events and Information	Remarks and references to Appendices
IN THE FIELD.	23.2.17	6PM	**Our Operations** Indirect fire was carried out on the following targets	
			Officiate	
		6PM to 6PM	2nd Lt. HARLAND	
		10PM to 9PM	Lt. BARTON	
		24.2.17 12M.N.		
			Gun Pos. Target	MAP REF
			N.6.D.2/2.Y. LOUWAEGE FARM AND VICINITY (MUCH WORK GOING ON) 1000	TRENCH MAP
			N.12.A.14.36 TRAVERSE TRAMWAY BEHIND GRANDBOIS 1000	SHEET 28sw 1.10.000
		4.55PM	**Raid.** 8 Guns of the Company co-operated in raid made by the 10th Battalion Queens Royal West Surrey Regiment on the HOLLANDSCHESCHUUR SALIENT (N.18.B) ZERO hour was at 4.55 PM, and from this time until 6.20PM, the guns engaged, directed rapid fire on the enemy's lines. The object of our fire was (1) to isolate the area to be raided. (2) to demoralise the enemy. And with this purpose in view, the following targets were engaged:- OBLIGE ALLEY and the base of CROONAERT SALIENT. (O.4.C.) OBLIGE ALLEY, OBLIGE LANE and OBLIGE AVENUE. (O.13.A.) OBSTRUCTION LANE, SUNKEN ROAD and UNNAMED WOOD (O.13.C.) ZIG ZAG HEDGE ROW IN N.18.D. The majority of these targets were engaged in enfilade. Assistance was given by	

WAR DIARY or INTELLIGENCE SUMMARY

Army Form C. 2118.

No. 124 MACHINE GUN COMPANY.

(Erase heading not required.)

Instructions regarding War Diaries and Intelligence Summaries are contained in F. S. Regs., Part II. and the Staff Manual respectively. Title pages will be prepared in manuscript.

Place	Date	Hour	Summary of Events and Information	Remarks and references to Appendices
IN THE FIELD	24.2.17		Raid continued. The 48th MACHINE GUN COY with 4 guns and the 123 MACHINE GUN COY on our right and left respectively. The guns of the 48th MACHINE GUN COY established a barrage along NAIL ROW (N.18.B) and the N.W edge of GRAND BOIS — The guns of the 123RD MACHINE GUN COY searched thoroughly GRAND BOIS (O.13.A.B.) The raid was very successful, the nature of our MACHINE GUN FIRE was rapid, and 35,500 rounds of S.A.A. were expended by the guns of this Company. For further details see 124 Brigade Order No. 95. and the 20.No.39. attached. Enemy activity Retaliation very slight.	MAP REF TRENCH MAP SHEET 28.S.W 1/10,000
	24.2.17	6 PM	Casualties during last 24 hours NIL. See NOTE	
	24.2.17	6 PM	Weather during last 24 hours has been very misty, and little observation was possible during the above mentioned raid.	
	24.2.17	6 PM	Strength. The strength of the Company for week ending 24th inst. is as follows. OFF. O.RANKS 11 145 1 attached to 123 M.G. COY 2 " 124 T.M.B. 1 Course of Inst. 1 Leave 1 attached Ambulance	

124, MACHINE GUN COY.
M. G. O.

Army Form C. 2118.

WAR DIARY
or
INTELLIGENCE SUMMARY.
(Erase heading not required.)

No. 124
MACHINE GUN COMPANY.

No. ....
Date ....

Place	Date	Hour	Summary of Events and Information	Remarks and references to Appendices
IN THE FIELD	24.2.19	6 PM	Our Operations	MAP REF.
	TO		Indirect fire was carried out on the following targets	TRENCH MAP
	25.2.19	6 PM	Gun No.3. Target	SHEET 28 SW
		TO 10.30 PM	Officer i/c Hold fired CATTEAU FARM	1.10.000.
			Lt BARTON. N.6.D.2½.Y. 500 0.8.C.85.45.	
			" " 500 SEARCH TRENCH FROM	
				0.Y.D.6.5 TO JUNCTION OF TRENCH
				AT 0.14.A.10.80.
			Enemy Activity	
			Normal.	
	25.2.19	6 PM	Weather	
			The weather during last 24 hours	
			has been very dull and misty.	
	25.2.19	6 PM	Our Operations	
	TO		Indirect fire was carried out on the following targets	
	26.2.19	6 PM	Gun 108. Target	
			Officer i/c Holsfired SEARCH OBSTRUCTION LANE AND	
			LT WHITE N.12.A.2/4.2½ 500 OBVIOUS AVENUE FROM
				0.13.C.95.90 TO
				0.13.D.19.48.
			" " 500 SEARCH VICINITY OF 0.Y.D.44.45.
				AND TOWARDS POINT OF
				OBSTRUCTION AVENUE AT
				0.Y.D.96.48.

124, MACHINE GUN COY.
M.G.C.

Army Form C. 2118.

No. 124
MACHINE GUN COMPANY.
No. ....
Date ....

WAR DIARY
or
INTELLIGENCE SUMMARY.
(Erase heading not required.)

Instructions regarding War Diaries and Intelligence Summaries are contained in F. S. Regs, Part II. and the Staff Manual respectively. Title pages will be prepared in manuscript.

Place	Date	Hour	Summary of Events and Information	Remarks and references to Appendices
IN THE FIELD	25.2.17	6PM TO 8PM	Indirect fire continued. Officer i/c Gun 108. 2ND LT HARLAND N.11.C.6.4.	MAP REF TRENCH MAP SHEET 28 SW 1.10.000.
	26.2.17	6PM + 11PM	" "	
			Enemy Activity Artillery fairly active during morning. Machine Guns and Trench Mortars normal.	
	26.2.17	6PM	Casualties during last 24 hours. Nil. Sick. Nil.	
	26.2.17	6PM	Weather during last 24 hours has slightly improved much brighter.	
		6PM	Own Operations	
	26.2.17 TO 6PM 27.2.17		Indirect fire was carried out on the following targets Officer i/c Gun 108. I.T. BARTON N.6.C. 5½.½.	

Rods Fired
500.
500

Target
SEARCH NEW TRENCH UNDER CONSTRUCTION FROM 0.13.A.50.90. TO 0.13.B.10.90.
TRIANGLE FORMED BY TRENCH TRAMWAY AND TRENCHES AT 0.13.A.55.23.

Rods Fired
500
500

Target
(LONG RANGE SHOOT)
ENTRANCE TO DUGOUTS AT 0.13.C.5.5.
DUMP NEAR TRENCH TRAMWAY 0.13.C.9½.3½.

P.T.O.

Army Form C. 2118.

WAR DIARY
or
INTELLIGENCE SUMMARY.
(Erase heading not required.)

Instructions regarding War Diaries and Intelligence Summaries are contained in F. S. Regs., Part II. and the Staff Manual respectively. Title pages will be prepared in manuscript.

Place	Date	Hour	Summary of Events and Information			Remarks and references to Appendices
IN THE FIELD	26.2.17	6 PM TO 9 PM	Indirect fire continued			MAP REF TRENCH MAP SHEET 28 3 N.E. 1:10.000.
			Officer i/c	Gun Pos	Rds Fired	Target
			Lt WHITE	N.6.B.2½.4	500	SUSPECTED HEADQUARTERS AT. O.14. A.6.4/B.
		6 PM	"	"	250	ZERO HOUSE AT O.14.A.6.6/B.
		27.2.17 12 PM	"	"	260	SUSPECTED SIGNALLING STATION AT O.14.A.4/4.8.
		7.30 AM	2nd Lt HARFAND	N.11.C.6.4	500	SEARCH VICINITY OF DUMP NEAR JUNCTION OF ROAD AND TRAMWAY AT. O.13.C.9.0.
		"	"	"	500	SEARCH VICINITY OF HOSPICE O.19.A.4/2.8.
		11.30 AM	Enemy Activity Normal.			
	27.2.17	10.30 AM	2nd Army Commander inspected 10th Batt 2nd Surrey Regt and representatives of all other Units who took part in the raid which took place on the 24th Inst. The Company was represented by O.C. Company, 1 Sergeant and two Privates. The Army Commander spoke very highly of the raiders, also those who assisted in the operation.			
	27.2.17	6 PM	Weather during the last 24 hours the weather has been fine, Roads improving, and restrictions removed.			

VM O.O.
124. MACHINE GUN COY.
M. G. C.

Army Form C. 2118.

No. 124
MACHINE GUN COMPANY.
No..........
Date.........

WAR DIARY
or
INTELLIGENCE SUMMARY.
(Erase heading not required.)

Instructions regarding War Diaries and Intelligence Summaries are contained in F. S. Regs., Part II. and the Staff Manual respectively. Title pages will be prepared in manuscript.

Place	Date	Hour	Summary of Events and Information	Remarks and references to Appendices
IN THE FIELD	27-2-14 to 28-2-14	6PM 6PM	Our Operations. By the wish of G.O.C. 118T Division no indirect fire was carried out on the night of the 27th. A special programme has been arranged for 1-3-14. Enemy Activity. Normal.	
	28-2-14	12MN	Relief. No 4 Section relieved No 3 Section in the trenches and took over the following Gun Positions at GORDONS POST, TELFORD POST, SOUTHERN REDOUBT and WOODLEY POST. 2ND LT E. HERON relieved LIEUT G.H.R. BARTON at EASTERN BREASTWORK. For further details of relief vide sec O.O. 35 att to page 1.	MAP REF TRENCH MAP SHEET 28 SW 1.10.000.
	28-2-14	6PM	Casualties. Casualties during last 24 hours NIL Sick NIL	
	28-2-14	6PM	Weather. The weather during last 24 hours has been fine overcast at intervals Enemy Activity. Artillery slightly active	
	6PM 28-2-14 to 12MN 28-2-14		Our Operations. NIL	

OPERATION ORDER NO. 35.
BY
MAJOR W.H. DAVIS
COMMANDING 124th. MACHINE GUN COMPANY.
****

1. **RELIEF.**
   No. 4 Section will relieve No. 3. Section in the trenches on 1ST. FEB. and take up the following positions:-

   No. 1 Team will go to BEATON POST.
   No. 2   "   "   " " HARROWBY POST.
   No. 3   "   "   " " PRESCOTT'S POST.
   No. 4   "   "   " " FORT TORONTO.

2. **COMMAND.**
   2ND LT. HERON will relieve LT. BARTON at EASTERN BREASTWORK

3. **HANDING OVER.** and SPARE PARTS
   Relieving teams will take guns with them only, all other necessary equipment being handed over by the relieved Section.

4. **TIME TABLE.**
   8.45 am. Relieving teams and limbers leave Company H.Q.
   9.30 am. Guides from each team to be relieved will be at the ration barrier.

5. **INFORMATION.**
   All necessary information is to be given by outgoing teams
   Section Officers in particular will see that all orders regarding returns to be made are handed over, especially the return of ammunition expended during the week which must reach Company Hqrs. not later than 10 am. each Saturday.

6. **COMPLETION OF RELIEF.**
   Relief of each position must be completed by 12 noon.
   Each team when relieved will march independently to Company Hqrs. under the Senior N.C.O. who will report his arrival to the Orderly Room.
   Report of completion of relief will be telephoned from FORT TORONTO using the following code:- BOAT RACE STARTS AT   AM

   All limbers will wait at the barrier and bring back outgoing teams equipment and packs.

7. **RATIONS.**
   Relieved section will bring back with them the unexpired portion of the day's rations.
   Relieving Sections will take with them the unexpired portion of the day's rations.

8. **TRENCH FEET.**
   Officers will take particular care that all men rub their feet with oil and change their socks daily, one pair of socks per man to be sent to Company Headquarters in exchange.

9. **GUM BOOTS.**
   Relieved teams will bring their gum boots out with them and relieving teams will take their gum boots with them.

10. **STRAGGLING.**
    O.C. Company has noticed with much displeasure that the relieved teams when returning to Company Hqrs. straggle all over the roads. This must cease. The N.C.O. of each team will be responsible for the collecting of all his men and marching them down in a proper, soldierlike manner.

                                    Lieut. & Adjt.
                                    124th. M. Gun Company.

OPERATION ORDER NO. 36
BY
MAJOR W.H. DAVIS
COMMANDING 124th. MACHINE GUN COMPANY.
****

No. 124
MACHINE GUN
COMPANY.
No...........
Date..........

1. **RELIEF.**
    No. 3. Section will relieve No. 2. Section in the trenches on 10TH FEB. and take up the following positions:-

    No. 1 Team will go to GORDONS POST
    No. 2   "   "   "   " TELFORD POST
    No. 3   "   "   "   " SOUTHERN REDOUBT
    No. 4   "   "   "   " WOODLEY POST

2. **COMMAND.**
    2ND LT CROWDER will relieve LT WHITE at WESTERN REDOUBT
    RIDDLES   2ND LT HARLAND at FORT TORONTO.

3. **HANDING OVER.**
    and SPARE PARTS
    Relieving teams will take guns with them only, all other necessary equipment being handed over by the relieved Section.

4. **TIME TABLE.**
    8.45 am. Relieving teams and limbers leave Company H.Q.
    9.30 am. Guides from each team to be relieved will be at the ration barrier.

5. **INFORMATION.**
    All necessary information is to be given by outgoing teams
    Section Officers in particular will see that all orders regarding returns to be made are handed over, especially the return of ammunition expended during the week which must reach Company Hqrs. not later than 10 am. each Saturday.

6. **COMPLETION OF RELIEF.**
    Relief of each position must be completed by 12 noon.
    Each team when relieved will march independently to Company Hqrs. under the Senior N.C.O. who will report his arrival to the Orderly Room.
    Report of completion of relief will be telephoned from FORT TORONTO using the following code:- LUNCH WILL BE AT   AM.

    All limbers will wait at the barrier and bring back outgoing teams equipment and packs.

7. **RATIONS.**
    Relieved section will bring back with them the unexpired portion of the day's rations.
    Relieving Sections will take with them the unexpired portion of the day's rations.

8. **TRENCH FEET.**
    Officers will take particular care that all men rub their feet with oil and change their socks daily, one pair of socks per man to be sent to Company Headquarters in exchange.

9. **GUM BOOTS.**
    Relieved teams will bring their gum boots out with them and relieving teams will take their gum boots with them.

10. **STRAGGLING.**
    O.C. Company has noticed with much displeasure that the relieved teams when returning to Company Hqrs. straggle all over the roads. This must cease. The N.C.O. of each team will be responsible for the collecting of all his men and marching them down in a proper, soldierlike manner.

Lieut. & Adjt.
124th M.Gun Company.

VERY SECRET.

OPERATION ORDERS 39.
BY
MAJOR W.H.DAVIS
COMMANDING 124th.MACHINE GUN COMPANY.
****

1. GENERAL IDEA.

   A raid on the HOLLANDSCHESCHUUR SALIENT will be made by a Battalion of the Brigade about 5 pm. on the 24th. February with the object of taking prisoners, inflicting loss on the enemy, and destroying dugouts and defences.

   Precise ZERO HOUR will be notified later and watches will be synchronised at 3 pm. on day of raid by means of a runner send from Headquarters.

2. MACHINE GUN CO-OPERATION.

   The following guns will participate and will be under the command of the Officers and N.C.Os. indicated:-
   - (A) COCKATOO TRENCH..........2/Lt.HENRY.
   - (B) BARROWBY POST............SGT.NORRIS.
   - (C) MAJORS COPSE.............2/LT.HARLAND.
   - (D) PRESCOTT POST............2/Lt.RIDDLES.
   - (E) WOODLEY POST.............SGT.HARRIS.
   - (F) BREASTWORK...I F ....2/LT.HERON.
   - (G) MANTHORPE....I F.........LT.BARTON.
   - (H) GORDONS POST.............2/LT.CLOWDER.

3. NATURE OF FIRE.

   Fire will be opened at ZERO HOUR and will be continued until ZERO HOUR plus 2hrs.30 min. and will be in the nature of "RAPID".

   Targets to be "SEARCHED" will be dealt with by bursts of from 20-30 rounds and targets to be "TRAVERSED" will be dealt with by slow swinging TRAVERSE. Precise instructions as to targets, ranges and elevations will be issued to each gun Commander and labelled A. B. C., etc.as per para.(2) of these orders.

4. AMMUNITION SUPPLY.

   A reserve of 7 filled belt boxes and 5,000 S.A.A. will be kept in hand in case of enemy possible counter attack and the "RAPID FIRE" will need to be regulated by this consideration. All spare numbers will be occupied in filling belts.

5. POSITION OF READINESS.

   Guns concerned will be in a position of readiness at 15 Minutes before ZERO HOUR and extreme precautions will be taken to conceal all preparations from the enemy.

6. WITHDRAWAL.

   Guns will revert to their normal positions and functions at ZERO plus 3 hours.

7. CLEANING.

   Guns will be cleaned as follows:-
   - A.C. & F.......ZERO plus 3 hours.
   - B.D. & G...... "   "   3 hours 30 min.
   - E............. "   "   4 hours.
   - H............. "   "   4 hours 30 min.

8. Guns not actually firing will be ready to
"STAND TO" from ZERO - 30 mins. to ZERO plus 3 hours.
FORT GRANTHAM. The whole team with except sentry
will be in the dugout throughout operations.
S.REDOUBT & TELFORD POST. The tripod will be mounted
on the emplacements and the gun near by.
MCDONALDS POST. A state of vigilance will be maintained,
tripod in position, gun in dugout, sentry by dugout.

9. EQUIPMENT.
All ranks will wear skeleton equipment.

10. Position of O.C. Coy. will be in COCKATOO TRENCH
at N 11 c 5.1.

11. REPORTS.
Gun Team Commanders will send written reports
by their own runners to FORT MORROW as soon after operations
as possible. These reports will record number of rounds
fired, any observations of importance, and any casualties
that may occur.

12. RESERVE GUNS.
The four guns in reserve will be distributed as follows:-
The one at present in use in the front line will be brought
to MAJORS COPSE. The three others will remain at Company
Headquarters. All personnel of the section in relieve will
remain at Company Headquarters under the Command of Lieut.
WHITE.

W H Davis

Major,
Commanding 124th.Machine Gun Company.

20/2/17.

ADDITIONS TO O.O. NO.39.

1. Should the enemy discover the concentration of the raiding Battalion in our front line trenches, O.C. Raid is empowered in order to avoid casualties to commence the raid before ZERO HOUR. He will announce this decision to all concerned by firing a RED ROCKET from the front line trench and the new ZERO will be 15 minutes after the RED ROCKET goes up. Gun Commanders will have all preparations made and teams will be standing to from 2.30 pm. onwards. In the event of the raid being precipitated therefore, the RED ROCKET will be the signal to get the guns mounted.

2. APPENDIX "H".
    Amended and issued herewith with this order.

3. ZERO will be notified to all concerned by the following code "WORKING PARTY" will arrive at   pm."

4. MOVEMENT.
    Throughout the afternoon movement will be concealed as much as possible; no working parties will be out after 12.30 pm.

5. RATIONS, - will arrive at the Barrier at 10.30 pm.

                                (Sd) W.H. DAVIS, Major,
                                Commanding METAPHOR.

                    ****

OPERATION ORDER NO.44.
by
MAJOR W.H.DAVIS, COMMANDING 124th.MACHINE GUN COMPY.

INFORMATION. The 57th.Brigade Machine Gun Coy. will relieve the 124th.M.G.Coy. on the morning of the 21st. inst.

GUIDES. Guides from each gun position will be at the daylight barrier at 9.30 am. By 6 pm. as much gun equipment as possible, e.g. 6 Belt boxes per gun should be brought down to the dump, ~~where two limbers will be in attendance~~, care being taken that nothing is sent down prior to relief which is essential for the proper working of the gun. One man will be left on guard over this equipment 2/Lt. Riddles will detail runner from Fort Morrow for this duty.

HANDING OVER. All Trench Stores will be handed over to the incoming teams and all necessary information regarding the positions given
A list of Trench Stores is sent herewith. The positions must be left clean and tidy. Each team will bring a pick axe with them. "Very" Light Pistols will also be brought out.

CERTIFICATES. Each gun team commander will make out in duplicate a list of such stores handed over by him. One copy signed both by the relieved and relieving N.C.Os. will be handed over to the relieving Team Commander and the other signed copy to be handed into the Orderly Room immediately on arrival at Coy. Headquarters.

LIMBERS. On arrival at the ~~team~~ Dump each Team will pack their gun equipment in one of the limbers which will be found there, and then proceed to Coy. Headquarters under their Gun Team Commander. Two teams equipment will be packed in each limber.
On arrival at Coy. Headquarters the limbers will be repacked in the proper manner ready to move off. Each man will carry his pack to Coy. Headquarters.
Lieut. C.V.WHITE will be on duty at the dump.

TELEPHONES. Section Officers at MAJORS COPSE and MANTHORPE POST will arrange to have the telephones at their dugouts disconnected and brought to Company Commanders. H.Q. A Signaller will be sent up for this purpose.

RATIONS. Rations, except the dinner ration, will be issued as usual. Dinner will be served on arrival at new area.

BLANKETS. Blankets will be made up in rolls — and labelled one roll for each gun team — and brought to the limbers by 6 am.

ROUTES. Teams will relieve according to the following routes:-
P. & O. & BRASSERIE - GORDONS POST, TELFORDS POST & BEGGARS REST.

CHICORY LANE & BRASSERIE.   - SOUTHERN REDOUBT.

Via CAPTAINS POST   - MANTHORPE POST, BREASTWORK, MC DONALDS POST.

No. 124 MACHINE GUN COMPANY.
No.............
Date............

These teams singly at intervals regulated by O.C. Section.

POPPY LANE - WOODLEY POST, PRESCOTTS POST, FORT GRANTHAM.

By nearest route   -   HARROWBY POST, BELTON POST.
avoiding VIERSTRAAT

Routes for incoming teams will be the same except that teams for MANTHORPE POST, BREASTWORK and MCDONALDS POST will proceed via BRASSERIE and GRIGORY LANE. O.C. Section will instruct guides.

TIME.   Relief must be completed by 11 am. and the Company moves to its new area by motor lorries at 11.30 am.

Watkins
Major,
Commanding 124th. Machine Gun Coy.

After Orders

The Relieving Company do not intend to take over the following positions:- Prescott Post, Telford Post, Breastwork and Belton Post. As soon as the neighbouring teams have been relieved, the teams at these positions can make their way to the Daylight Barrier.

A limber will be at the Daylight Barrier at 9am and by that hour all Officers kits must be at the Dump. Officers' Servants can then accompany the limber to H.Q and complete the packing of kits.

W

Army Form C. 2118.

No. 1.A
MACHINE GUN
COMPY. Army
No. M.G. 382
Date 1 - 4 - 1917

WAR DIARY
or
INTELLIGENCE SUMMARY.
(Erase heading not required.)

Vol 10

Place	Date	Hour	Summary of Events and Information				Remarks and references to Appendices
							MAP REF SHEET 28 S.W. 4.A. 1:10.000
FIELD	1-3-17		Our Operations				
			Indirect fire was carried out on the following targets				
			from Pos.				
			Officer i/c	Gun Pos.	Rds fired	SPECIAL SHOOT. Target	
		6 P.M.	2nd Lt HARLAND	N.11.C.6.4.	500	SEARCH THOUGHLY UNNAMED WOOD	
	to		"	"	500	DUGOUTS AT 0.13.A.3½.5.	
		11.30 P.M.	"	"	250	DUMP AT 0.13.C.9¼.3½.	
		6. P.M.	" HERON	N.12.A.14.96.	500	DUGOUTS AT 0.13.B.6½.5.	
	to		"	"	500	ENFILADE OBSTRUCTION LANE FROM TRIANGLE 0.13.A.55.85. TO TRENCH JUNCTION AT 0.13.C.90.	
		12 M.N.	"	"	250	SEARCH VICINITY OF LOUVAEGE FARM 0.Y.D.80.30.	
		7 P.M.	LIEUT BARTON	N.6.C.5½.1½.	1000	SEARCH ROAD 0.13.C.30.85 TO 0.13.C.45.10.	
	to		"	"	250	DUGOUTS AT 0.13.A.4.3.	
		10.30 P.M.	"	"			
		6 P.M.	" WHITE	N.6.D.2½.4.	500	SEARCH VICINITY OF CHATEAU FARM 0.8.C.	
	to		"	"	500	DUGOUTS AT 0.14.A.4¾.9.	
		12 M.N.	"	"	250	ZERO HOUSE 0.14.A.55.65.	
		6 P.M.	2nd Lt CROWDER	N.11.A.9.9.	500	SEARCH VICINITY OF RED CHATEAU N.18.B.90.05.	
	to		"	"	500	SERIES OF DUGOUTS AT 0.13.A.4.3.	
		11.30 P.M.	"	"	250	SEARCH ROAD FROM 0.13.A.0.10 TO 0.13.C.25.90.	

WAR DIARY
or
INTELLIGENCE SUMMARY.
(Erase heading not required.)

Army Form C. 2118.

MACHINE GUN COMPANY

Place	Date	Hour	Summary of Events and Information	Remarks and references to Appendices
FIELD	2.3.17		Indirect fire continued	MAP REF
			Officer i/c Gun No. Rds fired Target	SHEET 28 SW. 4 A
		11 PM	2ND LT RIDDLES N.12.A.2/4.2/2. 500 SEARCH OBVIOUS AVENUE O.13.C.96.40 TO O.13.D.32.32.	1.10.000.
		TO	" " 500 DUGOUTS AT O.Y.D.4.1/2. AND SEARCH VICINITY	
		1 AM.	" " 250 DUMP AT O.13.B.2.3/4. 3/4.	
		12MN	LIEUT HENRY " 500 SEARCH OBSTRUCTION AVENUE FROM O.13.A.4/4.3 TO O.13.B.05.22. HOSPICE AND VICINITY	
		TO	" " 500 DUGOUTS AT O.19.A.8.8.	
		3 AM.	" " 250 O.13.C.5 1/2. 4 1/2.	
		11 PM	2ND LT. RILEY N.11.B.4.4 1/2. 500 CONSTANTLY USED DUGOUTS O.19.B.4.4 1/2.	
		TO	" " 250 BEND IN ROAD AND VICINITY O.13.C.30.88.	
		3 AM.	" " 500 OBVIOUS AVENUE O.13.C.05.55. TO O.13.C.32.33.	
	2.3.17		O.C. Company was present during the above operations	
			Weather fine, roads improving. Casualties nil Sick 1 O.R.	
			Work done wiring continued in front of gun positions	

WAR DIARY
or
INTELLIGENCE SUMMARY.
(Erase heading not required.)

Army Form C. 2118.

No. 124
MACHINE GUN
COMPANY

Place	Date	Hour	Summary of Events and Information	Remarks and references to Appendices
FIELD	2.3.14		Our Operations	
			Indirect fire was carried out on the following targets	MAP REF
			Officer i/c Target Rds fired	SHEET.
		7 PM TO 9.30 PM	2nd Lt. HERON N.19.A.14.96. 500	ENFILADE TRENCH FROM O.Y.D.4.3/4 TO O.8.C.0.3½.
			" " 500	DUGOUTS AT O.13.B.4.4½
		9 PM TO 12 MN.	" HARLAND N.11.C.6.4. 500	SEARCH TRENCH TRAMWAY FROM 0.15.A.4.4¾ TO O.13.A.3¾.3½. 28SW¼A
			" " 250	NEW WORK GOING ON AT O.Y.C.31.2.4. 1:10,000.
			" " 250	CROSS ROADS AT O.13.C.3.9.
	3.3.14		Enemy Activity	
			Normal.	
			Work done.	
			A new alternative emplacement constructed at SOUTHERN REDOUBT N.12.B.2.1/4.3¾.
	3.3.14		Casualties nil Sick nil	
	3.3.14		Weather fine, sharp frost in morning, series of dangerous showers	
	3.3.14		Officers for week ending 3rd inst. is as follows.	F.G.C.M.
			OFFICERS 7. including the undermentioned casuals.	O.C. Coy presided at
			OTHER RKS. 195. including the undermentioned casuals.	F.G.C.M. at MURRUM-
			1 attached to 123 M.G. Coy.	BRIDGES CAMP.
			1 " Field Ambulance	
			2 Course of Instruction	
			2 Employed away from Company	

(M.T)

Army Form C. 2118.

No. [...]
MACHINE GUN
COMPANY.
No. ....
Date ....

WAR DIARY
or
INTELLIGENCE SUMMARY.
(Erase heading not required.)

Instructions regarding War Diaries and Intelligence Summaries are contained in F.S. Regs., Part II. and the Staff Manual respectively. Title pages will be prepared in manuscript.

Place	Date	Hour	Summary of Events and Information	Remarks and references to Appendices
FIELD	3-3-19		**Our Operations**	
			Indirect fire was carried out on the following targets	MAP REF
			Officer i/c Gun No. Rds fired Target	TRENCH MAP
	3.3.19 11 PM TO 4.3.19 1 AM		LT. HENRY N.6.D.2/2.4. 300 DUMP AT O.8.C.84.42.	SHEET 28 SW
			" " 500 GROUP OF DUGOUTS NEAR CATTEAU FARM O.Y.D.30.02.	4.A
			2ND LT. HERON N.12.C.14.96. 250 NEW WORK AT O.Y.D.Y3.Y8. DUGOUTS AT O.13.B.05.80.	1,10,000.
			" " 600 TRAVERSE BETWEEN O.Y.D.Y2.Y8 AND A POINT OF OBSTRUCTION AVENUE AT O.Y.D.Y3.48. NEW TRENCH BEING DUG.	
	4.3.19 1 AM		O.C. COY visits Gun Positions. Work done wiring commenced in front of TELFORDS POST N.12.B.10.9.	
			Enemy activity Artillery slightly active **Strength** No.1931 Sgt 19 Taylor 10.	
	4.3.19		**Casualties** nil sick 1 other rank. transferred from No.9 M.G. Company	
			Weather fine, sharp frost during early hours of morning	Taken on strength of Coy Appointed L/cpl 9

Army Form C. 2118.

No. 124 MACHINE GUN COMPANY.
No................
Date..............

WAR DIARY
or
INTELLIGENCE SUMMARY.
(Erase heading not required.)

Instructions regarding War Diaries and Intelligence Summaries are contained in F. S. Regs., Part II. and the Staff Manual respectively. Title pages will be prepared in manuscript.

Place	Date	Hour	Summary of Events and Information	Remarks and references to Appendices
FIELD	4.3.17		Our Operations	MAP REF.
			Indirect fire was carried out on the following targets	TRENCH MAP
			Officer i/c Gun Pos. Target	SHEET 28 SW
	4.3.17	8 PM	2ND LT HARLAND. N.11.C.6.4. SEARCH NEW TRENCH FROM 500	
		TO	" O.13.A.50.90 TO O.13.B.10.90.	
		4 PM.	" SEARCH UNNAMED WOOD 500	
			" O.13.C.	
			" DUGOUT UNDER 500	
			" CONSTRUCTION AT 0.13.A.2/4.1/4.HA.1:10,000.	
	5.3.17	10 AM	O.C. Company visits all gun positions	
	5.3.17		Enemy Activity. normal. Casualties nil. Sick 1 other Rank.	
	5.3.17		Work Done. Wiring between Telford's Post and Support line	
	5.3.17	8 AM	Weather. Snow fell heavily during the morning, roads bad.	
	5.3.17		Our Operations	
			Indirect fire was carried out on the following targets	
			Officer i/c Gun Pos. Target	
		8.30 PM	" AT HENRY. N.12.A.2/4.2.1/2. SEARCH OBSTRUCTION LANE AND 500	
		TO	" OBVIOUS AVENUE FROM	
		11-30 PM	" 0.13.C.73.89 TO 0.13.D.08.55.	
			" SEARCH TRENCH RAILWAY FROM 500	
			" 0.13.B.00.25 TO 0.13.B.13.15.	

WAR DIARY
or
INTELLIGENCE SUMMARY.
(Erase heading not required.)

Army Form C. 2118.

No. 124
MACHINE GUN COMPANY.
No. ....
Date ....

Instructions regarding War Diaries and Intelligence Summaries are contained in F. S. Regs., Part II. and the Staff Manual respectively. Title pages will be prepared in manuscript.

Place	Date	Hour	Summary of Events and Information	Remarks and references to Appendices
FIELD	5.3.17		Our Operations	
			Indirect fire continued	MAP REF
			Officer i/c — Gun No — Pds fired — Target	TRENCH MAP SHEET 28 S.W. 1:10,000.
		10 PM TO 12 MN.	2nd Lt HERON — N.6.D.2/2.Y. — 500 — LOUWAEGE FARM O.Y.D.91.35. SEARCH OBSTRUCTION DRIVE FROM JUNCTION O.13.B.00.25 TO O.13.B.13.13.	
			" — " — 500 — TRENCH TRAMWAY JUNCTION O.13.C.51.69.	
		9 PM TO 12 MN.	" HARLAND — N.11.C.6.4. — 500 — " "	
			" " — " — 500 — DUMP AT O.13.A.51.12.	
			O.C. Company visits line in the afternoon.	
			Enemy Activity	
			Artillery slightly active all day.	
	6.3.17		Relief	
		11 AM.	No 3 Section relieved No 2 Section in the trenches and took over the following gun positions at the BREASTWORK, McDONALDS POST, BEGGARS REST, AND MANTHORPE POST. LIEUT WHITE relieved 2nd LIEUT HARLAND AT FORT TORONTO and 2nd Lt CROWDER ATT. relieved LIEUT HENRY AT WESTERN REDOUBT.	SEE O.O. 140
			Work Done	
			Wiring in front of TELFORDS POST continued	
			Casualties Nil Sick 3 OR	
			Weather fine all day.	(MT)

Army Form C. 2118.

No. 124
MACHINE GUN COMPANY.

WAR DIARY
or
INTELLIGENCE SUMMARY.
(Erase heading not required.)

Instructions regarding War Diaries and Intelligence Summaries are contained in F.S. Regs., Part II. and the Staff Manual respectively. Title pages will be prepared in manuscript.

Place	Date	Hour	Summary of Events and Information	Remarks and references to Appendices
FIELD	7.3.17		Our Operations	
			Indirect fire was carried out on the following targets	MAP REF
			Officer i/c Gun No. Target. Rds Fired	TRENCH MAP
	7.3.17	11-30PM	2nd Lt CROWDER. N.6.D.2½.y. SUSPECTED ENTRANCE 500	SHEET 28 SW
		TO	" " TO TUNNEL 0.8.D.y¾.y. 500	H.A.1.10,000.
	8.3.17	2AM.		ON RAET FARM AND DISTRICT. 0.14.A.23.05.
	7.3.17	7PM	LIEUT C.V. WHITE N.11.C.6.4. HOSPICE AND VICINITY 500	
		TO	" " 0.19.A.y½.8½. 500	
		12MN.	" " DUMP ON TRENCH TRAMWAY 0.13.C.9¼.3½. 500	
	7.3.17	9PM	2nd LT E. HERON N.12.C.14.96 DUMP AT JUNCTION OF TRENCH TRAMWAY 0.13.C.9.0. 500	
		TO	" " CONSTANTLY USED DUGOUTS	
	8.3.17	1-15AM		0.13.B.4.4½.
				RENTY FARM AND VICINITY 0.13.B.90.55.
	8.3.17	10AM	O.C. Company visits line. Enemy activity normal.	
			Casualties nil sick 1 other rank	
			Weather Snow fell at intervals during day.	

Army Form C. 2118.

No. 124
MACHINE GUN COMPANY.
No..........
Date..........

WAR DIARY
or
INTELLIGENCE SUMMARY.
(Erase heading not required.)

Instructions regarding War Diaries and Intelligence Summaries are contained in F. S. Regs., Part II. and the Staff Manual respectively. Title pages will be prepared in manuscript.

Place	Date	Hour	Summary of Events and Information	Remarks and references to Appendices
FIELD	6-3-17		<u>Our Operations</u> No Indirect fire was carried out on the night of the 6th inst. <u>Enemy Activity</u>	MAP REF TRENCH MAP SHEET 28 SW 4A 1:10,000.
	7-3-17		Machine Guns and Snipers active otherwise normal. O.C. Company visits all gun positions in the line	
		11 AM	Lieut. J. M. Lawson proceeded to STEENVOORDE on a course of tactical handling of machine guns. Lieut. H. Inskaren Henry takes over the duties of Adjutant during the absence of Lieut. Lawson. Lieut. L. R. Barton completed course of instruction at the 41ST DIVISION GAS SCHOOL. <u>Casualties</u> Nil. Sick 3. o'ranks. <u>Weather</u> fine, wind very high, cold, roads dry.	

WAR DIARY
or
INTELLIGENCE SUMMARY

(Erase heading not required.)

No. 124
MACHINE GUN COMPANY.

Army Form C. 2118

Place	Date	Hour	Summary of Events and Information	Remarks and references to Appendices
FIELD	8-3-17		**Our Operations**	
			No Indirect fire was carried out on the night of the 8th inst.	
	9-3-17		**Enemy Activity**	
			Artillery and M.G's very active all day.	
			Weather Snow fell at intervals during day	
			Casualties nil **Sick** nil	
			Work Done Wiring still continued in front of TELFORDS POST	
	9-3-17		**Our Operations**	
			Indirect fire was carried out on the following targets	MAP. REF.
				TRENCH MAP
				SHEET 28 SW
				1.10.000.
		Officer i/c	Gun Pos.	Target	Rds Fired
		8 PM TO 12 MN.	2ND LT HARLAND	N.11.A.99.		500	TRAVERSE TRACK FROM 0.13.A.40.30. TO 0.13.A.45.85.
		8 PM TO 11.30 PM	LT WHITE	N.11.C.6.4.		"	DUMP AT 0.13.A.5½.1½. AND SEARCH OBSTRUCTION LANE IN VICINITY.
		9 PM TO 1 AM	2ND LT RIDDLES	N.11.B.7.4½.		500	SEARCH UNNAMED WOOD (WORK REPORTED GOING ON HERE) FROM XROADS AT 0.13.C.3.9. DOWNWARDS
		10-3-17 1 AM	"	"		500	SEARCH UNNAMED WOOD FROM 0.13.C.1.4. UPWARDS
		9-3-17 10 PM TO 10-3-17 2 AM	2ND LT. HERON.	N.12.C.19.96.		500	0.Y.D.4.1 TO 0.Y.D.2½.4. SEARCH TRAM WAY FROM SUSPECTED ENTRANCE TO TUNNEL 0.8.D.7¾.Y.
						500	ONRAET FARM AND DISTRICT 0.14.A.23.05.

WAR DIARY
or
INTELLIGENCE SUMMARY

(Erase heading not required.)

Army Form C. 2118.

No. 124 MACHINE GUN COMPANY.

Place	Date	Hour	Summary of Events and Information	Remarks and references to Appendices
FIELD	9-3-17		Indirect fire continued	
			Officer i/c Gun No. Rds fired Target	
		8.30PM TO 11.30PM	2nd Lt CROWDER. N.6.D.2½.4. 1000. DUMP AT CATTEAU FARM O.8.D. 84, 82. AND TRAVERSE CATEN DRIVE IN VICINITY	MAP REF TRENCH MAP SHEET 23 SW. 2. 1:10,000
	10.3.17		Enemy Activity	
			Artillery slightly active Casualties nil Sick nil	
			Weather	
			Fine during the morning, overcast during the afternoon.	
		6 PM	The strength of the Company for week ending 10th inst- is as follows.	
			Officers Other Ranks	
			11 196 Including the undermentioned casuals.	
			1 Attached to 123 Fd. Amby for duty	
			4 Field Ambulance	
			4 Course of Instruction	
			1 att to 124 T.M.B.	
			1 " to 413th Divisional Train	

WAR DIARY
or
INTELLIGENCE SUMMARY

Army Form C. 2118.

No. 124 MACHINE GUN COMPANY.

Place	Date	Hour	Summary of Events and Information	Remarks and references to Appendices
FIELD.	10.3.17		Our Operations	
		7 PM to 11 PM	Indirect fire was carried out on the following targets	
			Officer i/c Lt. WHITE	Gun Pos. Rds Fired Target.
				N.11.C.6.4. 500 SEARCH UNNAMED WOOD IN O.13.C.
			"	" 500 BLACK COT AND SEARCH VICINITY
				MAP REF TRENCH MAP SHEET 28 SW2 1/10,000.
	11.3.17		Casualties normal. hit sick 1 OR rank	
			Enemy Activity normal.	
			Weather very dull, much rain, roads very muddy.	
	11.3.17		Our Operations	
			Indirect fire was carried out on the following targets.	
			Officer i/c	Gun Pos. Rds Fired Target
		9.30PM to 12 MN.	2ND LT HERON	N.6.D.2/2.7. 500. TWO LARGE DUGOUTS AT O.B.C.8/2.3 AND SEARCH VICINITY
			"	" 500. DUMP AT CATTEAU FARM O.8.C.85.
		6.30PM to 9.30PM	2ND LT CROWDER	N.12.A.2 1/4. 2 1/2. 500. DUGOUTS (IMPORTANT POINTS) O.13.C.2.6.
			"	" 500. DUMP ON TRENCH TRAMWAY O.13.C.9 1/4. 3 1/2.
	12.3.17		Enemy activity normal Casualties hit sick 1 OR.	

WAR DIARY
or
INTELLIGENCE SUMMARY

(Erase heading not required.)

Army Form C. 2118.

No. 124 MACHINE GUN COMPANY.

Place	Date	Hour	Summary of Events and Information	Remarks and references to Appendices
FIELD	12.3.17		Lieut J.N. Lawson rejoined Company from course of Instruction and took over the duties of Adjutant.	
			Weather — very changeable some rain at intervals	
	12.3.17		Our Operations	
			In direct fire was carried out on the following targets	MAP REF
			Officer i/c Gun No.s Rds fired Target	TRENCH MAP
	13.3.17	1AM to 3AM	LIEUT WHITE N.11.C.6.4. 260 JUNCTION OF ROAD AND TRENCH TRAMWAY AT O.13.C.9.0.	SHEET 28 SW2
				1, 10,000.
			" " " 250 ENFILADE NEW TRENCH FROM O.13.A.14.1/4.9/14 TO O.13.B.O.9/2.	
	12.3.17	6-10.30PM to 9-15PM	LIEUT BARTON. N.6.C.5½.½. 250 DUMP ON TRENCH TRAMWAY AT O.13.A.5½.½.	
			" " 250 SEARCH SUNKEN ROAD FROM O.13.C.J.8½ TO O.13.C.63/4.2/4.	
		9-PM to 12-MN	2ND LIEUT CROWDER. N.6.D.2½.4. 250 DUGOUTS AT O.9.D.1½.8.	
			" " 260 RENTY FARM AT O.13.B.9½.5½.	
			Casualties nil sick nil	
			Enemy activity normal.	
	13.3.17	2 PM	O.C. Company visits line.	
			Weather dull and overcast	

No. 124
MACHINE GUN COMPANY

Army Form C. 2118.

WAR DIARY
or
INTELLIGENCE SUMMARY
(Erase heading not required.)

Place	Date	Hour	Summary of Events and Information	Remarks and references to Appendices
FIELD	13.3.17		Our Operations	MAP REF
			Indirect fire was carried out on the following targets	TRENCH MAP
				SHEET 28 S.W.
			Officer i/c Gun Pos. Rds fired Target	1/10,000.
		9 PM to 11.30 PM	LIEUT WHITE N.11.C.6.4. 260 SEARCH VICINITY OF POINT 0.13.A.5.3.23 MANY DUGOUTS.	
			" " 250 JUNCTION OF ROADS AND TRENCHES 0.13.C.3.8½.	
		8.30PM TO 12 MN	LIEUT BARTON N.12.A.14.96. 260 SEARCH OBSTRUCTION LANE AND OBVIOUS LANE FROM 0.13.A.8½.13¼ TO 0.13.D.9½.6¾.	
			" " 250 TRENCH TRAMWAY JUNCTION AT 0.13.C.5¼.4.	
	14.3.17	10 AM	O.C. Company accompanied by O.C. No 9th M.G Coy and 4 Section officers of the same Company visited all Vickers Gun Positions in 124th L.B. Sector.	
			Enemy Activity normal Casualties nil Sick 1 O.R.	
			Weather very changeable, fine at intervals	

WAR DIARY
or
INTELLIGENCE SUMMARY
(Erase heading not required.)

Army Form C. 2118.

No. 104
MACHINE GUN COMPANY

Place	Date	Hour	Summary of Events and Information	Remarks and references to Appendices
FIELD	14.3.14		Our Operations.	MAP REF.
			Indirect fire was carried out on the following targets	TRENCH MAP
				SHEETS 28 SW2
			Long Range Shoot.	1/10.000
			Officer i/c Gun No. Rds fired Target
		14.3.14 7PM TO 10 PM	2nd Lt CROWDER. N.6.D.2½.2.4. 250. ONRAGE FARM. O.14.C.2.½.
			" " 250 BLUE FARM O.14.C.6.4.½.
		15.3.14 1.AM.	LIEUT BARTON N.6.C.5½.1/2. 500 HOSPICE O.19.A.8.8½.
		14.3.14 9-PM TO 12-MN	LIEUT WHITE N.N.C.6.4. 250 HOSPICE O.19.A.8.8½.
			" " 250 ROW OF DUGOUTS FROM O.13.C.5½.4.½. TO O.13.C.3½.4.6.
			Enemy Activity normal. Casualties nil Sick 1 O/R.
			Weather fine generally. roads improving
	15.3.14		Our Operations
			No indirect fire was carried out on the night of the 15th inst.
	16.3.14		Enemy activity normal Casualties nil sick nil
			Weather fine
	16.3.14	9 AM.	OC Company visits all guns in the line Wiring in front of TELFORD'S POST
			continued Observation good.

Army Form C. 2118.

No. 1.4
MACHINE GUN
COMPANY.
No.......... Date..........

WAR DIARY
or
INTELLIGENCE SUMMARY
(Erase heading not required.)

Instructions regarding War Diaries and Intelligence Summaries are contained in F. S. Regs., Part II. and the Staff Manual respectively. Title Pages will be prepared in manuscript.

Place	Date	Hour	Summary of Events and Information			Remarks and references to Appendices
FIELD	16-3-17		**Day Operations**			
			Indirect fire was carried out on the following targets			
			Officer i/c	Gun Pos.	Rds. fired	Target
		6.45 PM to 9.45 PM	LIEUT WHITE	N.12.A.2¼.2½.	250	GROUP OF DUGOUTS AT O.13.B.6½.5.	MAP REF
		"	"	"	250	SEARCH. OBSTRUCTION & INF. AND OBVIOUS AVENUE FROM O.13.C.Y3.8 TO O.13.D.08.35.	TRENCH MAP
		9 PM to 11.30 PM	2ND LT. CROWDER	N.6.D.2½.4.	250	SUSPECTED ENTRANCE TO TUNNEL O.8.D.Y¼.Y.	SHEET 28 SW2
			"	"	260	SUSPECTED WIRELESS STATION O.14.A.7¾.8.	1/10,000.
		8.30 PM to 11 PM	2ND LIEUT BARTON	N.12.A.14.96.	260	NEW YORK AT O.Y.D. Y3.98.	
			"	"	250	TRAVERSE BETWEEN O.Y.D. Y2.Y8 AND POINT OF OBSTRUCTION AVE AT O.Y.D. Y3.H-8.	
			Enemy Activity normal			
			Casualties nil	seek nil		
	17-3-17	6 PM	2ND LIEUT HERON proceeded to STEENVOORDE training area with billeting party.			
			Strength of Company for week ending 17th inst= is as follows			Weather fine, good visibility
				Officers	Other Ranks	
				11	145	including the undermentioned casuals
					3	Brigade H.Q.
					3	Batt. H.Q.
				1	2	Employed on duty away from Coy.

WAR DIARY or INTELLIGENCE SUMMARY

(Erase heading not required.)

Army Form C. 2118.

No. 124 Army MACHINE GUN COMPANY.

Instructions regarding War Diaries and Intelligence Summaries are contained in F. S. Regs., Part II. and the Staff Manual respectively. Title Pages will be prepared in manuscript.

Place	Date	Hour	Summary of Events and Information	Remarks and references to Appendices
FIELD	14/3/17		Our Operations	MAP REF.
			Indirect fire was carried out on the following targets	TRENCH MAP
				SHEET 28SW2
				1/10,000.
			Officer i/c Gun No. Rds fired Target	
		4 PM	2ND LT CROWDER N.6.D.2½.4. 250 BRANCH OF TRAMWAY	
		TO	" " 250 O.8.D.H.Q. DUGOUT AT O.Y.D.H.Q.	
		10 PM	" " 250 SUPPLY DUMP AT O.13.B.6.4.	
		9.30 PM	LIEUT WHITE N.11.C.6.4. 250 DUMP ON TRAMWAY O.13.A.5½.1½.	
		TO	" " 250 PLATEAU FARM N.18.D.5.6.	
		11.15 PM	" " 250 DUGOUTS AT O.13.A.2.6.	
			Enemy Activity — normal. Casualties nil. Sick 2 O.R.	
	15.3.17	11-4 AM	Relief. No 1 Section relieved No 2 Section in the trenches and took over gun posts at Gordons Post, Telfords Post, Southern Redoubt, and Woodley Post. 2nd LT RIDDLES relieved LT WHITE at MAJORS COPSE and 2ND LT HARLAND relieved 2ND LT CROWDER at WESTERN REDOUBT. For further details of relief orders see O.O. att to page 1.	
			Weather fine visibility good.	

WAR DIARY
or
INTELLIGENCE SUMMARY

(Erase heading not required.)

Army Form C. 2118.

No. 124 MACHINE GUN COMPANY.

Place	Date	Hour	Summary of Events and Information	Remarks and references to Appendices
Flêtre D.	18.3.17		**Our Operations** No indirect fire was carried out on the night of the 18th inst-	
	19.3.17	6.40am to	Indirect fine was carried out in conjunction with 41st Divisional Artillery, and Trench Mortars on the HOLLANDSCHESCHUUR SALIENT	MAP REF TRENCH MAP SHEET 28SW2 1/10,000
			Gun Pos. Rds fired Target	
			Officer i/c	
			LT BARTON N.12.A.14.96 1,250 As above.	
			2ND LT RIDDLES N.11.C.84.3 500 DO	
			" COCKATOO TRENCH 500 DO	
			2ND LT MARLAND N.12.A.14.96 1,000 DO	
		9am	**Enemy Activity** normal.	
			Casualties nil sick nil	
		10am	O.C. Company visits line. **Weather** dull, very high wind, rain at intervals	

Army Form C. 2118.

NO. 124
MACHINE GUN
COMPANY.

WAR DIARY
or
INTELLIGENCE SUMMARY
(Erase heading not required.)

Place	Date	Hour	Summary of Events and Information	Remarks and references to Appendices
FIELD	19-3-19		**Our Operations** No indirect fire was carried out owing to a very high wind	
	20-3-19	10 AM	O.C. Company accompanied by O.C. 54th Machine Gun Company resident hut.	
			Enemy Activity normal. Casualties nil. Sick 2 o/ranks.	
			Weather much rain & snow, very windy.	
	20-3-19		**Our Operations** No indirect fire was carried out on the night of 19th inst.	
	20-3-19		54th Machine Gun Company took over gun positions from Company, the relief was completed by 1 p.m. For further details of relief see O.O.144 attached. On completion of relief Coy proceeded in Motor Lorries to billets in	O.O. 144 att.
			STEENVOORDE. Casualties nil. Sick nil.	
			Weather fine overcast at intervals	

Army Form C. 2118.

No. 124
MACHINE GUN
COMPANY.

WAR DIARY
or
INTELLIGENCE SUMMARY
(Erase heading not required.)

Instructions regarding War Diaries and Intelligence Summaries are contained in F.S. Regs., Part II. and the Staff Manual respectively. Title Pages will be prepared in manuscript.

Place	Date	Hour	Summary of Events and Information	Remarks and references to Appendices
FIELD	22-3-17		Reorganising of Sections was carried out. Weather showery and overcast.	
	23-3-17		Company was inspected by 2nd Army Commander. Weather fine.	
	24-3-17		Company training carried out. Weather showery & overcast.	
	25-3-17		— do —	
	26-3-17		— do — Weather raining all day.	
	27-3-17		— do — Weather fine. Sick 1.O.R.	
	28-3-17		— do — Weather overcast, showery.	
	29-3-17		— do —	
	30-3-17		G.O.C. 124 Infantry Brigade inspected Company in the following, Gun Drill, Elementary Drill, and action from Limbers. Sick 1.O.R. Weather fine, showery.	
	31-3-17		Sections attached to units as follows:- No1 Section 32ND ROY FUSRS. No 2 Section 21ST KRR. No 3 Section 10TH QUEENS No 4 Section 26TH ROY FUSRS. Training was carried out with the above units. Weather very windy. Some rain. Sick 1.O.R.	

2ND LIEUT W.M. HARLAND GAZ. LIEUT 1-3-17.

WAR DIARY
or
INTELLIGENCE SUMMARY

(Erase heading not required.)

Army Form C. 2118.

No. 124
MACHINE GUN
COMPANY

Place	Date	Hour	Summary of Events and Information	Remarks and references to Appendices
FIELD	31-3-17		Strength of Company for week ending 31st inst is as follows.	
			Officers 11 O/Ranks 142 including the undermentioned casuals.	
			Att to 123 M Coy. 1	
			Hospital Base 3	
			Field Amb. 4	
			Sick train 1	
			Course of Instruction 3	

OPERATION ORDER NO....
BY
MAJOR W.H.DAVIS
COMMANDING 124th. MACHINE GUN COMPANY.
############

1. **RELIEF.**
   No. 3. Section will relieve No. 2. Section in the trenches on 6TH MARCH and take up the following positions:-

   No. 1 Team will go to BREASTWORK
   No. 2 " " " " McDONALDS POST
   No. 3 " " " " BEGGARS REST
   No. 4 " " " " MANTHORPE POST

2. **COMMAND.**
   2ND LT CROWDER will relieve LT HENRY at W. REDOUBT.
   LT WHITE   do   2ND LT HARLAND at FORT TORONTO.

3. **HANDING OVER.**
   Relieving teams will take guns with them only, all other necessary equipment being handed over by the relieved Section.

4. **TIME TABLE.**
   8.45 am. Relieving teams and limbers leave Company H.Q.
   9.30 am. Guides from each team to be relieved will be at the ration barrier.

5. **INFORMATION.**
   All necessary information is to be given by outgoing teams
   Section Officers in particular will see that all orders regarding returns to be made are handed over, especially the return of ammunition expended during the week which must reach Company Hqrs. not later than 10 am. each Saturday.

6. **COMPLETION OF RELIEF.**
   Relief of each position must be completed by 12 noon.
   Each team when relieved will march independently to Company Hqrs. under the Senior N.C.O. who will report his arrival to the Orderly Room.
   Report of completion of relief will be telephoned from FORT TORONTO using the following code:- HOT SOUP AT   AM.

   All limbers will wait at the barrier and bring back outgoing teams equipment and packs.

7. **RATIONS.**
   Relieved section will bring back with them the unexpired portion of the day's rations.
   Relieving Sections will take with them the unexpired portion of the day's rations.

8. **TRENCH FEET.**
   Officers will take particular care that all men rub their feet with oil and change their socks daily, one pair of socks per man to be sent to Company Headquarters in exchange.

9. **GUM BOOTS.**
   Relieved teams will bring their gum boots out with them and relieving teams will take their gum boots with them.

10. **STRAGGLING.**
    O.C. Company has noticed with much displeasure that the relieved teams when returning to Company Hqrs. straggle all over the roads. This must cease. The N.C.O. of each team will be responsible for the collecting of all his men and marching them down in a proper, soldierlike manner.

John W Lawson Lieut. & Adjt.
124th M. Gun Company.

No. 124
MACHINE GUN
COMPANY.
No. C3. 42/4
Date 1-5-17

From O.C. 124 M.G Comp
To 124 I.B. Hqs.

Herewith War Diary for the month
of April 1917.

John M Lawson Lieut & adjt
for O.C.
124, MACHINE GUN COY.
M. G. C.

Army Form C. 2118.

WAR DIARY
or
INTELLIGENCE SUMMARY.
(Erase heading not required.)

No. 124 MACHINE GUN COMPANY

Place	Date	Hour	Summary of Events and Information	Remarks and references to Appendices
FIELD SIEGVOORDE	1-4-17 to 2-4-17		Sections attached to Infantry Battalions for training. No 1 Section was attached to the 32nd Roy Fusiliers, No 2 Section to the 21st R.R.W. boys No 3 Section to the 10th Queens and No 4 Section to the 26th Roy Fusiliers. Weather much rain, very dull, roads very bad. Sick 2 other ranks.	
	3-4-17		Brigade practise attack 16 Vickers guns co-operated in the 124th Infantry Brigade practise attack. For further details see Brigade orders on 1st 50 and 1.59 and 1.59	copy 38
	4-4-17		Company training carried out.	
	5-4-17		Company training and carried out and preparations made for moving to forward area.	
	6-4-17		Relief. 8 Vickers guns relieved 8 Vickers guns of 123 Machine Gun Company in the ST ELOI SECTOR. On completion of relief the disposition of guns were as follows: I-B.14. O.32. c.1½. 5/4; I-B.16. I.31. C.8¼. 9; I-B.14. 1-31. A. 1-½. 5/4; I-B.18 I.31. C.6.2½; 26A. SCOTTISH WOOD RIGHT N.5.B.25.96. 22. SCOTTISH WOOD LEFT M.30. C.H6.80, ECLUSE TRENCH I.32.A.1½.2, CANAL BANK 1.32. B. 30. 140. The relief was completed by 3-30 p.m.	Map Ref trench map

Army Form C. 2118.

WAR DIARY
or
INTELLIGENCE SUMMARY.
(Erase heading not required.)

Instructions regarding War Diaries and Intelligence Summaries are contained in F. S. Regs., Part II. and the Staff Manual respectively. Title pages will be prepared in manuscript.

No. 124
MACHINE GUN COMPANY

Place	Date	Hour	Summary of Events and Information	Remarks and references to Appendices
FIELD	6-4-19	6-30 AM	The Company less 9 gun teams proceeded by march route to Lamafat	
MORBAC			H. 31. B. 3. 4.	
CAMP	7-4-19	9 AM	O.C. Company accompanied by Lieut JGR C Henry visits line in STEEFSECTOR	
H.31.B.3.4.			Casualties nil. Sick 2 of ranks. Weather fine	
	8-4-19	9 AM	O.C. Company accompanied by Lieut JGR.L. Henry made further reconnaissance of Vickers gun positions in ST ELOI SECTOR.	
		4 PM.	G.O.C. 124th Infantry Brigade accompanied by Staff Captain inspected company's Billets etc.	
		2 PM.	G.O.C. 41st Division inspected Company's horses and mules.	
			Casualties nil. Sick 1 Rank. Weather fine	
			Lieut J.C. Lawson visits line on a reconnaissance	
	9-4-19		Casualties nil. Sick nil. Weather very dull, little rain	
	10-4-19		Lieut J.W. Layton accompanied by O.C. 122. Machine Gun Company visits all gun positions in ST ELOI SECTOR. Weather fine at intervals, some snow.	
			Casualties nil. Sick nil.	

Army Form C. 2118.

WAR DIARY
or
INTELLIGENCE SUMMARY.
(Erase heading not required.)

No. 124 MACHINE GUN COMPANY.

Place	Date	Hour	Summary of Events and Information	Remarks and references to Appendices
FIELD	11/4/17		Major W.R. Davis relinquishes the command of Company, and proceeds to Machine Gun Corps School of Instruction, Camiers.	
			Lieut. J.W. Lawson takes over the command of Company and Lieut Hart Hony takes over the duties of 2nd in command. Weather enough, some rain.	
			Casualties nil sick 1 Evac.	
	12/4/17		Preparations made for relief. Casualties nil sick 1 Evac. Weather fair, rain at intervals	
	13/4/17	6 P.M.	Relief. Company relieved 122 Machine Gun Company in the ST ELOI SECTOR SEE 00 43 further details and disposition of guns see Operation Orders attached Enemy activity Artillery slightly active	attached sheet 28.
			Casualties nil Sick 2 evac 3 to Rest Weather fine overcast. Observation of Ref. Operations nil Enemy activity Artillery slightly active	
	14/4/17		Casualties nil sick nil. Observation Moderate Operations nil approaches to gun positions & emplacements carried out. Weather clinging cold, rain.	

Army Form C. 2118.

WAR DIARY
or
INTELLIGENCE SUMMARY.
(Erase heading not required.)

Instructions regarding War Diaries and Intelligence Summaries are contained in F. S. Regs., Part II. and the Staff Manual respectively. Title pages will be prepared in manuscript.

No. 124.
MACHINE GUN COMPANY

Place	Date	Hour	Summary of Events and Information	Remarks and references to Appendices
FIELD	14.4.17		**Strength** — The strength of Company on the 14th inst. was as follows:—	
VOORMEZEELE			Officers Other Ranks	
			Effective strength 11 171	
			Unfit for duties:—	
			Hospital — Casuals — At Works	
			Ammunition Carriers — 50.	
			11 221.	
			Infantry	
			K.G. Start of 9 Companies 1. — 1.	
			Lieutenant from	
			attached to 123rd Coy. 1. — 1.	
			2 10.	
	15.4.17		Our operations nil. Enemy activity artillery active all day, machine guns	
			very active at night. Casualties nil. Sick nil.	
			Work done. General improvements to gun positions, reconstruction of gun	
			emplacements and wiring in front of gun positions. Weather fine, rain at intervals.	
			Our Operations. Indirect fire was carried out on the following targets:—	Map Ref Sheet 28
			Officer Gun Position Target	
		9 PM TO 1 AM	ANDITHERON 500 DUMP at O.8.D. CO. 85.	
			500 CATTEAU FARM.	

Army Form C. 2118.

No. 124
MACHINE GUN
COMPANY.

WAR DIARY
or
INTELLIGENCE SUMMARY.
(Erase heading not required.)

Place	Date	Hour	Summary of Events and Information	Remarks and references to Appendices
FIELD	16/4/17		Enemy activity. Artillery slightly active. Casualties nil. Sick nil.	
		Our own. General improvements to emplacements, clearing approaches to gun positions, and wiring continued at all gun positions. Weather very wet, visibility poor.	
	17/4/17		Our Operations. Indirect fire was carried out on the following targets.	
			Officers.	
			Lieut Parker. Gun Position MARTENS FARM. Hits Fired Target 500.	
	17/4/17	10·30 to 11·30 am	Lieut Parker " DUMP at O.8.A.85·33. 250.	
	17/4/17	7pm to 9pm	" " DOME HOUSE. 250.	
	17/4/17	9pm to 10pm	" Skyline Farm " HIELF FARM. 500.	
	17/4/17	10pm to 11pm	" " CATTEAU FARM. 500.	
			" " AERO HOUSE O.14.A.60.65. 500.	
			Enemy Activity. Artillery very quiet. Machine Guns slightly active. Intended Offa rounds 1. Seek 2 other ranks one from cordite poisoning. Casualties.	
			Our Own. General improvements all round. Weather fine, very windy.	

WAR DIARY or INTELLIGENCE SUMMARY

Army Form C. 2118.

Place	Date	Hour	Summary of Events and Information	Remarks and references to Appendices
FIELD	18.4.17		Our Operations. Indirect fire was carried out on the following targets. Has exploded.	
DICKEBUSCH			3000. Targets. CATTEAU FARM, HILLE FARM, DUMP at O.9.C.65.40. ESTAMINET TRACK. O.9.C.30.40, O.9.C.4.9. O.9.C.4.4.½. ANGLE OF ROAD. O.4.D.20.05. RAVINE WOOD. TRENCH TRAMWAY at O.10.A.8.9.	Any Rif. Shelters
			No Retaliation. General improvements at all positions. Casualties nil. Sick 1 O.R. Weather fine. Good visibility.	
			Our Operations. Indirect fire was carried out on the following targets. Has exploded 3000. Targets. CATTEAU FARM, HILLE FARM, RAVINE WOOD. DUMP ON TRENCH TRAMWAY O.10.B.20.10. X ROADS at O.10.B.60.60. Enemy activity very quiet.	
	19.4.17		Company was relieved in the St. Eloi Sector by the 122 Machine Gun Company. relief was complete by 2 a.m. On completion of relief Company less transport proceeded to Ontario Camp at RENINGHELST and formed part of 41st Division reserve Brigade, for further details of relief orders see appendix.	See O.O.4.44. attached.

Army Form C. 2118.

WAR DIARY
or
INTELLIGENCE SUMMARY.
(Erase heading not required.)

Instructions regarding War Diaries and Intelligence Summaries are contained in F. S. Regs., Part II. and the Staff Manual respectively. Title pages will be prepared in manuscript.

No. 156 MACHINE GUN COMPANY

Place	Date	Hour	Summary of Events and Information	Remarks and references to Appendices
FIELD.	20.11.17		Company training carried out.	
NIEUWHEIST.	21.11.17		Company training carried out.	
		11-30AM	O.C. Company attended conference of Battalion Commanders at Brigade Hq.S. Inst. Ref. In the Conf. The following subjects were discussed, Instruction for coming Offensive on 2nd Army front, and reconnaissance for troops in the SE E1.01 SECTOR.	Shut 23.
			Strength. The strength of the Company on the 21st inst was as follows.	
			Officers Other ranks	
			Attached for duty 11 — 142.	
			33 Grooms & Drivers A.S.C.	
			11 — 220.	
			Field Ambulance — 10.	
			Course of Instruction 1 1.	
			Base. Off. Servant 1.	
			Servant (Officer) 1.	
			Leave. 1.	
			1 14.	

WAR DIARY
or
INTELLIGENCE SUMMARY.
(Erase heading not required.)

Army Form C. 2118.

Place	Date	Hour	Summary of Events and Information	Remarks and references to Appendices
FIELD	22.4.17		Church Parade.	
UNUBECTS	23.4.17		Preparation for trenches.	
	24.4.17	3 AM	Relief. Company relieved 122 Machine Gun Company in the ST. ELOI SECTOR. For distribution of guns and further details of relief see appendix.	See O.O. 145 att.
			Weather fine, good visibility. Casualties nil.	
		10 PM	Our Operations. Indirect fire was carried out on the following targets. Rounds expended 2,450. Targets engaged. OUWAEGE FARM, STRONG POINT O.8.D.9.4. HOF of DUGOUTS O.8.C.8.4.30, SIGNAL ST. N.O.14.A.4.4.80, TRENCH & DUGOUTS from O.8.D.20.12 to Trel. 28. DUGOUTS O.8.C.8.4.30, MARTENS FARM, O.8.D.60.05, DUGOUTS O.8.D.6½.½. C.14.C. 28.83, MARTENS FARM, O.8.D.60.05, DUGOUTS O.8.D.6½.½.	
	25.4.17		Enemy Activity. Machine Guns, Artillery very quiet. Work going strong and general improvement at all wheeled gun positions.	
			Casualties. 1 O.R. wounded.	

Army Form C. 2118.

WAR DIARY
or
INTELLIGENCE SUMMARY.
(Erase heading not required.)

Instructions regarding War Diaries and Intelligence Summaries are contained in F. S. Regs., Part II. and the Staff Manual respectively. Title pages will be prepared in manuscript.

Place	Date	Hour	Summary of Events and Information	Remarks and references to Appendices
VOORMEZEELE	2/11/14	1 PM	Our Operations. Indirect fire was carried out on the following targets from O.P. fixed 2.5ft. Targets engaged. Searched trench O.I.H.B.0.8 to O.I.H.B.10.38, supports and track O.8.C.80.08 to O.I.H.A.90.96, O.8.D.84,50, O.9.C.H.9, O.10.A.1826.	
		to	Enemy Activity. slightly active during day. Casualties nil.	
		5 PM	Work done. General improvements to ground.	
	3/11/14	1.7 PM	Our Operations. Indirect fire was carried out on the following targets. Rounds fired 250. Targets engaged. DUMP O.I.H.B.25.3H.; ORTHE CRESCENT searched O.I.H.B.I.0.8.	
		to	40. O.I.H.B.10.38.; EVANS FARM. O.I.H.B.32.20.; SEARCHED TRENCH O.I.H.B.36.38.15	Sheet Ref.
		6 PM	O.I.H.B.35.10.; SEARCHED ROAD O.P.C.78.16. to O.I.H.A.65.65.; Traversed O.I.H.B.38.38. to Sheet 28.	
			O.I.H.B.65.35.	
	3/11/14		Enemy Activity. Artillery very active at intervals during day.	
			Casualties. nil.	
			Work done. reconstruction of L. wheel for Emplacements, and general improvements to	
			F.O.C. 12H. Infantry Brigade accompanied by O.C. Company reviewed enfiladed gun positions	
	4/11/14	3 AM	at MOATED GRANGE, FORT, OOSTOEK FARM,	

WAR DIARY
or
INTELLIGENCE SUMMARY

Army Form C. 2118.

No. 124 MACHINE GUN COMPANY

Place	Date	Hour	Summary of Events and Information	Remarks and references to Appendices
100 R. MEZEELE	23/4/17	6 PM	Our operations. Indirect fire was carried out on the following targets. Hele Trench 2000 targets engaged. DUMP. O.G.A.Y.5.60., DUGOUT O.G.D.9.1.12., SEARCHED TRENCH O.G.D.20.22., O.O.1.H.B.25.85., SEARCHED TRENCH O.C.85.38., O.O.S.D.OC.15., SEARCHED	Appx Ref. Phot 28.
	23/4/17	1 PM	TRENCH O.1.H.A.23.72. O.O.1.H.A.40.32. Enemy operations. Artillery shelled NORMEZEELE with high velocity shells. about 1 P.M., Machine Guns more active during night. Infantry shot fire. wiring in front of gun positions. Casualties nil.	
	24/4/17		Weather fine, good visibility. Major W. B. Lacy returned to Company from leave & assumed Command of Company. Lieut J.O. Lawson relieved the duties of 2/C and Adjutant.	
	25/4/17		Strength of the company on the 28th inst. was as follows. Officers Other Ranks. 11. 173. Including the undermentioned appeals Officers Other Ranks. Course of instruction 1. 1. Hospital. 6. Divisional Train 1. Leave 1.	

T2134. Wt. W708—776. 500000. 4/15. Sir J. C. & S.

WAR DIARY
or
INTELLIGENCE SUMMARY.
(Erase heading not required.)

Army Form C. 2118.

No. 124 MACHINE GUN COMPANY

Place	Date	Hour	Summary of Events and Information	Remarks and references to Appendices
VOIRMEZEEL		6 P.M.	Our operations. Indirect fire was carried out on the following targets. Hots fired.	
	28/4/17		5000 targets engaged. SEARCHED ROAD O.8.D.88.62. O.8.D.94.06.	
	To	10 P.M.	Combined shoot on PHEASANT WOOD, Hand and Dump O.9.c.60.90.to O.9.c.90.10. half-left	
	29/4/17		Enemy Activity. Artillery fired a few high velocity shells to be F.O.R.M.P.I.E.N.R.E. Sheet 28.	
	29/4/17		about 8.30 A.M. Machine Gun very active during night of 28th inst.	
			Hostile swung in front of gun positions, but general improvements to	
		6 P.M.	emplacements and mens dugouts. Casualties nil.	
			Our Operations. Indirect fire was carried out on the following targets. Hots fired.	
	29/4/17		2000 targets engaged. STRONG POINT O.8.D.90.45. SEARCHED TRENCH O.8.C.85.38.	
	To		to O.8.D.05.15. DUGOUTS O.8.D.25.02. TRENCHY DUGOUTS O.8.D.20.12 to O.14. E.A.R.S.	
	12/9/17		Enemy activity. Artillery very active, machine guns again very active during	
	30/4/17		night of 29th inst.	
			Work done. swung and general improvements at gun positions	
			Casualties nil.	

SECRET.   Copy No. 1

OPERATION ORDER NO. 143.
by
LIEUT. J.W. LAWSON,
Commanding 124th. Machine Gun Company.   11/4/17.

1. No.124th.M.G.Coy. will relieve No.122nd.M.G.Coy. in the ST.ELOI Sector on Friday 13th. inst.

2. On the night of the 12/13th. the Transport Officer will arrange to take all guns, tripods, spare parts, etc. at present at Coy.Headquarters (MICMAC CAMP) to VOORMEZEELE at ration time and will leave them in charge of the guard of this Company at CANTEEN POST.

3. Company will parade outside the Camp on 13th.inst.at 10.45am. and proceed to the trenches via DICKEBUSCH, where guides from 122nd.M.G.Coy. will meet them at the Y.M.C.A. at 11.30am. Each subsection and Coy.Headquarters will march at 100 yds. intervals.

4. On arrival in VOORMEZEELE each team will be met by guides. Each team will draw its equipment in turn (waiting in the communication trench until the preceding team is clear) and proceed to its allotted position.

5. The usual handing over Certificates will be received.

6. Arrangements have been made to relieve guns at MOATED GRANGE (L.B.2) and OOSTHOEK (L.B.9) on the night of 12/13th.

7. On completion of relief the following will be the position of sections:-
No.1 Section will occupy position held by No.1 Section of 122nd.
    M.G.Coy., viz. L.B.2, L.B.14, L.B.16, and L.B.17.
No.2 section will occupy positions held by No.3 section of 122nd.
    M.G.Coy., viz. L.B.1, L.B.3, L.B.4, L.B.5.
No.3 section will occupy positions held by No.2 section of 122nd.
    M.G.Coy., viz. L.B.6, L.B.7, L.B.8 and L.B.9.
No.4 section will occupy positions held by No.4 section of 122nd.
    M.G.Coy., viz. L.B.15, L.B.18, and 2 guns in G.H.Q.2nd.line.

8. 2 men from each gun team will be detailed nightly to fetch rations from the dump. Rations will arrive at 9.30 pm.

9. One servant per section will be left at Camp in charge of Officers kits. These kits should be reduced to a minimum and will be taken to VOORMEZEELE by ration limbers at night.

Issued at 9 pm.   JWLawson. Lieut.
                                             Commanding 124th.M.G.Coy.

Copy No. 1 Original   War Diary   Copy No. 6 O.C.No.4 Section.
    "   2 Duplicate   do   "   7 Transport Officer.
    "   3 O.C. No. 1 Section.   "   8 O.C. 122nd.M.G.Coy.
    "   4 O.C. No. 2 Section.   "   9 Xth.Corps M.G.Officer.
    "   5 O.C. No. 3 Section   :   10 Spare.

*****

17/4/17.

SECRET.

Copy No. 2.

OPERATION ORDER NO.44
by
LIEUT.J.W.LAWSON, COMMANDING METAPHOR.

1. No.124 Machine Gun Coy. will be relieved by No.122 Machine Gun Coy. in the ST.ELOI SECTOR on 19th.inst. (except as in para.2).

2. The guns at L.B.9 (OOSTHOEK FARM) and L.B.2 (MOATED GRANGE) will be relieved by 122 M.G.Coy.on the night of 13th. inst. On relief these teams will report to Coy.Headquarters,VOORMEZEELE, with guns, spare parts, tripods, etc.and proceed to MICMAC CAMP. A limber will be at Coy. Headquarters at 1.0am.on 19th.inst. to take these teams, guns, etc. to CAMP. On the morning of the 19th. these teams will relieve the two guns of 122 M.G.Coy.engaged in Anti-aircraft defence.

3. Lieut.White will attend at MICMAC CAMP at 7.45am. on 19th. inst. and take over the camp and anti-aircraft guns.

4. The usual handing over certificates will be given and received, and copies sent to this office. These certificates will contain a statement to the effect that all emplacements, dugouts, latrines, cookhouses, etc. were handed over in a clean condition.

5. On relief the gun equipment (except as in para.2) will be dumped in large dugout opposite CANTEEN POST, and a guard of 8 men and 1 N.C.O. from Sec.4 will be left in charge and act as loading party to the limbers which will withdraw the gun equipment at night. Section officers will report relief complete to Coy. Headquarters, VOORMEZEELE, and gun teams will proceed independently to MICMAC CAMP and report to Lieut. White.

Lieut.
Commanding 124th.M.G.Coy.

Copy No.	1	War Diary.
"	2	Duplicate.
"	3	O.C. No.1 Section.
"	4	O.C. No.2 Section.
"	5	O.C. No.3 Section.
"	6	O.C. No.4 Section.
"	7	Transport Officer.
"	8	O.C. 122nd.M.G.Coy.
"	9	Spare.
"	10	Xth.Corps, M.G.Officer.

SECRET.   Copy No. 9
OPERATION ORDER NO.45
by
LIEUT.J.W.LAWSON, COMMANDING METAPHOR.   22/4/17.
****

1.   No.124th.Machine Gun Company will relieve No.122nd. Machine Gun Coy. in the ST.ELOI SECTOR on the night of 23/24th. inst.

2.   The following will be the position of sections after the relief.

        No.1 Section will occupy positions L.B.6, L.B.7, L.B.8 & L.B.9.
        No.2   "   "   "   " L.B.2, L.B.14, L.B.16 & L.B.17
        No.3   "   "   "   " L.B.1, L.B.3, L.B.4, & L.B.5.
        No.4   "   "   "   " L.B.15, L.B.18 and two guns
                                            in G.H.Q. 2nd. line.

        122nd.M.G.Coy. will provide guides for the positions to be occupied by Sections 2 and 3.
        ALL belt boxes and gun equipment will be taken.

3.   Sections in rotation will parade at half hour intervals commencing with Section 1 which will parade at 7.30 pm.
        Headquarters will bring up the rear.
        All limbers will have been loaded previously.
        Officers' kits will be put on their Sections' Limbers.

4.   The usual handing over certificates will be given and received.

5.   Officers will hand in ration strength of each team by 11 am. 23rd. inst.

6.   Completion of relief will be reported to Company Headquarters as follows :-

                "O. O. No. 45 complied with......(Time)."

7.   ACKNOWLEDGE.

                                                        Lieut.
                                                Commanding METAPHOR.

                Copy No. 1 Original War Diary.
                     "   2 Duplicate
                     "   3 O.C. No.1 Section.
                     "   4 O.C. No.2 Section.
                     "   5 O.C. No.3 Section.
                     "   6 O.C. No.4 Section.
                     "   7 Transport Officer.
                     "   8 122nd.M.G.Coy.
                     "   9 Spare.

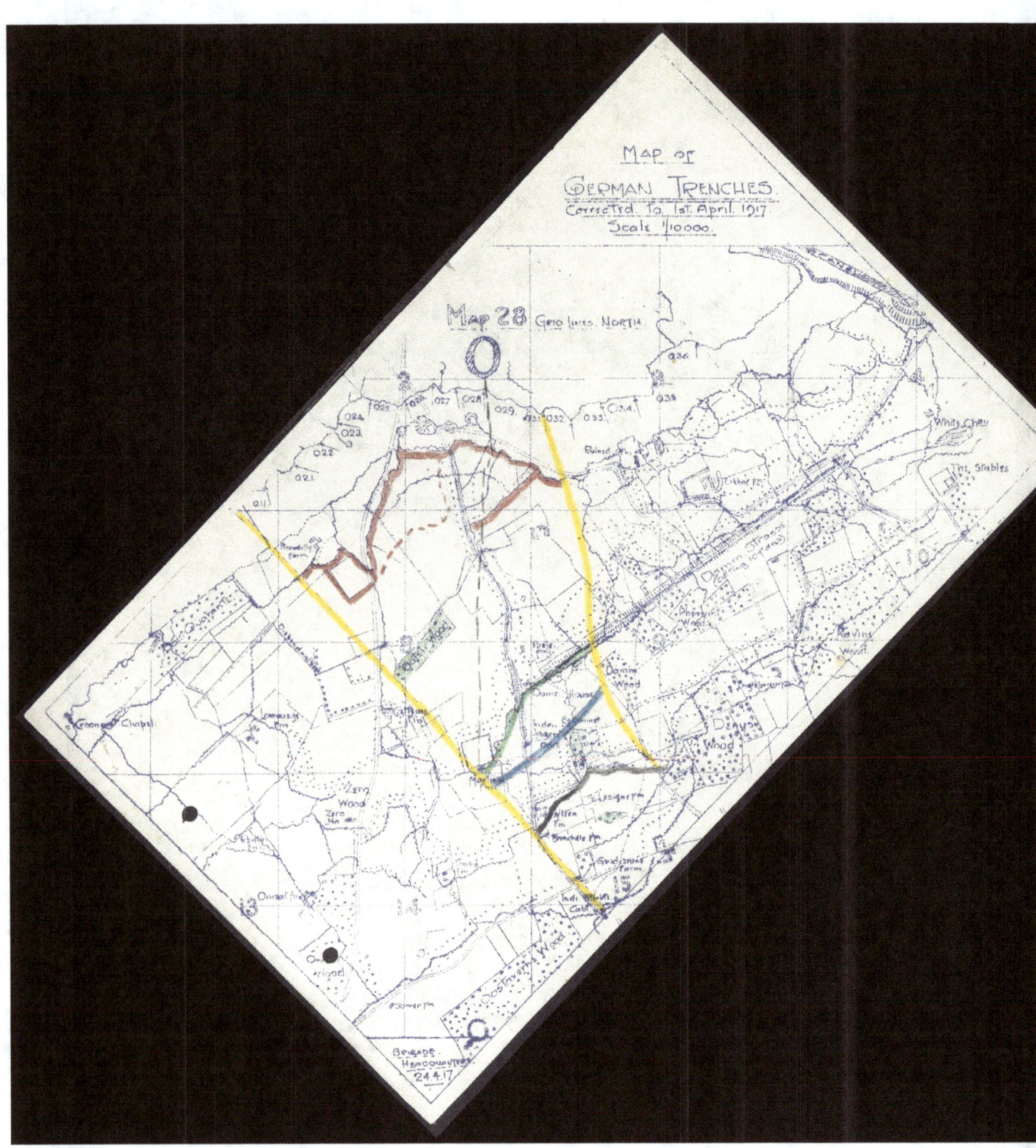

Army Form C. 2118.

No. 194 MACHINE GUN COMPANY
M.G. 4.5.4.

WAR DIARY
or
INTELLIGENCE SUMMARY.
(Erase heading not required.)

Instructions regarding War Diaries and Intelligence Summaries are contained in F. S. Regs., Part II. and the Staff Manual respectively. Title pages will be prepared in manuscript.

Vol 12

Place	Date	Hour	Summary of Events and Information	Remarks and references to Appendices
VOORMEZEELE	30.4.14	9 PM to 11.30 PM	2,500 rounds were fired on the following targets :- TRAMWAY O.9.C. 78.45. to O.9.C. 90.10. C.T. O.9.C. 113.12. to O.9.C. 66.96. DUMP AT DEL BSKE FARM O.10.B. 20.25. TRAMWAY O.9.C. 30.42. to O.9.C. 76.46. COPSE O.9.A. 48.142. to O.9.A. 90.15.	Map 16 / Scale
	1.5.14	6 PM	The enemy heavily bombarded the vicinity of ENGLISH ROAD causing a violent explosion. After the explosion three enemy aeroplanes reconnoitred the vicinity and returned to their lines. These planes were not fired on. Enemy Machine Guns were rather quiet last night. This afternoon about 4.30 PM the enemy presumably in relation of our bombardment fairly shelled our SUPPORT and RESERVE LINES	
	6.7.4	9 PM to 1.5.14	Afterwards sending a number of high velocity shells into VOORMEZEELE VILLAGE. 2,000 rounds was fired on the following targets :- RENTY FARM. TRENCH O.8.C.85.58. to O.8.D.05.15. EVANS FARM O.14.B.32.20. ROAD O.8.B.D.82.52. to O.8.B.D.98.05. TRAVERSE O.14.B.32.20. to O.14.B.05.35.	
		3 AM 6 PM	VOORMEZEELE VILLAGE was shelled with H.V. Bangs between 6 AM and 8 AM	
	2.5.14 to 3.5.14	10 AM 6 PM	Company was relieved in ST ELOI SECTOR by 193 Machine Gun Company. On destruction of guns and other details of relief see appendix.	See C.O. N.B. attached
	3.5.14 to 5.5.14		On completion of relief Company proceeded to Billets in RENINGHURST.	

Army Form C. 2118.

WAR DIARY
or
INTELLIGENCE SUMMARY.
(Erase heading not required.)

Instructions regarding War Diaries and Intelligence Summaries are contained in F. S. Regs., Part II. and the Staff Manual respectively. Title pages will be prepared in manuscript.

No 124 MACHINE GUN COMPANY.

Morris L.
124, MACHINE GUN COY.

Place	Date	Hour	Summary of Events and Information	Remarks and references to Appendices
RENINGHELST	3.5.14		Company training carried out.	
	4.5.14		Company training carried out. N.C.O's lectured on map Reading by O.C. Company. Field work carried out.	
	5.5.14		Company training carried out. N.C.O's instructed to make calculations out for indirect fire. GOEDEWAERSVELDE INF. BDE lectured all officers and signals in the theatre RENINGHELST. Field work carried out. Company lectured by O.C. about offensive spirit.	
	6.5.14		Company training carried out. N.C.O's received further instruction on Map Reading and use of Compass.	
	7.5.14		Field work carried out on left flank trenches.	
	8.5.14		Company training carried out. N.C.O's received further instruction on indirect fire. Route march, and company training.	
	9.5.14		Scheme carried out. G.O.C. 41ST DIVISION lectured all officers and N.C.O's or plans obtained on recent operations.	
			The strength of the Company for week ending 12th inst is as follows Officers 5 O.Ranks 144 Including the undermentioned Corporals NCOs 3 ORs 2ND ARMY rest Camp H.O.R. courts of trial 1 Off 6 ORs.	

Army Form C. 2118.

WAR DIARY
or
INTELLIGENCE SUMMARY.
(Erase heading not required.)

Instructions regarding War Diaries and Intelligence Summaries are contained in F. S. Regs., Part II. and the Staff Manual respectively. Title pages will be prepared in manuscript.

No. 124 MACHINE GUN COMPANY.

124. MACHINE GUN COY.

Place	Date	Hour	Summary of Events and Information	Remarks and references to Appendices
RENINGHELST	13.5.17		Church Parade and Kit Inspection.	
	14.5.17		Field Work carried out.	
	15.5.17		Company training carried out. LT. COL. G. GWYN THOMAS DSO 26TH ROYAL FUSILIERS lectured officers and Sergeants. Subject: Attacks of localities by a small Unit. (v.g.)	
			Halton on Company. O.C. Company proceeded on leave to England	
	16.5.17		Company training carried out. Lieut. f. W. Lawton takes over command of Company	
	17.5.17		Company dies transport proceeded to Abeele and bivouaced there for the night.	
	18.5.17		Company entrained at BEERE for GANSPETTE training area.	
GANSPETTE TRAINING AREA.	19.5.17		Company training carried out. The strength of the Company for week ending 19th inst. is as follows. Officers 10 Tanks. 144. including the un-obsolete oracles NE. 2 Off 4 OR's 2nd ARMY rest camp 4 OR's Leave 1 Off. hower of instr 2. Company Billeted in HEILEBROUCQ K 35. A. 40. 9.5.	myself Shak ya / 29,005.

T2131. Wt. W708—776. 500000. 4/15. Sir J. C. & S.

Army Form C. 2118.

No. 124 MACHINE GUN COMPANY.

WAR DIARY
or
INTELLIGENCE SUMMARY.
(Erase heading not required.)

Instructions regarding War Diaries and Intelligence Summaries are contained in F.S. Regs., Part II. and the Staff Manual respectively. Title pages will be prepared in manuscript.

Place	Date	Hour	Summary of Events and Information	Remarks and references to Appendices
GANSPETTE	20.5.17		Church Parade. Ceremonial Drill. Kit Inspection.	
TRAINING AREA	22.5.17		Route march with pack mules. 2 Section's Range. 2ND LT. P.S. HODGKINSON JOINED FOR DUTY.	
	23.5.17		Company training carried out. Section Sergeants instructed on the use of the Graph. Company training carried out. Section Sergeants instructed in the use of compass. O.C. Company lectured officers and Sergeants. Lieut C.V. White lectured junior N.C.O.'s on Map reading.	
	24.5.17		Company on Range. O.C. Company lectured all officers on coming operations. Lieut C.V. White admitted to Hosp. sick.	
	25.5.17		Company training carried out. All gun team commanders lectured by O.C. Company on coming Operations. 2/Lieut A.H. Duff returned from leave and rejoined.	
	26.5.17		Company training carried out. Major W. B. Bows 126th C/Pound Company from leave and took over command of the Company from Capt. J.H. Lawson who resumed the duties of 2nd in command and Adjutant.	
	27.5.17		Church parade.	
	28.5.17		Company took part in prize to attack by 15th Brigade. 15 rifles and for this purpose the Sections were attached to the Units as follows. Hot. Section attached	

Army Form C. 2118.

Lemans, Meyer O.O.
124, MACHINE GUN COY.
M. G. C.

WAR DIARY
or
INTELLIGENCE SUMMARY.
(Erase heading not required.)

Instructions regarding War Diaries and Intelligence Summaries are contained in F.S. Regs., Part II. and the Staff Manual respectively. Title pages will be prepared in manuscript.

Place	Date	Hour	Summary of Events and Information	Remarks and references to Appendices
GONNEHEM	28.5.17		to 32nd Battalion Royal Fusiliers, No 3 Section to 10th Queens, 2 guns of No 2 Section to 26th Battalion Royal Fusiliers and 2 guns to 21st King's Royal Rifles. No 4 Section under the command of 2nd Lt. W. Henry carried out Barrage work. L.O. 41st Division and G.O.C. 124th & 123rd Bde were present during operations.	
TRAINING AREA	29.5.17		Sent programme carried out as on 28th inst.	
	30.5.17		Sent programme carried out as on the 26th and 29th inst. The 2nd Army Commander accompanied by G.O.C. 41st Division, G.O.C. 123rd Bde. and I Corps commander were present during operations.	Map Ref. Sheet 24.5 N.E. 1/20,000
ARNEKE	31.5.17		Company leave La Motte Training Area and proceed by march route to ARNEKE. The strength of the Company on the 31st inst was as follows—	
			Officers 11.	
			Effective Sgts. 11. 172. This includes the undermentioned extra Co.	
			Attached 142. Source of Instruction 1. O.R.	
			Leave to U.K. 4. O.R.	
			Hospital 2 off. 6. O.R.	

WAR DIARY or INTELLIGENCE SUMMARY

Army Form C. 2118.

No. 124 MACHINE GUN COMPANY.

Vol 13

Place	Date	Hour	Summary of Events and Information	Remarks and references to Appendices
ARNEKE	1-6-17	9 AM	Company entrain at ARNEKE for 41st Divisional Area detrained at POPPERINGHE 11 AM	
		1 PM	Company arrived at QUEBEC CAMP and billeted in tents	
RENINGHELST	2-6-17		Sections 2 and 3 relieved a Section of 123 Machine Gun Company in the ST ELOI SECTOR and took up 4 gun positions	
	4-6-17		The remainder of the Company proceeded to the ST ELOI SECTOR and took over from 123 Machine Gun Company the Machine Gun positions in the 124th Infantry Brigade Battle Area	
	5-6-17		Second Lieutenant R. ? Allen reported to duty. General preparations, including building of Emplacements for Barrage Guns were made in view of the attack by the Second Army front to be made on the YPRES-	
	6-6-17		Sections were attached to the units of the Brigade and proceeded to their Assembly Places as follows:— No 1 Section was attached to 2nd Battalion Royal Fusiliers. No 3 Section was attached to the 26th Battalion Royal Fusiliers. No 2 Section to 10th Battalion R.W. Surreys. No 4 Section was detached for Barrage work under the command of the Acting Divisional Machine Gun Officer.	
	7-6-17		The 124th Infantry Brigade participated in the attack of this date of the	

J.M. Mans O.C.
124, MACHINE GUN COY.

WAR DIARY
or
INTELLIGENCE SUMMARY.
(Erase heading not required.)

Army Form C. 2118.

No. 124 MACHINE GUN COMPANY.

Place	Date	Hour	Summary of Events and Information	Remarks and references to Appendices
	7.6.17		Second Army on the enemy's position on the WYTSCHAETE - MESSINES RIDGE. The frontage allotted to the Brigade was that portion of the enemy's defences NOE WYTSCHAETE between PICCADILLY FARM (O.8.A.28.45) and a point O.13.c.25.30. At 3.10 am a mine was sprung & at the attacking left was launched. Three objectives were allotted to the Brigade (1) RED LINE, BLUE LINE, and BLACK LINE. The following were the dispositions of the infantry prior to the attack :- On the right 10th Batn. Queens (R.W. Surreys) have assembly trenches O.14.a.25 the DIEPENDAAL BEEK to the junction of trails O.24.a.0.22. 21st Batn. R.W.K. Coys from the junction of trenches O.24 and O.22 to the junction of trenches O.24 and O.25. On the left 32nd Batn. Royal Fusiliers from trench O.24 to trench O.22.C. joined the 32nd Batn Royal Fusiliers in the same trench. Three sections of this company were disposed of by detaining the machine gun barrage (The four sections being engaged in barrage fire). The following was the role allotted to the guns following up the attack :- (1) To engage hostile machine guns (2) to support attacking infantry (3) to assist the consolidation of the Captured positions and repulse enemy counter attacks (4) to secure	

A6945 Wt. W11422/M160 350,000 12/16 D. D. & L. Forms/C./2118/14.

WAR DIARY or INTELLIGENCE SUMMARY

Army Form C. 2118.

No. 124 MACHINE GUN COMPANY.

Remarks and references to Appendices: 3

Place	Date	Hour	Summary of Events and Information	Remarks and references to Appendices
	7.6.17		...... the strong points constructed in rear of captured positions. Whit...	
			These objects in view the following orders were issued from 124 I.B. Hqrs.	
			"A" Four guns will move over in the initial attack with the 10th Queens. Two of	
			these will come into action about PICK-DILLY FARM and fire S.E. These two guns support	
			will be installed in 2 strong points made by 10th Battn Queens and 21st Battn K.R.R.C.	
			half an hour before the Battalions advance from the RED LINE.	
			"B" Four guns will go over with the 26th Royal Fusiliers and will come into action	
			on the capture of the BLUE LINE. (a) 2 m.g. the junction of the tram road and	
			the DAMMSTRASSE and (b) just behind DAMM WOOD. One gun from each of these	
			two will follow 21st Battn KRRC after the Battn have passed through the BLUE	
			LINE and will come into action on the BLACK LINE in the sector of the 21st Battn KRRC.	
			"C" Four guns will go over with the 32nd Battn Royal Fusiliers - (a) two of these	
			will remain on the RED LINE and occupy the two strong points made by the 32nd	
			Battn 32nd Royal Fusiliers (b) the other two will move forward behind the	
			32nd Battn Royal Fusiliers and will come into action on the BLACK LINE in	
			the sector of the 32nd Battn Royal Fusiliers	

O.C.
124, MACHINE GUN COY.
M.G.C.

WAR DIARY or INTELLIGENCE SUMMARY

Army Form C. 2118.

No. 124 MACHINE GUN COMPANY.

Place	Date	Hour	Summary of Events and Information	Remarks and references to Appendices
	7.6.17		The following was the manner in which the operations were carried out. 1st Objective - Red Line - Vickers guns were detailed to occupy strong points in rear of REDLINE. The section officer concerned reconnoitred but could not find any these. However the two guns detailed for the S.B. in the vicinity of O.3.c.1.3 were destroyed by shell fire in NO MANS LAND on the right one gun was left near PICCADILLY FARM by 2nd Lieut E. HERON in accordance with instructions the lift of two guns on the left was reported to O.C. COMPANY about 6AM. He applied to the D.M.G.O. for a gun which was sent up to the REDLINE. Acquired from a gun was also brought into action in the neighbourhood of PICCADILLY FARM and the fourth gun which should have remained in the REDLINE was taken forward to the BLACK LINE as the officers commanding could not find the strong points. 2nd Objective Blue Line. In accordance with instructions your Vickers guns under the command of Lieut W.H. HARLAND and LIEUT A.W. LUPTON accompanied the 16th Battn Royal Fusiliers to the BLUE LINE where tactical positions were taken up to cover the work of consolidation. 2 guns on the right, exposed flank and two guns on left of the Brigade sector - and fixed as	

Arthur Howard Capt.
124 MACHINE GUN COY.
M.G.B.

Army Form C. 2118.

No. 124
MACHINE GUN
COMPANY.

No. ....
Date ....

WAR DIARY
or
INTELLIGENCE SUMMARY.
(Erase heading not required.)

Place	Date	Hour	Summary of Events and Information	Remarks and references to Appendices
	4.6.17		Observed in the practice attack.	
			"C" third offensive - Blocking. The six guns detailed to proceed to the final objective in addition to the one detailed for the strong point on the RED LINE all reached the BLACK LINE under the command of 2/Lieut F.S. HODGKINSON. Lieut W.H. HARLAND and 2nd Lieut E. HERON immediately on arrival those guns were distributed tactically under the direction of Lieut W.H. HARLAND. About 4pm one of the guns was destroyed by a shell, the gunners being killed. A certain amount of firing was done by the BLACK LINE guns. Soon after the arrival, the BLACK LINE, the enemy were seen with-out two (2) field guns and unlimbered at about 800 yds 3 Lewis guns engaged them and they were compelled with-in two minutes to retire. A body of Germans were engaged as they retired from BAYNE WOOD. Lieut W.H. HARLAND reports that casualties were caused and that the enemy suffered heavily. Individual Germans were sniped by Vickers guns but the fire was so continuous throughout the [?] the ammunition had to be reserved [?]	

[signature] Capt.
O.C. 124, MACHINE GUN COY.

Army Form C. 2118.

WAR DIARY
or
INTELLIGENCE SUMMARY.
(Erase heading not required.)

Instructions regarding War Diaries and Intelligence Summaries are contained in F. S. Regs., Part II. and the Staff Manual respectively. Title pages will be prepared in manuscript.

No. 124 MACHINE GUN COMPANY.

Place	Date	Hour	Summary of Events and Information	Remarks and references to Appendices
	7.6.17		counter attack. O.C. Company visited the gun positions in the course of the day. The attack was successful right through all objectives were gained up to time and little resistance experienced. Casualties were light. The casualties sustained by this company were as follows:— 2nd Lieut AM. LUPTON wounded. Killed 3 other ranks. Wounded 10 other Ranks. Missing 10 Rank.	
	8.6.17		The guns were relieved by 143 Machine Gun Company and Company went into camp at VOORMEZEELE	
	9.6.17 TO 10.6.17		These days were spent in rest & re-equipment and re-organization.	
	11.6.17		The Company relieved 8 guns of No 12 Machine Gun Company. Five Company guns amount to guns of 123 Machine Gun Company in the captured positions in the BLACK BLUE, and GREEN LINES taken over on the 7th inst. One section was in reserve in the DAMMSTRASSE.	
	12.6.17 to 24.6.17		These days were occupied in consolidation of the line, making emplacements and extending dugouts. The enemy artillery that been very active over front-area, and his aircraft showed great activity, flying very low and firing M.G. on our trenches.	

124, MACHINE GUN COY.
M. G. C.

WAR DIARY
or
INTELLIGENCE SUMMARY.
(Erase heading not required.)

Army Form C. 2118.

No. 124 MACHINE GUN COMPANY.

Place	Date	Hour	Summary of Events and Information	Remarks and references to Appendices
	6.7.17 10.6.17 to 17.6.17		Work of consolidation continued & guns were employed in barrage fire to assist in attack by the 13th Bgde on the left. 119 102 S.13. 16,500 rounds expended.	
		6PM 6PM	No. 3 Section relieved No. 4 Section in the Front Line system. Enemy artillery much [?]	
	15.6.17 16.6.17		Quiet. Nothing of great importance to report. Enemy Artillery has been very active over back areas reviving some attention	
		6PM 16.6.17	of our Artillery has been causing annoyance by firing into our trenches this flying aircraft has been close to the emplacements of our gun emplacements and much [?] has been done to [?]	
			[?]	
			2nd Lieut J.M. HUTTON reported to duty	
	17.6.17		2nd Lieut J.R. MARSHALL " "	
		12 noon 2pm	2nd Lieut W.M. HARMAND was relieved by 2nd Lieut E. HERON and proceeded to [?] [?] — Lieut's to UK leave of going on the 22nd inst.	
	21.6.17		2nd Lieut R.P. ALLEN [?] and wounded by shell. 2nd Lieut J.R. HORSFALL are proceeded to Transport lines to rest. Enemy hostility and Aircraft have again been active on explosions of his been suffered with the hostile shelling but great progress	
			and been made	

[signature] Capt.
O.C.
124, MACHINE GUN COY.

WAR DIARY or INTELLIGENCE SUMMARY

Army Form C. 2118.

No. 124 MACHINE GUN COMPANY.

Place	Date	Hour	Summary of Events and Information	Remarks and references to Appendices
	23.6.17	6 pm	Lieut. G.G. CROWDER rejoined from leave and proceeded to trenches to take charge of the guns doing indirect fire. Owing to sight of the Lieutenant indirect fire was carried out in various vantage points on the enemy's lines.	
			Two rounds was expended. Much work has been carried out on the improvements of the positions. The enemy's artillery and aircraft still very active.	
	25.6.17	6 pm	Artillery has been somewhat quiet. Indirect fire was carried out on alleyways, tramways & enemy's lines. 1000 rounds expended owing to the numbers of sporting lads it would be advisable to keep in touch with the enemy. It has now been deemed advisable to try and get into touch by a series of sentry posts and machine guns which that the occupies his front line.	
	24.6.17	6 pm	Digging a strong point was found.	
			The enemy artillery was specially lively at night and shelled the whole of the Brigade sector vigorously through. Several hostile guns had lately been employed on the aircraft duties against low flying enemy machines. One aircraft was brought down by our gun fire. O.C. 14.2.	
			Machine Gun Company billeted in many Headqrs. HQs in the DÄMMSTRASSE	

124, MACHINE GUN COY.

WAR DIARY or INTELLIGENCE SUMMARY

Army Form C. 2118.

No. 124 MACHINE GUN COMPANY.

Place	Date	Hour	Summary of Events and Information	Remarks and references to Appendices
	6PM 28.6.14		To make arrangements in view of approaching relief. Had no enforcements and construction of two new gun-aircraft positions to proceeding.	
	29.6.14		During the period under review the attitude of the enemy has been very quiet. Two officers of the Machine Gun Company visited our HQ to make final arrangements for relief which takes place on the night of 30.6.14-1.7.14	
	TO		The weather which has been very sultry all day finally broke down cool-9	
	6PM 30.6.14	6PM	heavy thunderstorm ensued.	
	30.6.14		Two officers and wother Ranks of 142 Machine Gun Company reconnoitred gun positions and stopped at the various gun positions on the night of the 29th inst.	
	TO	7PM	Artillery and aircraft still very active.	
	30.6.14		Company started to be relieved by 142 Machine Gun Company. Relief was completed by 1-30AM 1-7-14. On completion of relief company proceeded to MURRUMBITZEE CAMP.	
	TO 1.30AM 1.7.14	1.30AM 1.7.14	During the period of holding the line from 11-6-14 to 30-6-14 the following casualties occurred:- 2Lieut P.S. HODGKINSON Shown died killed:3 other ranks. Several cases of Shell Shock also occurred.	
			Wounded:- 3 other Ranks	

[signature] CW
124, MACHINE GUN COY.
M.G.C.

Army Form C. 2118.

WAR DIARY
or
INTELLIGENCE SUMMARY.
(Erase heading not required.)

No. 124 MACHINE GUN COMPANY.

Place	Date	Hour	Summary of Events and Information	Remarks and references to Appendices
	30.6.17		The strength of the Company on the 30th inst was as follows. Officers: Other Ranks 12 : 191. During the time the Company was in action 34 Reinforcements were received and from this number 11 were transferred to 123 Machine Gun Company. Total casualties for the month of June are as follows:-	
			Killed Wounded Missing Shock Sick	
			OFF. OR. OFF. OR. OFF. OR. OFF. OR. OFF. OR.	
			NIL 8 2 15 NIL NIL NIL 3 2 16	
			[signature] Capt. O.C. 124 MACHINE GUN COY. M.G.C.	

WAR DIARY
or
INTELLIGENCE SUMMARY.
(Erase heading not required.)

Army Form C. 2118.

Place	Date	Hour	Summary of Events and Information	Remarks and references to Appendices
METEREN	1-7-18		Company arrived in the METEREN AREA.	
	2-7-18		Time was devoted to reorganising and re-equipping Company	
	3-7-18		The remainder of the time the Company was in the METEREN AREA was	
			devoted to carrying out including the use Barrage drill	
	10-7-18		In carrying out operations the 2nd and 3rd sections assisted in	
			the withdrawal of the Vickers Guns after it had been arranged that	
			the whole Lewis M.G. survey when the bombardment and at METEREN increased	
			to the line, the 1st Section to construct machine Gun Barrage Positions	
			& 4 Sec to improve the Barrage Bank for which this Company	
			was responsible.	
	11-7-18		MAJOR N.H. DAVIS M.C. effected change of command to BERTHEUIL and to	
			assist him in his duties.	
			LIEUT. J.W. LEFFREY proceeded on leave and joined the base sick of company.	
			LIEUT. M. MENZIES appointed Col. Ellmore M.C.	
			O.C. had listen inspected Company informing & comfort and congratulating	
			the Company their smart and clean turn out. He spoke kindly	

WAR DIARY
or
INTELLIGENCE SUMMARY.
(Erase heading not required.)

Army Form C. 2118.

Place	Date	Hour	Summary of Events and Information	Remarks and references to Appendices
METEREN	12-7-17		of say the company behaved and the work they did during June operations. After the inspection 2nd Lt E. HERON was presented with the MILITARY CROSS and 24725 Pte Stansfield A. no 301516 Pte Smith F. were presented with	
			MILITARY MEDAL. 2nd Lt A.W. LUPTON was awarded the Military Cross and No. 30106 Pte Fraser J. the Military Medal but were not at the presentation. All the above awards were for gallantry in action during June operations	
			of 2nd ARMY FRONT.	
	18-7-17		Company leave METEREN AREA and proceed to camp at WEST OUTRE.	MAP REF
	19-7-17		General preparations made for going into the line	HOLLEBEKE
	20-7-17		O.C. Company and Section Offrs proceed on a reconnaissance of gun positions held	MAP
			by 142 M Coy in the RYVE SECTOR. In view of coming relief arrangements were made	
			by "CC" 124 and 142 Coys. LIEUT Col WHITE joined for duty from Base Depot.	
	21-7-17		Company proceeded to the trenches and took over gun positions held by 142 M.G. Coy.	
	22-7-17		No. 1 Section in reserve were relieved by a section of the Divisional	Sixth Day 233 Class
			Machine Gun Company.	

WAR DIARY
or
INTELLIGENCE SUMMARY.

(Erase heading not required.)

Army Form C. 2118.

Place	Date	Hour	Summary of Events and Information	Remarks and references to Appendices
TRENCHES	22/4/17		Coy proceeded to the trenches at WEST OUTRE [illegible] to Gun Company at WEST OUTRE.	
"	23/4/17		Reconnaissance of all firing & map points for No 1 & No 2 more positions.	
Sectors 7.8.	24/4/17		Coy Coy A.B. relieved in the line by 123 M.G. Coy. Coy relief of Sections 2,3 and 4 proceeded to Barrage positions during the relief of 2 "A" Coy 123 Machine Gun Company and Left of 700 CATERPILLAR CRATER by heavy hostile shelling. Those two gun team & were relieved by two teams of No 2 section 2nd LT J.T.B. HOBSFALL O/C No 2 Section came in on what had happened to these two gun teams left side to his rear. CATERPILLAR CRATER search found on the unaccounted for the remainder of the Company to lay and maintain wire to normal teams to call for more of this.	
			were in position was heard from or until information was received that [illegible] for the duty Lubricating N.C.O.'s in charge of No 2 Section had been killed by the enemy shells and the remainder had been damaged or been forced to retire.	13 BRX 4/4/17 MILL 60.
	25/4/17		No. 2 No. 2 of T.B. HOBSFALL and Sergeant [illegible] had been Killed by hostile shelling TANK DRIVE (1.35.B. +C.55) they had both been Killed by hostile [illegible] also [illegible]	56.172
	26/4/17		Continued preparations at Barrage positions [illegible] the guns of [illegible] [illegible] during [illegible] had been hit	

Army Form C. 2118.

WAR DIARY
or
INTELLIGENCE SUMMARY.
(Erase heading not required.)

Instructions regarding War Diaries and Intelligence Summaries are contained in F. S. Regs., Part II. and the Staff Manual respectively. Title pages will be prepared in manuscript.

Place	Date	Hour	Summary of Events and Information	Remarks and references to Appendices
TRENCHES	16.4.17		Shot No. 1 Sex Nightingale in a complete position against this new line.	
	17.4.17	5PM	Nos 2 and 3 Sections and Headqrs moved back to RIDGE WOOD	
BIVOUACS			Section No remained in Bivouacs for the purpose of carrying out Instruction and Harassing fire on the Enemy Communications &c.	
	25.4.17		2ND LT G.T. THOMAS rejoined from leave to U.K.	
	30.4.17		Lt Parson left L.H.Q. on 5 days Leave to England W.E.F.	
	4.4.17-16.4.17		Nothing toward at Bezage Politics. This laid down between Enfay and Back Headquarters as for diagram.	

RIGHT GROUPPHONE.

[Diagram showing: BDE. HQRS (red), R. GROUP HQRS (blue), "A" BATTY HQRS (orange), "B" BATTY HQRS (yellow), connected by lines]

| | | | The laying system laying perfect establishing. Only this system worked communication was a constant source of anxiety to the Operators | |

WAR DIARY
or
INTELLIGENCE SUMMARY.
(Erase heading not required.)

Army Form C. 2118.

Place	Date	Hour	Summary of Events and Information	Remarks and references to Appendices
TRENCHES	28/7/17		Work continued at Barrage Batteries	
DO. DO.	29/7/17		No 1 Section opened Company and all three Sections W. & 9. & 3. and Company Headquarters moved forward. The Sections going to Barrage Positions 2 + 3 from 12 to 13th Battalions	
SECTOR	30/7/17		Final Preparations made at Barrage Positions. O.C. Company held conferences with Section Officers at RIGHT GROUP HQRS.	
	31/7/17		On this date the 41st Division made an attack on the enemy positions immediately north and south of the YPRES-COMINES CANAL. This Company formed a said "Z" Batteries and to support the attack with the Officers i/c the Companies 18, 142 and 194 full given a Barrage of 6 whites from the attack. The Barrage was in two stages the first 6 last from ZERO to ZERO+10 in the case of "A" Battery. Both Batteries then lifted and continued firing till ZERO+40 after which they stood by to answer S.O.S. calls and suchlike. The Barrage proved to be most successful and received great praise from the Infantry. The following is a table showing amount of ammunition...	MARKER SHEET HOLLEBEKE

Montgomery Col.

Army Form C. 2118.

WAR DIARY
or
INTELLIGENCE SUMMARY.
(Erase heading not required.)

Instructions regarding War Diaries and Intelligence Summaries are contained in F. S. Regs., Part II. and the Staff Manual respectively. Title pages will be prepared in manuscript.

Place	Date	Hour	Summary of Events and Information	Remarks and references to Appendices
TRENCHES	31-7-14		Expected:- Barrages- 58,450 - S.O.S. calls 6 3,160 - Smoke 3 - 20,450.	
BLUFF			Casualties during operations killed hit wounded officers 1 2nd Lt E. HERON	
SECTOR			O.R.'s	
			Two Guns were put out of action during operations.	
			Notes	
		1.	During the period the Company was in the line i.e. 21.7.14 to 31.7.14. Killed and Wounded Park was transferred to enemy's communications and Rly. dumps and other hostile armaments, and accordingly to information received from Captured German Prisoners, fire was very effective and demolished nightly for this purpose was very considerable amount of ammunition expended nightly for this purpose was 4,000 — at least one round to keep up communication.	
		2.	It was found out during operations on the 31st inst that 6 Squadies at least are required to keep up communication.	
		3.	Casualties during the month of June are as follows Killed officers 1 2nd LT J.T. HORSFALL Wounded Officers 2 2nd LT E.HERON & 2nd LT R.P.ALLEN Killed O.R. 1 Wounded O.R.	

[signature] Capt

Army Form C. 2118.

WAR DIARY
or
INTELLIGENCE SUMMARY.
(Erase heading not required.)

Place	Date	Hour	Summary of Events and Information	Remarks and references to Appendices
TRENCHES	31/7/16		The strength of the Company for month ending 31st June.	
			Officers 9 O.R's 168.	
			38 men attached from Infantry attainment to Corps	
			Reinforcements received from Base Depot during trip to R.	
			Officers 2 O.R's 10	

WAR DIARY or INTELLIGENCE SUMMARY

Army Form C. 2118.
No. 124 MACHINE GUN COMPANY.

Vol 15

Place	Date	Hour	Summary of Events and Information	Remarks and references to Appendices
TRENCHES PLUFF SECTOR.	1-8-17		Our guns were continually called up during the day by the S.H. S.O.S to enemy S.O.S calls 148,000 rds were expended for this purpose. The ground everywhere was knee deep in mud and much difficulty was experienced in getting to gun positions	JW
	2-8-17		During the night of the 1st/2nd inst intense fire was maintained on enemy's communications and HOLLEBEKE CHATEAU etc. During the early hours of the morning the enemy counter attacked at HOLLEBEKE and on the call of the S.H. S.O. Sig Staff the guns put up a barrage on their SOS lines. The attack was at first successful but our immediate counter attack drove the enemy out during the day the company answered several SOS calls, some little delay however was caused owing to the SOS signal not being seen, the actual SOS being received though the S.H. S.O. Ammunition expended during the night of the 1st/2nd inst was 35,500 rds. Excellent communication was maintained between Brigade, Group and Battery Headquarters. The weather was almost as bad as it could be and considering the conditions the morale of the Officers and men was splendid much difficulty was also	HOLLEBEKE MAP JW JW [signature] Capt

Army Form C. 2118.

No. 124
MACHINE GUN COMPANY.

No..................
Date................

WAR DIARY
or
INTELLIGENCE SUMMARY.
(Erase heading not required.)

Instructions regarding War Diaries and Intelligence Summaries are contained in F. S. Regs., Part II. and the Staff Manual respectively. Title pages will be prepared in manuscript.

Place	Date	Hour	Summary of Events and Information	Remarks and references to Appendices
TRENCHES	2-8-17		experienced in getting rations up to the men, also to keep the guns going owing to the hills being soaking wet.	W.
BLUFF				
SECTOR	3-8-17		Our guns were kept very busy during the night of the 2nd/3rd inst. Indirect fire was carried out on enemy's communications as arranged for by the G.H.Q. Several S.O.S. calls were answered. Ammunition expended 24,000 rds	W.
	4-8-17		The weather continued to be very wet and mist especially at early morning when the mist was very thick. 15,000 Rds expended on Indirect Fire and S.O.S. calls. 2nd Lieut. F. MAUD found for duty from Base Depot.	W. W.
	5-8-17		10,000 Rds expended on Indirect fire etc. About 10-30 am the enemy put over a considerable number of H.E. shells evidently searching for a Battery of Field Guns close by. One of these shells burst near one of our guns wounding the Battery Commander 2nd Lieut R.R. ALLEN and 4. O.R.	W.
	6-8-17		Indirect fire was carried out on a new series of targets arranged for by the G.H.Q. 6. 11,500 rds being expended. The weather improved a little but there was plenty of mud about.	W.

[signature]

Army Form C. 2118.

No. 124 MACHINE GUN COMPANY.

No. ....
Date ....

WAR DIARY
or
INTELLIGENCE SUMMARY.
(Erase heading not required.)

Instructions regarding War Diaries and Intelligence Summaries are contained in F. S. Regs., Part II. and the Staff Manual respectively. Title pages will be prepared in manuscript.

Place	Date	Hour	Summary of Events and Information	Remarks and references to Appendices
TRENCHES BLUFF SECTOR.	7.8.17		8,000 rds expended to prevent fire etc. Nose began to pull again making things worse than ever. During this spell of fact weather it was impossible to observe enemy body beyond 15 yds. 2/Lieut N.C. CLIFFORD joined for duty from North Army Machine Gun Corps.	
	8.8.17		Company was relieved in the line by the 123 Coy M.G. Corps. On completion of relief Company moved back to camp at RIDGEWOOD. During the relief the enemy heavily shelled the vicinity where our limbers were waiting to be loaded with gun equipment. All the limbers cleared off except one which got stuck as a shell hole and was left fast. This limber would have no doubt been smashed up if it had not been for the gallantry and disregard to danger of No 90917 Pte Walker of this company who seized the limber fatigue and off course struggling with his mules uncoupled the rear half of the limber after some considerable time and trouble which enabled the mules to gallop off. For this act Pte Walker was awarded the MILITARY MEDAL.	
	9.8.17		Time was devoted to reorganising and re-equipping the Company.	

WAR DIARY or INTELLIGENCE SUMMARY

Army Form C. 2118.

No. 124 MACHINE GUN COMPANY.

Instructions regarding War Diaries and Intelligence Summaries are contained in F. S. Regs., Part II. and the Staff Manual respectively. Title pages will be prepared in manuscript.

(Erase heading not required.)

Place	Date	Hour	Summary of Events and Information	Remarks and references to Appendices
RIDGE	10-8-17		General cleaning up of guns, tripods etc.	
WOOD			Captain F.W. Lawson proceeds on leave to UK. Lieut H.A. Henry assumes the command of the Company and Lieut S.H. Morland assumes duties of 2nd i/c. The weather improved and ground shows signs of drying up.	
TRENCHES	11-8-17		The Company relieved 123 Coy M.G. Corps in the line on the night of the 11/12th inst and took over positions as previously held. 8,000 rds were expended on a new series of targets as arranged for by the D.H.Q.O.	
BLUFF	TO			
SECTOR	12-8-17			
	13-8-17		Goods was expended on night firing. Work commenced with regard to the completion of gun emplacements, drainage of dug outs which was in most cases knee deep in water. Very little work could be carried out at the forward positions as they were in full view of the enemy, what work could be done had to be done at night.	
	14-8-17		Indirect fire carried out and work continued at all positions. Ammunition was got up to some positions to form a reserve in case of emergency.	
	15-8-17		The Company was relieved in the line by 141st Company M.G.C. on completion of relief the Company moved back to RIDGE WOOD	see co.33 attached

Army Form C. 2118.

No. 124
MACHINE GUN COMPANY.

No...........
Date..........

WAR DIARY
or
INTELLIGENCE SUMMARY.
(Erase heading not required.)

Instructions regarding War Diaries and Intelligence Summaries are contained in F. S. Regs., Part II. and the Staff Manual respectively. Title pages will be prepared in manuscript.

Place	Date	Hour	Summary of Events and Information	Remarks and references to Appendices
RIDGE	16.8.17		Company proceeded to camp between MONT-DES-CATS in Motor Lorries	
WOOD.	17.8.17		G.O.C. I CORPS accompanied by G.O.C. 41st DIVISION inspected the 122nd Infantry Brigade including this company. After the inspection the CORPS	
THIEUSHOUCK			COMMANDER addressed the Brigade and expressed his gratitude for the good work and the way the officers and men stuck it out during the rough weather which followed the offensive operations which commenced on the 31st July	MAP HAZEBROUCK
	18.8.14		G.O.C. 2nd Army accompanied by G.O.C. 14th DIVISION inspected the 122 & 123 including this Company.	
MONT-DES-CATS.	19.8.17		Preparations made for G.O.C. 122 & 13 inspection of Guns, Tripods, and equipment etc.	
	20.8.17		G.O.C. 122 Infantry Brigade inspected Company's Guns, Equipment etc.	
	21.8.17		General Training carried out.	
	22.8.17		Ditto.	
	23.8.17		Ditto.	
	24.8.17		O.C. Company rejoined Company from leave and resumed Command of the [signature]	

Army Form C. 2118.

No. 124 MACHINE GUN COMPANY.

No. ....
Date ....

WAR DIARY
or
INTELLIGENCE SUMMARY.
(Erase heading not required.)

Instructions regarding War Diaries and Intelligence Summaries are contained in F. S. Regs., Part II. and the Staff Manual respectively. Title pages will be prepared in manuscript.

Place	Date	Hour	Summary of Events and Information	Remarks and references to Appendices
NRNT-DES	24.8.17		Company Lieut 76 Sr Henry resumes the duties of 2/c Laboratories much for the move to TATTINGHEM AREA.	
CATS				
STAPLE	25.8.17		Company march with 124 Infantry Brigade to WALLEN-CAPPEL AREA and billet at STAPLE for the night of 25th/26th inst.	hay loft
ST MARTINS	26.8.17		Company forced by march route to TATTINGHEM AREA and billet at ST. MARTINS - UL - LAERT.	tents
UL-LAERT	27.8.17		General training carried out.	2, 2.4.2. S.C.
	28.8.17		Ditto	
	29.8.17		Ditto	
	30.8.17		Ditto	
TATTINGHEM	31.8.17		The commander-in-chief inspected the 124th Infantry Brigade including this company. After the inspection the Brigade marched past the C. in Chief. O.C. Company was congratulated by the G in Chief on the clean and smart turn out of the company. 5 O.R. Reinforcements joined from Base Depôt.	

Keith Lawson Capt

Army Form C. 2118.

No. 124 MACHINE GUN COMPANY.

No............
Date............

WAR DIARY
or
INTELLIGENCE SUMMARY.
(Erase heading not required.)

Instructions regarding War Diaries and Intelligence Summaries are contained in F. S. Regs., Part II. and the Staff Manual respectively. Title pages will be prepared in manuscript.

Place	Date	Hour	Summary of Events and Information	Remarks and references to Appendices
ST. MARTINS	31.8.17		The strength of the Company at the end of the month was as follows.	
AU - LAERT			Officers 9 ORKs 163.	
			Officers 11 — ORKs 163.	
			Total casualties for August.	
			OFFICERS ORKS	
			WOUNDED 1. KILLED 1. WOUNDED 6.	
			Total Reinforcements received Officers 3. ORKs 22.	
			Total Sick evacuated to Base. Officers nil ORKs 14.	
			[signature] Capt.	

SECRET   COPY No. 2

OPERATION ORDER NO 53. BY O.COMMANDING 124 COY. M.G.C
REF. 124 I.B. O.O. 128.

1. INFORMATION

The 119TH M.G. Coy will relieve the 124TH M.G. Coy in the sector immediately North of the Canal on the 15TH and night of 15TH/16TH inst.

2. GUIDES.

Guides for incoming teams will be provided by the 124TH M.G. Coy and will be at Coy Hqrs. BLUFF TUNNELS at the following times:-

"B" Batty Positions		8 AM.	15TH INST.
TRIANGULAR BLUFF N° 14 POS.		"	"
BATTLE WOOD N° 10 POS		"	"
CATERPILLAR CRATER N° 13 POS	9 AM	"	"
RAILWAY CUTTING N° 11 POS.		"	"
BUFFS BANK N° 8 AND 9 POS	7 PM	"	"
RAILWAY EMBANKMENT N° 2 AND 3 POS		"	"
LEFT FRONT LINE N° 4 AND 5 POS	7.30 PM	"	"
KLEIN ZILLEBEKE N° 12 AND 13 POS	"	"	"

All guides will be provided from men at Coy Hqrs.

3. EQUIPMENT

All Belt Boxes, S.A.A. in bulk, Petrol Tins etc, will be handed over to incoming teams. All teams will bring out Guns, Tripods, Spare Parts, except gun positions at Nos 2, 3, 4, and 6 positions who will hand over their Tripods to the incoming teams

TRANSPORT

Outgoing teams will carry all equipment to the crossing station at the corner of CLARKENCHTRENCH where a guide of the incoming Battery will be posted to indicate positions of limbers. After equipment has been placed on limbers each team will proceed independently to the camp last occupied by us near GORDON FARM.

HANDING OVER

Officers handing over will impart all information possible and explain the tactical situation of the position, water supply, rationing arrangements, communications, work in hand, maps, Barrage lines, SubRS Tables, Indirect Fire programme and S.O.S. signals will be handed over to incoming Officer.

RATIONS

The teams at the Battery Positions Nos 14, 15, 16 and 17, 18 will carry the unexpired portion of the rations for the 15th inst back to Camp.

RELIEF COMPLETE

Officers will report personally at Hd Qrs when their relief is complete.

14-8-17

Issued at: 7pm

Copy 1. File.
"   2. War Diary.
"   3. Duplicate.
"   4. Co. HQ. M.G. Coy.
"   5. Transport Officer.

Copy 6. Lt White
"   7. Lt Brower
"   8. Lt Thomas
"   9. "   Clifford
" 10. "   Williamson
" 11. "   Hutton
" 12. "   D.C. G.O.

Army Form C. 2118.

WAR DIARY
or
INTELLIGENCE SUMMARY.
(Erase heading not required.)

No. 124 MACHINE GUN COMPANY.

95/6

Place	Date	Hour	Summary of Events and Information	Remarks and references to Appendices
TATINGHEM TRAINING AREA	1-9-17 to 4-9-17		General training was carried out as follows. Gun drill, Gas warfare schemes carried out. Revolver practice and Range work. Captain J.W. Lawson O.C. Company was attached to 124 Bde Hdqrs as Assistant Staff Captain. Lieut H. Honey took over the command of Company and Lieut W. Marland assumed the duties of 2/c.	AppA AppA
	6.9.17		In the event of further offensive operations on the 2nd Army front which the 124 Infantry Brigade were going to take part a practice attack was carried out by the 124 Infantry Brigade in which the Company took part. The attack was carried out precisely as similar operations as the Brigade would go only to the carrying of operations	AppA MAP REF SHEET 21 9E
	7.9.17		General training was carried out.	AppA
	10.9.17		A Further Brigade Practice attack was carried out.	AppA
	11.9.17 to 15.9.17		General training was carried out as follows, Lectures to officers, L.60°, and men on carrying of operations.	AppA
	16.9.17		The 124 Infantry Brigade in charge of the Company left the TATINGHEM AREA and proceeded to the THIEUSHOUK AREA halting for the night in	AppA

Army Form C. 2118.

No. 124 MACHINE GUN COMPANY.
No..........
Date..........

WAR DIARY
or
INTELLIGENCE SUMMARY.
(Erase heading not required.)

Instructions regarding War Diaries and Intelligence Summaries are contained in F. S. Regs., Part II. and the Staff Manual respectively. Title pages will be prepared in manuscript.

Place	Date	Hour	Summary of Events and Information	Remarks and references to Appendices
WALLEN	14-9-17		The 14th/15th not in the WALLEN - CAPPEL AREA.	
CAPPEL	15-9-17		The company arrived in the THIEUSHOUK AREA AT 5 P.M.	
AREA	16-9-17		The company proceeded to RIDGE WOOD. 4 guns of Section 1 under the command of Lieut. Thomas proceeded to the line and took over the guns of Section 4 near SHREWSBURY FOREST in the 39th Divisional front.	
WOOD		6 P.M.	Intimations were made for active operations. The guns in the line carried out harassing fire on targets arranged for by the 4th M.G. Bn. 39. D.D.	
	17-9-17	6 P.M.	The dispositions of machine guns for the attack were as follows: — GREEN LINE GUNS. Teams 3 and 4 of Section 3 under the command of Lieut. A. Willoughby were attached to the 3×4 Royal Fusiliers and to accompany the attack and take up positions approximately T.26.B.9.18 and to fire magnetic E.3. Teams 1 and 2 of Section 4 under the command of 2/Lieut. H. E. Clifford to accompany the 26th Royal Fusiliers and take up positions approximately T.24.A.18.45 and fire magnetic N.E. S.E.	
	18-9-17	6 P.M.	SUPPORT GUNS (Between BLUE & GREEN LINES) Teams 3 and 4 of Section 4 under the command of Lieut. L.G.S. Thomas to accompany the 26th Roy. Fus.	

Army Form C. 2118.

No. 124 MACHINE GUN COMPANY.

WAR DIARY
or
INTELLIGENCE SUMMARY.
(Erase heading not required.)

Instructions regarding War Diaries and Intelligence Summaries are contained in F.S. Regs., Part II. and the Staff Manual respectively. Title pages will be prepared in manuscript.

Place	Date	Hour	Summary of Events and Information	Remarks and references to Appendices
SHREWSBURY FOREST			a.m. take up positions approx J.26.B.90.90 and line magnetic N. & N.E. Sections 1 & 2 of Section 3 under the command of 2nd Lt. G.E. Crowsley to accompany the 21st K.R.R.C. and take up a position approx J.26.B.50.45 and fire magnetic S. & S.E.	MAP REF. FULL TEXT. MAP.
			RED LINE GUNS. Teams 1, 2, 3 and 4 of Section 2 will accompany the 21st KRRC under the command of 2/Lt. Thackeray and take up a position as follows. Teams 1 & 2 J.26.A.65.85. Teams 1 & 2 to fire magnetic N.E. & E. Teams 3 & 4 J.26.A.52.50. Teams 3 & 4 to fire magnetic E. & S.E.	
			RESERVE GUNS. Teams 1, 2, 3 & 4 of Section 1 occupied positions near SHREWSBURY FOREST under the command of Lieut. B.V. White.	
			COMPANY HEADQUARTERS were established in CANADA ST TUNNELS &c.	
			MOUNT SORREL. Sections 2, 3, and 4 joined the Battalions to which they were attached and moved forward to place of assembly.	MAP

WAR DIARY or INTELLIGENCE SUMMARY

Army Form C. 2118.

No. 124 MACHINE GUN COMPANY.

Place	Date	Hour	Summary of Events and Information	Remarks and references to Appendices
	20.9.17	5.40am	The 124 Infantry Brigade in conjunction with 123 Brigade on the left	MAP
SH. REINSBERG			and the 121 Brigade on the right attacked the enemy's trenches and strong	
FOREST			points on the right of the 41st Division front. There were three objectives viz.	
			1ST Objective RED LINE	
			2nd Objective BLUE LINE	
			3RD Objective GREEN LINE	ZILLEBEKE
			These objectives within the 124 Infantry Bde area ran as follows:-	MAP
			RED LINE - J.20.C.85.00 - J.26.A.85.22. - J.26.A.20.00 - J.26.a.65.00	See att
			BLUE LINE - J.20.D.60.00 - J.26.B.30.55. - J.26.B.20.00.	h.q.
			GREEN LINE - J.21.C.60.00 - thence along trench enclosing to J.23.B.20.66 for Bde	
			- J.26.D.68.90.	boundary
			At ZERO the whole Brigade moved forward, the Battalions detailed	+ objectives
			to take the RED LINE continued to go forward whilst the remainder of the	
			attacking forces formed up behind the German front line owing to heavy	
			machine gun fire the Battalions who had gone forward to take the RED LINE	
			had to fall back to the before the remainder of the brigade were attending.	

Army Form C. 2118.

WAR DIARY
or
INTELLIGENCE SUMMARY.

(Erase heading not required.)

No. 124 MACHINE GUN COMPANY.

No...........
Date..........

Instructions regarding War Diaries and Intelligence Summaries are contained in F. S. Regs., Part II. and the Staff Manual respectively. Title pages will be prepared in manuscript.

Place	Date	Hour	Summary of Events and Information	Remarks and references to Appendices
SHREWSBURY FOREST	20.9.17		Without delay the infantry again went forward and captured the RED LINE and later on captured the BLUE LINE. This was only held for a short time owing to heavy artillery and machine gun fire the infantry had to drop back to the RED LINE. Vickers guns took up positions between the RED and BLUE LINES and came into action as soon as the infantry fell back to the RED LINE. By this time all the offrs. of the company had become casualties, also 5 gun team commanders. About 10 am O.C. Company received information that the casualties in the Company were very heavy and offr. consulting the Brigade Major Sent C.I. White and 2 gun teams of No.1 Section in Reserve went forward and took up positions the RED LINE. In the meantime the infantry had again gone forward and taken the BLUE LINE and started to consolidate. The distribution of Vickers guns were now as follows. 4 Guns in the RED LINE and 3 Guns between the RED and BLUE LINES. The guns were kept busy during the remainder of the day firing at small parties of Germans who were seen moving about on the Ridge in front and any hits were observed later in the day the guns played a prominent part in repulsing a strong	MAP MAP REF LILLE ZELL MAP

WAR DIARY
or
INTELLIGENCE SUMMARY.
(Erase heading not required.)

Army Form C. 2118.

No 124
MACHINE GUN COMPANY.

Place	Date	Hour	Summary of Events and Information	Remarks and references to Appendices
SBRENSBURY	20/9/17		Enemy counter attack. The casualties during the day were as follows	MAP REF
FOREST			Killed 2 officers viz. 2/Lieut I hurst and 2/Lieut L.J.T. Thomas. O.R. 8.	ZILLEBEKE
			Wounded 3 officers viz. Lieut R. Willoughby, Lieut J.G.L. Knowles and 2/Lieut	MAP
			Lt. L. Clifford O.R. 30. During the attack several gun numbers took over the	
			command of their teams and there were old some good work for which they	
			have been recommended for awards.	
	21/9/17		The enemy delivered a strong counter attack during the early hours of the	1/24
			morning but were repulsed with heavy losses. There was considerable	
			rifle and artillery activity on both sides.	
	22/9/17		Four Vickers guns were relieved in the line by 4 guns of 118th Coy the go on relief.	MMA
			The Company proceeded to Camp at RIDGE WOOD.	
	23/9/17		The remainder of the company were relieved in the line by 118th Coy the G.C.	MMA
			and on completion of relief moved back to Camp at RIDGE WOOD.	
	24/9/17		The Company proceeded to BORRE (HAZEBROUCK AREA) in motor Lorries	MMA
			4 officers and 30 O.R. reinforced the company from the G.C. Base depot.	
	25/9/17		Reorganizing and the distribution of company was carried out.	MMA

Army Form C. 2118.

No. 124 MACHINE GUN COMPANY.

No............
Date...........

WAR DIARY
or
INTELLIGENCE SUMMARY.
(Erase heading not required.)

Instructions regarding War Diaries and Intelligence Summaries are contained in F. S. Regs., Part II. and the Staff Manual respectively. Title pages will be prepared in manuscript.

Place	Date	Hour	Summary of Events and Information	Remarks and references to Appendices
BORRE.	25.9.14		General cleaning up of gun equipment etc.	M.G.A.
HAZEBROUCK	26.9.14		General training was carried out.	M.G.A.
AREA	27.9.14		Ditto	M.G.A. MAP REF
			Preparations made for the move to join the Army transport proceeded by march route to GHYVELDE XV CORPS AREA	DUNKIRK
			Halting for the night of the 27th/28th inst at WOORMOUT.	12
	28.9.14		Company proceeded on Motor Busses to GHYVELDE.	M.G.A.
	29.9.14		Ditto	M.G.A.
	30.9.14		General training carried out	M.G.A.
			The strength of the Company at the end of current month was as follows:—	
			Officers 10	
			Ranks 164.	

W Whelan Lieutenant.

124, MACHINE GUN COY.
M. G. C.

MESSAGE MAP

Scale 1/5,000

September 1917.

N°2

LEGEND

Approx 700 guns here to the up in this advance, Direction to fire Reserve guns.

Reference
Machine gun
Trench Mortar
Dugouts
Wire
Tracks

MESSAGE FORM

No.

To:—

Note:—Either give Map Reference or mark your position by a 'X' on the Map on back.

1. I am at..........
2. I have reached limits of my Objective.
3. My Platoon is at.......... and is consolidating.
   Company
4. My Platoon is at.......... and has consolidated.
   Company   (Place where you are).
5. Am held up by (a) M.G.
                 (b) Wire at..........
6. Enemy holding strong point.......... on Right at ....
                                          Left.
7. I am in touch with.......... on Right.
                                   Left.
8. I am not in touch with..........
9. Am shelled from.—
10. Am in need of:—
11. Counter Attack forming at..........
12. Hostile (a) Battery
            (b) Machine Gun active at..........
            (c) Trench Mortar
13. Reinforcements wanted at..........
14. I estimate my present strength at.......... rifles.
15. Add any other useful information here:—

Time.......... m.   Name..........
Date.......... 1917.   Platoon..........
                                       Company..........
                                       Battalion..........

(A) Carry no maps or papers which may be of value to the Enemy.
(B) Give no information if captured, except the following, which you are bound to give:—
    Name, Rank, ~~Company and Regiment~~
(C) Collect all captured maps and papers and send them in at once.

Army Form C. 2118.

NO. 124
MACHINE GUN
COMPANY.

WAR DIARY
or
INTELLIGENCE SUMMARY.
(Erase heading not required.)

Vol 17

Instructions regarding War Diaries and Intelligence Summaries are contained in F. S. Regs., Part II. and the Staff Manual respectively. Title pages will be prepared in manuscript.

Place	Date	Hour	Summary of Events and Information	Remarks and references to Appendices
GHYVELDE	1-10-17		General training carried out. 10 Reinforcements for from Base kept.	
	2-10-17		General training carried out. Revolver practice on range.	
	3-10-17		Company spent day on range, stoppages and range practices carried out.	
	4-10-17		General training carried out. O.C. Company visits O.C. 126 Coy the G.Corps at COXYDE	MAP REF
			BAINS and arrangements were made for the relief of 126 Coy in the Coast Defence Sector.	COXYDE
	5-10-17		Preparations made for Company moving to the forward area.	SHEET 1.A.
	6-10-17		Company proceeded by march route to SURREY CAMP, COXYDE BAINS. On arrival 8 guns	
			relieved 8 guns of the 126th Coy M.G.C. in the Coast Defence Sector. The remaining	
			8 guns remained in reserve at SURREY CAMP.	
			Owing to both aeroplane bombing trouble recently, work was carried out to protect	
			the huts, tents and stables i.e. Sandbagging round the outside to a height of 3 feet.	
			4 guns of No 3 section under the command of 2/Lieut _____ relieved 4 guns of	
			No 124 Coy M.G.Corps in the line.	
			Considerable amount of work was carried at all gun positions on Coast Defence	
			And in the line by a strong wind blowing the sand in dugouts and gun	
	8-10-17		emplacements. Gun positions in the dunes were shelled at intervals.	

(A.883.) Wt. W60/M1672 350000 4/17 Sch. 52a. Forms/C/2118/14 D. D. & L., London, E.C.

Army Form C. 2118.

No. 124 MACHINE GUN COMPANY.

No................
Date................

WAR DIARY
or
INTELLIGENCE SUMMARY.
(Erase heading not required.)

Instructions regarding War Diaries and Intelligence Summaries are contained in F. S. Regs., Part II. and the Staff Manual respectively. Title pages will be prepared in manuscript.

Place	Date	Hour	Summary of Events and Information	Remarks and references to Appendices
COYDE BAINS	27.4.17		O.C. Company & his 2.O. and 2 h. 2.O. went out on a reconnaissance. Information was received that the following N.C.O.s and men of the Company have been awarded the MILITARY MEDAL for gallantry in action on the 20th September 1916. No 43586 Sgt Yarn R.C., No 31486 Cpl Roch W.H., No 24416 A/Cpl Chambers W., No 43583 Pte Lawler J., No 43659 Pte Joyce L. The awards were given except in the case of Pte Lawler, for finding men now and after all the officers in the Company had been casualties in the case of Pte Lawler, for getting his officer to a place of safety and then proceeding to bring the enemy hostile shell with a very important message.	
	30.10.17		O.C. Company attended a conference at the 118th Div. H.Q.s H.Q.s. A.L. Henry Webring instructor paid a visit to Company and after visiting a cork-house said everything was quite satisfactory. The gun positions in the line were very heavily shelled during the day and caused 1 gun team to work position after losing 1 of the section the emplacement was totally destroyed.	
	31.10.17		Lieut H.W. Henry returned from leave and resumed command of the Company Lieut W.Th. Hartland assumed the duties of 2/C.	

Army Form C. 2118.

WAR DIARY
or
INTELLIGENCE SUMMARY.
(Erase heading not required.)

Instructions regarding War Diaries and Intelligence Summaries are contained in F. S. Regs., Part II. and the Staff Manual respectively. Title pages will be prepared in manuscript.

No. 124 MACHINE GUN COMPANY.

Place	Date	Hour	Summary of Events and Information	Remarks and references to Appendices
COXYDE	10.10.17		Nine new flue emplacements were constructed by section 3 in the line	
BAINS			Enemy activity normal. The section in reserve in SURREY CAMP continued the sand bagging of huts etc.	
	13.10.17		Normal. The section went relieved on the coast defence sector by the 123 Coy by Bn Glort.	
	14.10.17		On completion of relief all tanks who had been on coast defence proceeded to Coy Hqrs at SURREY CAMP. The Company relieved the 231st Coy Bn Glorts in the NIEUPORT BAINS SECTOR. Section 1 under the command of 2nd Lieut Ellingworth relieved a section of 123 Coy on coast defence and two guns on the reserve line.	
	15.10.17		Section 2 under the command of 2nd Lieut Wright relieved a section of the 123 Coy in the left front sector. Section 3 under the command of 2nd Lieut Jones in reserve, the town and of facing their relieved a section of 123 Coy in the right front sector. Section 3 in the Bn was again relieved by a section of 123 Coy and on completion of Hq went into reserve at left transport lines near COXYDE BAINS. Nothing of much importance happened on this date.	
	16.10.17		Quiet and machine guns were very active. Artillery normal	

Army Form C. 2118.

No. 124 MACHINE GUN COMPANY.

No. ....
Date ....

WAR DIARY
or
INTELLIGENCE SUMMARY.
(Erase heading not required.)

Instructions regarding War Diaries and Intelligence Summaries are contained in F. S. Regs., Part II. and the Staff Manual respectively. Title pages will be prepared in manuscript.

Place	Date	Hour	Summary of Events and Information	Remarks and references to Appendices
NIEUPORT	18/10/17		No 3 Section under the command of Lieut C.V. Muir relieved a section of 182 Coy	
BAINS			at in right reserve positions	
SECTOR	19/10/17		Normal.	
	20/10/17		Our guns on anti-aircraft work fired 2,000 Rds on hostile aircraft whenever very active. Such work has been carried out since the Company have been in the line with regard to the construction of new open emplacements, dugouts etc.	
	21/10/17		About 3·15 p.m. one of our airplanes came under fire of hostile A.A. guns and was hit. The plane crashed to the ground in the enemy's lines. Our guns on A.A. work fired 1,500 rounds during the night of 21/22nd. Our guns carried out harassing fire in the vicinity where one of our planes had been brought down during the day. This was done to hinder the enemy from taking the plane away.	
	22/10/17		Normal.	
	23/10/17		During the night of 22nd/23rd Indirect fire was carried out on enemy's comm'n, cross-roads and tracks. 2,500 rounds were expended. Enemy activity normal	
	24/10/17		Indirect fire was carried out on hostile armaments etc. 3,000 Rounds fired. General surveillance have been carried out at all our positions in the line.	

WAR DIARY
or
INTELLIGENCE SUMMARY.
(Erase heading not required.)

Army Form C. 2118.

No. 124 MACHINE GUN COMPANY.

Place	Date	Hour	Summary of Events and Information	Remarks and references to Appendices
NEUPORT BAINS SECTOR.	25.10.17		Hostile snipers and machine guns were active throughout the night & dawn. Our guns fired 2500 rounds on enemy's communications.	
			The whole day was spent in clearing away sand drifts from dug-outs and emplacements.	
	26.10.17		Enemy activity normal. Our guns commenced firing during the night but owing to wind and sand firing was stopped.	
	27.10.17		Our guns fired 2,000 rounds on hostile front - roads dug-outs etc. The enemy's artillery was very active at intervals.	
	28.10.17		Enemy activity normal.	
			The Company were relieved in the NIEUPORT BAINS SECTOR by the 160th Coy M.G.C. On completion of relief the Company proceeded to billets at TETEGHEM.	
NR. GHYVELDE	29.10.17		During the morning reliefs were sent to take the Company did not reach billets until the morning of 29th. The men were allowed to rest for the remainder of the day. All ranks on leave to England were recalled.	
	30.10.17		Harrasing [?] training up.	
	31.10.17		O.C. inspected Company. General training carried out.	

Army Form C. 2118.

WAR DIARY
or
INTELLIGENCE SUMMARY.
(Erase heading not required.)

No. 124 MACHINE GUN COMPANY.

Instructions regarding War Diaries and Intelligence Summaries are contained in F. S. Regs., Part II. and the Staff Manual respectively. Title pages will be prepared in manuscript.

Place	Date	Hour	Summary of Events and Information	Remarks and references to Appendices
TITGHEM	30/10/17		During the month of October there were very few casualties and not much sickness.	Nil
			Casualties during month 1 O.R. wounded.	Reinforcements 14.
			Sick evacuated to Hos. 1 OFFICER. 14 O.R.	
			Sick discharged from " 9 O.R.	
			Sick Evacs. C.C.S. 4 O.R.	
			The strength of the Company on the 31-10-17 was as follows	
			10 Officers 140 O.Ranks	

O.C.
124 MACHINE GUN COY.
M. G. C.

W095/26495

S/4492/5

41ST DIVISION
124TH INFY BDE

TRENCH MORTAR BTY
JLY-AUG 1916

41 July
Army Form C. 2118.
124 T.M.B

WAR DIARY
or
INTELLIGENCE SUMMARY
(Erase heading not required.)

124 Bde Trench Mortar Battery   VOL 1

Place	Date	Hour	Summary of Events and Information	Remarks and references to Appendices
	1/7/16	7 a.m.	2Lt Liddell relieved 2Lt Barker at Lancaster Support Farm (U 27 c 11½)	
		10 a.m.	Lieut Eaves relieved 2Lt Birch at London Bridge (U 21 d 2.6)	
		11 a.m.	2Lt Birch & Barker returned to rest billets at Bapaume	
		12 noon	Lieut Eaves transferred to Lancaster Support Farm and 2Lt Liddell to London Bridge and Lancaster Support Farm as the registered H.Q. of the half battery in the line.	
		3 p.m.	Explosion in bomb store at U 26 a 1.9 caused during cleaning of shells by a purely fly off fuzen. 20 pounds of ammunition were destroyed and also the gun emplacement but no casualties resulted.	
		7 p.m.	250 rounds of ammunition brought up from Maricourt 16/75. (U 26 c 6/25) to central bomb store at U 29 B 1.2	MMB
	2/7/16	6 p.m.	Capt Bowen returned from course of instruction in Stokes Guns at Derbyshire to rest billets at Bapaume	MMB
	3/7/16	12 noon	Capt Bowen relieved 2Lt Liddell at London Bridge (U 21 d 2.6) and 2Lt Liddell returned to rest billets at Bapaume	MMB
	4/7/16	6 a.m.	Work started on new defensive emplacement at London Bridge (U 21 d 3.6) to fire on pt G U 21 b 5	MMB
		5 p.m.	Subsection 1 relieved by 123 T.M.B. at Lancashire Support Farm.	
		7 p.m.	Subsection 1, 124 T.M.B. took over St Yves sector handed 121 to T124. 2Lt Birch conformed to instructions dated 2/3/16	
	5/7/16	6 a.m.	Ammunition in store commenced at U 15 c d 5. to add 800 rounds-	
			Work on emplacement at U 21 d 3.6 continued	
	6/7/16	6 a.m.	[struck through] continued at U 15 c 4.6.	MMB
		9 a.m.	All work suspended owing to retaliation of enemy for tommi mortar bombardment-	MMB
	7/7/16	6 a.m.	Work carried on at all U 21 d 3.6 & U15-c-4.6.	
			[heavily struck through lines]	

2449 Wt. W14957/M90 750,000 1/16 J.B.C & A. Forms/C.2118/12.

Army Form C. 2118.

WAR DIARY
or
INTELLIGENCE SUMMARY
(Erase heading not required.)

124 Trench Mortar Battery

Instructions regarding War Diaries and Intelligence Summaries are contained in F. S. Regs., Part II. and the Staff Manual respectively. Title Pages will be prepared in manuscript.

Place	Date	Hour	Summary of Events and Information	Remarks and references to Appendices
	8/7/16		Work carried on all day on new bomb store with the assistance of left half battery	A172
	9/7/16		do	A172
	10/7/16	9 am	Right half battery relieved by left half battery and work on bomb store carried on	A172
	11/7/16		Work on defensive emplacement at U.21.a.2.4 and on ammunition store at U.15.c.6½ carried on. Headquarters of 124 T.M.B. in the line Denton Halt U.15.d.2.4½.	A172
	12/7/16		Work on defensive emplacement at U.21.a.3.4 carried on. Bomb store completed. Rest billets for half battery out of the line transferred to A.2.d.5.8. (Sheet 36)	A172
	13/7/16		Mortar stores emplacement commenced. New defensive emplacement to cover front line trench from U.15.d.5.5 to U.15.d.5½.3.2 commenced at U.15.d.13½.	A172
			Sights for new offensive emplacements at U.15.d.3.2.3.3. U.15.a.5.0 attacked and papers taken to German front line. All working parties cancelled between 12 noon + 6 pm by S.O.O. 11.27 amended by R.047. A working party of 1 NCO + 5 men was supplied by the 32nd R.B. for mortars U.15.d.13½.	
	14/7/16		One emplacement commenced at U.21 & 5½ & 6½ to fire on German front line saw U.21 & 7.5. 2 emplacements commenced at U.15.d.5.0. to cover from U.15.d.6.6 to U.21.& 8.5.	A172
	15/7/16		N.O.1.S.37 Cpl Ospug and/or 186 B.O. with absence Mortar Store carried on until the assistance of 30 men of the 32nd R.B. and 3 snipers.	A172
	16/7/16		do	A172
			294 rounds of ammunition taken up to store at U.15.c.4.6½.	
	17/7/16		Work on emplacements and shell store carried on.	A172

2449 Wt. W14957/M90 750,000 1/16 J.B.C. & A. Form/C.2118/12.

Army Form C. 2118.

WAR DIARY
or
INTELLIGENCE SUMMARY
(Erase heading not required.)

134 Trench Mortar Battery

Place	Date	Hour	Summary of Events and Information	Remarks and references to Appendices
	10/7/16		Work in the following carried on: 3 Gun Obs and Shell stores at U.21.d.9½.0. 1 Gun Obs U.21.b.6½.9½. 2 " U.15.d.5½.10½ 2 " U.15.c.5½.3½	MB
			81 shells fitted with fuses detonator gram cartridge all ready for use at U.15.c.4.5	
	14/7/16		Left Half Battery relieved by Right Half Battery at Cnr St Yves and London Bridge	MB
	20/7/16	10.30 am	Gun Obs ammunition stores U.21.d.9.5.0 completed Cleaning & transmitting ammunition	MB
	24/7/16		Gun Mortars gun cable carried at London Bridge completed	MB
	25/7/16		Rifle to Mortar shot at U.21.d.9.5.0. 6 had test detonator	MB
	26/7/16		Drink carried on Gun alternative emplacement	
	27/7/16		2" Ls Dijon hoisted to shine history	
	28/7/16	11.30 am	Don't twinkle out in Mortar emplacement	
			300 shells were fired from trench mortars at U.21.d.9.3.0 in to the enemy's store at U.22.c.33 MB	4/9
			Much damage was done, the parapet being blown in in several places + the mine damaged.	
	2/4/16	12.3 m	60 shells were fired from U.21.d.13½ on to the enemy's line at U.21.f.83 also 70 shells were fired on to U.21.d.13, & got enemys front line & supports trenches around U.21.d.97	963
		9 am	Section 2 12.47 MB Whizim Selecter 1 12.47 MB Section 1 to Yves Hiccan to Cathe	
		11 am	Work employment at U.15 d 13½ carried on. 2/Lt Barker distinguished himself by going out into No Mans Land in broad day light to bring in as many of the 10 R Bath. Batts who were wounded. Accompanied by Drummer Nelly of the 10 R Bath. Batts he successfully brought in the wounded men & stretcher

WAR DIARY or INTELLIGENCE SUMMARY

Army Form C. 2118.

124 Trench Mortar Battery

Place	Date	Hour	Summary of Events and Information	Remarks and references to Appendices
	28/7/16		Mortar emplacement at U.15.d.1.3½ carried on.	
	29/7/16		Sub Section at St Yves relieved by 123 Bde TMB and transferred to Lancrois Support Farm in relief of 123 Bde TMB. Front to be covered by 124 TMB from Trench 103 to 120. HQ of 124 TMB in the line to be transferred to Lancrois Support Farm (ShRy). Emplacements taken over at U.25.c.1½.9 (offensive) U.27.c.9.1½ (defensive) U.27.b.8½.5 defensive	
		12.50 am	2 Rds Barker fired from Stumpabort T U.21.d.8.5 & U.21.d.6.6 from 2 guns on enemy lines at U.22.c.38. 24 rounds were fired. There was no retaliation and no casualties received.	
	30/7/16		Emplacement at U.26.c.1½.9 improved. 2/Lt Barker took command of the section in the line so Lieut Birk was detailed for a course of M.M. instruction in Stokes mortars at Terdeghem.	
	31/7/16		Lieut Birk went to course of Stokes Mortars at Terdeghem (course lasting 1 week) Ammunition checked over and cleaned.	

To:- 41st Division A.

Reference your A.450 of 25/8/16, herewith War Diary of 124th Infantry Brigade Trench Mortar Battery, as requested.

E. Heath
Brigadier General,
Commanding 124th Infantry Brigade.

28/8/16.

A.G's Office,
Base.

Herewith War Diary of 124th Brigade, Trench Mortar Battery.

Reggie Court ?
Major,
DAA & QMG
41st Division.

29/8/16.

Army Form C. 2118.

Vol 1

Of 124th Inf. Bde.
Of Trench Mortar Bty.

WAR DIARY
or
INTELLIGENCE SUMMARY
(Erase heading not required.)

124th
TRENCH MORTAR
BATTERY.

Instructions regarding War Diaries and Intelligence Summaries are contained in F. S. Regs., Part II. and the Staff Manual respectively. Title Pages will be prepared in manuscript.

Place	Date	Hour	Summary of Events and Information	Remarks and references to Appendices
	1.8.16	10am	19 rounds were fired from T.119 in 87th BIRDCAGE. with good results. The Enemy did not retaliate. JB.	
	2.8.16		No firing owing to working parties. Officers day out at T.109 repairs. JB.	
	3.8.16	10.37hr	72 rounds were fired from T.113 at a suspected trench mortar battery located at U.22.c.7.1½.	
		10.59pm	A further 28 rounds were fired at U.22.c.7.1½. The Enemy retaliated with 35 crumps in the vicinity of T.115	JB.

WAR DIARY
or
INTELLIGENCE SUMMARY

Army Form C. 2118.

Place	Date	Hour	Summary of Events and Information	Remarks and references to Appendices
	4.8.16	4am	17 rounds were fired from T11B onto BIRDCAGE	J.B.
		10.20am	Section 2.124 T7 B.13. relieved Section 2.124 T7 B.13. Section 2 proceeded to rest billets at La Crèche. Officers in line Capt Ewen at Lancashire Support Farm & Lt Dippie at London Bridge. JMS
			Strengthening dug outs & overhauling ammunition.	
		9.15pm	Five rounds were fired from V28a 1.6 onto enemy line at V28a 7.9½. Enemy retaliated with 6 4.2 s at S1.107 doing no damage. JMS	
	5.8.16		Constructing a new gun emplacement at V28 a 1.6. JMS	
			No firing took place owing to working parties running patrols.	

Army Form C. 2118.

WAR DIARY
or
INTELLIGENCE SUMMARY
(Erase heading not required.)

Instructions regarding War Diaries and Intelligence Summaries are contained in F. S. Regs., Part II. and the Staff Manual respectively. Title Pages will be prepared in manuscript.

Place	Date	Hour	Summary of Events and Information	Remarks and references to Appendices
	6.8.16	7.57pm	30 rounds fired from emplacement at V20 a 1½.2 on to enemy's front line at V20 a 7.3½. Considerable damage was observed. Enemy retaliated with whiz bang on S1.107, S1.109. The crew. There were no casualties.	JMS.
		8.45pm	5-8 rounds were fired from on to enemy's line at V20 C.5.1. with poor results.	JMS.
	7.8.16	9.15pm	Preparing ammunition. Work on emplacement at V20c.1½.7.	JMS.
	8.8.16	11.a.m.	5-2 rounds were fired into enemy's front line at V20 c. 4½.1. Considerable damage was done the parapet being knocked down in several places.	JMS.
		6.45pm	87 rounds were fired at V20 a 1½.2 on to enemy's front line at V20 a 7.3½ yards ten rounds. The enemy's prompt down for a share of 50 yds. Retaliation was seven consisting of whiz bangs. K.9.5, S4.2.5.	JMS.

Army Form C. 2118.

WAR DIARY
or
INTELLIGENCE SUMMARY

(Erase heading not required.)

Instructions regarding War Diaries and Intelligence Summaries are contained in F. S. Regs., Part II. and the Staff Manual respectively. Title Pages will be prepared in manuscript.

Place	Date	Hour	Summary of Events and Information	Remarks and references to Appendices
	9/8/16	9.30 pm	60 rounds fired from U.21.b.2.3 into U.21 & U.6½.3 which was suspected to be a machine gun emplacement. Officer in charge Capt Ewen	A/3
	10/8/16		Work carried on or emplacement at U.28.a.1½.4½. No firing was permitted on account of wiring parties sent out by battalions in front line	A/3
	11/8/16	6.45 pm	At 6-45 P.M. 11/8/16 two guns one in emplacement at U.28.c.19.5 U.26.a.11½.4½ were registered onto U.28.a.3½. Registration was also carried out from U.26.a.11½.6 onto the spot U.28.c.4½.6. 60 rounds intended to fire 60 rounds at the spot and 60 rounds per gun into U.26.a.3½ during the bombardment at 10.20 pm. As the bombardment was cancelled and as the 10 R.Q were sent out patrols this was cancelled	A/3
	12/8/16		Left section 134 S'd M.B relieved right section 134 D.M.B in firing. Relief started at 6 am from La Brade. S.S wagon to convey stores etc at La Brade at 5.30 am. Relief completed 10.30 am. On completion of relief disposition of officers was as follows:	
			Lieut Drinkle "The Ruby" Lancaster Support Farm (Headquarters on the line)	
			2 Lieut Barker — Garden Bridge U.21.a.2.7½	
			2 Lieut Ewen — Stokes In School La Brade	
			2 Lieut Pittier — do do	
			No machine was fired on account of patrols and wiring parties.	
	13/8/16		New offensive emplacement commenced at U.28.a.16½ and U.22.c.11½. No firing as our own hostile artillery was inactive and observers patrols and wiring parties were out and the D.H.O was requested to refrain from stirring up hostile retaliation	A/3

2449 Wt. W14937/M90 750,000 1/16 J.B.C. & A. Forms/C.2118/12.

Army Form C. 2118.

WAR DIARY
or
INTELLIGENCE SUMMARY
(Erase heading not required.)

Instructions regarding War Diaries and Intelligence Summaries are contained in F. S. Regs., Part II. and the Staff Manual respectively. Title Pages will be prepared in manuscript.

Place	Date	Hour	Summary of Events and Information	Remarks and references to Appendices
	14/8/16	3.15 pm	All blankets returned.	A/13
	15/8/16		Work carried on in emplacements at U.28 a.1.5½ and U.22 c.11½. No ammunition expended for army reason on 13/8/16. Emplacement at U.28 a.1.5½ completed and at U.22 c.11½ almost completed. Ammunition checked over, cleared where necessary, and handing over statements prepared ready for relief by 70th D.B. D.M.B. O.C. 70th D.B. D.M.B. shown round trenches in preparation for relief.	A/13
	16/8/16	10.30am	124 S.M.B. relieved by 70 R. S/3 S.M.B. at Lancaster Support & comm. and London Bridge. Left half battery to relief met by S.S. Nugget at Haversley Station M.B. Railway went into billets along with Right Siege Battery (transferred from 2nd Brooks) to C. Coy mill 134 M.S. Coy at B.1.C.24 (Map 36)	Copy of handing over statement attached Refs. A/13 Attch A/13
	17/8/16	7 am	Batt. at B.1.C.24 struck and 124 S.M.B. moved to billets at F.12.a.55	A/13
	18/8/16		Drill, Inspection of Kit, Checking of Stores etc.	A/13
	19/8/16		Advanced Sec. Drill and Arms Drill at field at F.12.a.55	A/13
	20/8/16	9 am 12.45 pm	Route march route followed F.12.a.55, A.7.d.18, A.21.a.25, F.21.c.H.9. F.21.a.5.5., A.7.a.1.8. A reference Sheet 36a F Sheet 36a	A/13

WAR DIARY or INTELLIGENCE SUMMARY

Army Form C. 2118.

(Erase heading not required.)

Instructions regarding War Diaries and Intelligence Summaries are contained in F. S. Regs., Part II. and the Staff Manual respectively. Title Pages will be prepared in manuscript.

Place	Date	Hour	Summary of Events and Information	Remarks and references to Appendices
	20/5/16		Lieut Jory reconnoitred route to Baillens Neuf Station in accordance with	
		12.40 P.O. N.O.R.? Report	1 Route to Station F 12 a 65 Shut 36 a	
			A 7 d 17 36	
			A 2 c 60 36	
			S 25 b 64 26	
			2 Distance 13/4 miles	
			3 Time allowed for movement 1 hour	
			4 Position outside station for troop to Rail S25 b 92 (26x20)	A/13
	21/5/16		24 more men attached to 13# J x 13. 6 men from each battalion in the Brigade making total strength of 80.	
		9 am	Bathing Parade at Divisional Baths at X 20 a 28. Parade at 8am return at	
		10 am	11.30 am Return route via Outtersteene.	
		3 pm	Gun Drill	
		4.30 pm		Kit inspection for 24 new men	A/13 Report on Bath Parade attached
	22/5/16	8 am	12 mile route march	
		1 pm		
		2 pm	Drill Issuing of rations Packing of stores and kits ready for move	
		4.30 pm	No 22517 Pte A Knight sent to hospital with Rheumatism	A/13

Army Form C. 2118.

WAR DIARY
or
INTELLIGENCE SUMMARY
(Erase heading not required.)

Instructions regarding War Diaries and Intelligence Summaries are contained in F. S. Regs., Part II. and the Staff Manual respectively. Title Pages will be prepared in manuscript.

Place	Date	Hour	Summary of Events and Information	Remarks and references to Appendices
	23/8/16	5 a.m.	Marched with transport via route reported on 20/8/16 to Bailleul Meat Station	
		11.30 am	Entrained at 11.30 am 4 officers 77 O.R.	
		9.50 pm	Arrived Pont Remy Station 9.50 p.m.	
	24/8/16	12.10 AM	Unloading completed 12.10 AM.	
		3.50 am	Marched with transport (18 handcarts) to Troisffleurs arriving at 3.50 A.M.	1A/3
	24/8/16	3 P.M.	Arrangement of Billets, unloading of stores and general inspection of battery.	2/3
	25/8/16		Gun Drill, Arms Drill, Preliminary fuzing instns	
	26/8/16		Divisional Rest Day.	
			Paraded at 4.30 P.M. and marched to Encourt arrived at 8.8 p.m.	R/1/3
	27/8/16		for billeting. Place unsuitable for billeting, so returned at 6 P.M.	
			No 1 Subsection paraded with 21st A.R.B at Franvines for practice in attack of trenches	
			No 2 " " " 32nd R.B " " " "	
			No 3 " " " 10R Queen " Bulbury Abbs " "	
			No 4 Sub Secm as not required by 2 or R 3 for training moved stores etc to Vaurelles	
	28/8/16		Subsections paraded as on 27/8/16 for training in the attack	2A/3
			No 9966 Pte J. Parsons went to hospital 14 O.K.D.Q.	
			Weather so inclement no outdoor parade possible.	
	29/8/16		Inspection of all equipment, clothing etc.	
		3 P.M.	3 P.M. Battery moved from billets at Vaurelles to billets at Bellancourt as it was more central	2A/3

No. 10011 P/8 astrup 9 A/bb/14 P.D.A mit Barks
2449 Wt. Wx957/M90 750,000 1/16 J.B.C. & A. Forms/C.2118/12

APPENDIX 4.

Copy No 14

21st Battalion King's Royal Rifle Corps
Operation Order No 15.

1. The Battalion will be relieved on the night of the 24/25th by the 12th Bn. East Surrey Regiment and will proceed to billets at VOLPAGO.

2. Guides 1 Officer (to be detailed by O C D Coy) and 4 O.R. per Coy (1 per Platoon) will meet opposite numbers at the Cross Roads 4.91.06 at 5pm on the 24th inst.

3. Order of Relief
   Right Front Coy to be relieved by "C" Coy 12th Bn. East S. Regt.
   Left Front Coy   "   "   "   " "D" "   "   "   "   "
   Right Support Coy "   "   "   " "B" "   "   "   "   "
   Left Support Coy "   "   "   " "A" "   "   "   "   "

4. On Relief A and C Coys will use No 1 Road, B and D Coys will use No 2 Road. Companies will proceed independently to their new billets via GIAVERA - SELVA to VOLPAGO.

5. Maps, sketches, Trench Log Books and other Trench Stores will be handed over on Relief. O.C Coys will hand over a written statement showing all work in progress at present and proposed. Receipts will be obtained for all stores handed over. Hot Food Containers will also be handed over. The Quartermaster will obtain a receipt for those handed over by him. This receipt should be sent in to this Office.

6. 1 Officer for Bn. H.Q. 1 Officer, 1 NCO and 2 O.R. per Coy of the Relieving Unit will stay with their opposite numbers 24 hours previous to Relief. Similar personnel from this Battalion will remain for 24 hours after Relief.

7. 1 Officer (to be detailed by O C A Coy) and 1 NCO per Coy will proceed to VOLPAGO on the 24th inst to arrange

billets. They will leave the line in the early morning.

8. 1 Limber per Company and 2 for Battalion Headquarters will be at respective Headquarters at 6.30 p.m. to collect baggage etc. The packs of the men coming off the island will be dumped as follows:-

'B' Coy - Junction of No. 2 Road with the NERVESA - BAVARIA Road
'C' Coy - Junction of No. 4 Road with the BAVARIA - GIAVERA Road.

1 man per Coy will be left behind to guard these packs until collected. The Transport Officer will arrange to collect these packs at 12 midnight. He will also arrange for the horses of O.C's 'A' and 'D' Coys to be at the Church BAVARIA at 9 p.m. and the horses of H.Q. Officers and O.C. 'B' and 'C' Coys to be at the same place at midnight.

The Transport Officer will also arrange for Field Kitchen, Officers valises and mens surplus kit to be at the new billets on the arrival of the Battalion.

The Quartermaster will arrange to have a hot meal prepared on the arrival of Companies at VOLPAGO.

9. Relief Complete will be notified to Bn. HQ. by wiring SNOW followed by the Company Code name. Companies will report arrival in billets.

ADDENDUM

Ref. para 8. O's C. Front Line Coys will arrange for the packs of their Signallers to be carried on the Company Limbers.

Issued at 11.30 p.m.
22-12-17.

P. J. Smith
Capt. and Adjutant
21st K.R.R.C

Copies to:-
No 1. Commanding Officer
2. H.Q.
3. O C 'A' Coy
4. O C 'B' Coy
5. O C 'C' Coy
6. O C 'D' Coy
7. Transport Officer
8. Quartermaster
9. O.C. 12th Bn. East Surrey Regt.
No 10. RSM
No 11. War Diary
No 12. File.

Copy of report sent to 124 I.B.
2/8/16

From O.C. 124 T.M.B.
To H.Q. 124 Infantry Brigade

As the Trench Mortar Battery is now a
definitely established unit I should like to
suggest that a special cap badge be provided.

At the present time we have four different
units represented and although the men are naturally
proud of their present badges I consider that it
would foster esprit de corps in their present unit
if they wore the special badge of that unit.

I should be obliged if this could receive your
consideration.

R. H. Furth Lt
for O.C. 124 T.M.B.

Handed over by 124 2/nB to 70 R Bn 2nB

> 72th
> TRENCH MORTAR BATTERY.
> No................
> Date 16/8/16

Ammunition	No of Rounds	Green	Red
Offensive Gun Pit T 106	99		99
" J 110	111	51	60
Offensive Gun Pit store			
Junction of Borden Av. } ST 110	104	91	13
Defensive Gun Pit ST 107	78	78	
" ST 110	42	42	
Central Store			
Lancashire Support Farm }	556	44	{42 not filled}

150 Red Cartridges

3 Offensive Gun Pits complete & 1 almost complete
2 Defensive Gun Pits
5 Mens Dug Outs
1 Officers Dug Out
1 Cook House
3 Trench maps 1/10000 St Yves 1/10000 Ploegsteert Secret map F

Signed A S ForD Lt
124/2/nB

I certify that the above were handed over correctly and that the Dug Outs were left in order

signed A Shaw 2 Lt
70th Bn 2 MB.

Army Form C. 2118.

WAR DIARY
or
INTELLIGENCE SUMMARY
(Erase heading not required.)

Instructions regarding War Diaries and Intelligence Summaries are contained in F. S. Regs., Part II. and the Staff Manual respectively. Title Pages will be prepared in manuscript.

Place	Date	Hour	Summary of Events and Information	Remarks and references to Appendices
	30/8/16		Subsection paraded as on 27th for training to attack.	2/13
	31/8/16	9 am to 12 y 5 PM	Route march of 10 miles	
		2 PM to 5	NCO's instructed in map reading and use of compass at cross roads North of Espagne by Lieut Smith. Men instructed in map reading, trotting distance etc. No 9965 Qr Saroona J returned from hospital	2/13

724th TRENCH MORTAR BATTERY

www.ingramcontent.com/pod-product-compliance
Lightning Source LLC
Chambersburg PA
CBHW080832010526
44112CB00015B/2495